T0267189

THE DEACON

An Ancient Office For The Glory of Christ and His Church

ALLEN GARARD
MARK GARARD

Mustard Seed Foundation Press
Springfield, Missouri

Cataloging data:
Garard, Allen 1949
Garard, Mark 1955

1. Deacons, New Testament Church
2. Church Polity, Officers
3. Biblical Studies, United States, Deacons

ISBN 978-0-578-86736-6
eBook ISBN 978-1-66786-577-5

Printed and bound in the United States of America

CONTENTS

ACKNOWLEDGEMENTS

While we cannot acknowledge every contribution along the way (there have been many), and we run the risk of overlooking some, we nevertheless want to express our gratitude to a few individuals who made major contributions to the completion of this book.

First, we are thankful for our parents, both of whom are at home with our Lord. God blessed us with parents who lived out diaconal work before our eyes, showing kindness and extending hospitality for many who desperately needed their love and compassion.

Second, we must acknowledge and thank our wives, who have loved us, encouraged us, stood by us, and served with us these many years as we labor together in the work of the Lord.

Third, we express our indebtedness to the late Terry Wolever, the longtime editor of Particular Baptist Press. Terry was the first to read our original manuscript. He not only made early editorial contributions, but constantly encouraged us to finish the work, a work he said he was blessed to read.

Next, we want to acknowledge both Jonathan Garard and Mary Madearis for their financial contributions that made the printing of this book possible.

Above all, we are grateful to God who has burdened our souls for the well-being of the church. Our prayer is that the Head of the Church will use this material to encourage those who labor in the office of the Deacon. May He be glorified!

FOREWORD

This book is the fruit of many years of study, labor, and life of two men whom God has blessed to enjoy a very close relationship. Yes, they are brothers by birth and enjoy the blessing of family relation. But they are also blessed to be brothers by second birth, as well as united in faith and practice. It is really a unique blessing that has enabled them to work closely together on the subject of this present title, though not laboring together in the same church. They have both been grounded in solid biblical doctrine that is consistent with historic Baptist confessions.

Al and Mark Garard are lovers of Christ and lovers of His church. This has been demonstrated in their lives as they have been used over the years in planting new churches, renewing existing churches, and strengthening those that are more mature. Their hearts beat for building up the church of Jesus Christ. They have served in a number of local Baptist churches to this end and continue today to serve as elders with a heart for establishing sound New Testament church order.

With their collective years of experience working out the principles set forth in the Word of God and learned through intense reading and research, they have come together to put in print what they have compiled over the years. While this book is the result of intense work, it is truly a labor of love, as these brothers desire to pass along to other churches that which they have learned and practiced in their own ministries.

These men are not writing from merely a theoretical perspective. They are not short on academic study and diaconate theories, but they are not writing for academia. They are very aware of the varied perspectives that exist among various faith communities. They are driven not so much by setting forth arguments for a particular position as they are by helping churches develop men who are divinely equipped with proven character to carry out the vital function of the diaconate in a local congregation. They have come to see this office to be much more than a position in a church. It is a gift that Christ has given for the proper maturing of any New Testament church. They know that, if men serve well according to the principles set forth in the Scripture, the church will be edified in very practical ways and the elders will have liberty to give themselves to the tasks of prayer, preaching, and shepherding the flock.

Because of my respect for the character of these men and their proven love for the church, I can heartily recommend them and trust that what they have written will be of great benefit to the church. I know Al and Mark well enough to say without hesitation that their greatest joy will come from knowing that this volume has been a help to those who either aspire to serve or are already serving as deacons.

May the Lord give these brothers the desire of their hearts as you benefit from their written effort and your church is strengthened as a result.

For the glory of Christ, the Head of His Church,

Kyle White

Pastor of Community Baptist Church

Elmendorf, Texas

INTRODUCTION

Two thousand years ago, world leaders, project designers, engineers, architects, and builders collaborated to produce some of the most amazing structures ever built, ancient structures that once stood proudly as testaments to human achievement. Today, they either stand in ruins, or they are completely gone, eroded by time, natural elements, and human progress. There are a few that still stand, but they continue to erode, and one day, given enough time, they will exist only on the pages of books or in someone's fading memory.

There is one ancient structure, however, that continues to stand and defy the onslaughts of every effort to destroy her. That structure is the church. If the remnants of ancient buildings are landmarks to the genius of their human builders, then the church is a testament to her divine builder, Jesus Christ. Jesus declared, "I will build my church," and He serves as both the Cornerstone and Head of the church, to the eternal glory of the Father who designed it all.

The church has suffered attack, both from without and within, and Satan has attempted to bring her to her knees in defeat, yet she triumphantly continues to push back against every evil force hurled against her. Today, churches are being planted, renewed, and strengthened throughout the world and will continue to exist until that appointed day when God will draw all things to a close, Christ will be revealed from heaven, and the church will be presented in all her glory to the Father.

We are reminded of the words of that glorious hymn by Arthur Coxe, drawn from Isaiah 28:6, "O Where are Kings and Empires Now?" This hymn reminds us that, in contrast to the crumbling foundations of this world's kingdoms, the church has an unshakable foundation.

"I lay in Zion a stone for a foundation stone."

1. O where are kings and empires now
   Of old that went and came?
   But Lord, Thy Church is praying yet,
   A thousand years the same.

2. We mark her goodly battlements,
   And her foundations strong;
   We hear within the solemn voice
   Of her unending song.

3. For not like kingdoms of the world
   Thy holy Church, O God;
   Tho' earthquake shocks are threatening her,
   And tempests are abroad;

4. O Unshaken as eternal hills,
   Immovable she stands,
   A mountain that shall fill the earth,
   A house not made by hands. Amen.

Until that final day when God makes all things right, the church stands, built upon the foundation of the apostles and prophets—Christ Jesus himself being the Cornerstone. The apostles were first, then the prophets, then church planting evangelists, then pastor teachers, and finally, every member of the Body of Christ equipped to minister to one another so that the church grows, matures, and is strengthened to carry the spiritual battle forward (Eph. 4:11-13).

As the master designer and architect of the church, God has given the church two officers, one to oversee and lead the church spiritually (pastors) and one to lead by serving the church in practical matters (deacons). It is the practical office of the deacon that is the focus of this book.

Solomon said, "[O]f making many books there is no end; and much study is a weariness of the flesh" (Eccl. 12:12). Coming from the wisest of all men, it begs the question, "Why write another book on an old subject?" Briefly stated, here are our reasons.

We wrote this book, first of all, because we love the church. Perhaps the title of the book is a little misleading. Ultimately, this is a book concerning the church but not everything about the church. Specifically, it's about the office of the deacon. But the deacon functions in the context of the church. It is neither an independent office nor a para-church office. By opening the door into the office of the deacon, we will inevitably explore other church issues, like servanthood, love, mission, and unity. Everyone who loves the church ought to enjoy studying this often misunderstood and under-appreciated office.

Secondly, we wrote because we think it is needed. We're not throwing shade on every other book on the subject, not at all. There are a number of helpful books that need to be read by anyone who desires to know more concerning the person and work of the deacon. However, after many years of preaching and teaching through the Bible, teaching and reteaching on the offices of the church, planting churches, and installing both elders and deacons, we believe there is more to be said.

While we give priority to what is clearly stated in the Scriptures, we also give attention to what is left unstated. You will know this as the difference between the explicit and the implicit. We think the implicit—those things implied by the explicit statements—need to be explored more fully. This takes us into the world of the "missing details" that everyone wishes were explicitly stated. We do that in this book.

Thirdly, we wrote because of our suspicion that the days ahead will place a high demand on the church generally and the office of the deacon particularly. Whatever your view on final things, whether the Lord's return is imminent or far off, the world is spiraling downward at an alarming speed. While we have a positive view of the final outcome, we have a negative view of man's ability to get himself out of this mess, and the world will inevitably turn against the church.

Both world history and current events tell the story of the persecution of the church. We think the future will tell the same story. Hardships will come. While the spiritual leaders of the church will shepherd us through the attacks against our faith, the servant leaders of the church (deacons) will minister to us in the physical realm. Like the chosen seven in Acts 6, they will care for the needy and neglected. With these things in mind, we think the work of the deacon will be vital in the future. Therefore, preparation must be made in the present. This book is meant to help the church meet both present and future demands.

Finally, we wrote this book because we wanted a practical, how-to operations manual to put into the hands of our own deacons. You will find our suggestions for an Operations Manual in Chapter 5.

Our hope is that you will find this volume helpful as you flesh out every nuance of the office in your ministry. Whether you are a pastor looking for a training tool or a deacon looking for a more meaningful ministry, we think you will find help in this book.

God willing, we will carry our study into a second volume to explore various topics that cannot be covered in one book. To pack it all into one volume would only prove Solomon's point: it would be "weariness to the flesh." In Volume 2, we will cover such topics as serving with the right attitude, the necessary skills for diaconal work, the deacon and missions, the relationship between pastors and deacons, the deacon's reward, the question of deaconesses, the deacon in church history, social justice and the deacon, facing situational challenges, and a few more interesting subjects. Perhaps one of these topics will pique your interest.

As you can see, Volume 2 will deal primarily with practical issues related to the office. Think of it this way: Volume 2 will be like a second semester course on the office of the deacon, diving deeper into the subject than almost any other available study. Our goal, in both volumes, is to think and act biblically as we fulfill God's intentions for the office. May He be glorified!

CHAPTER 1

THE NATURE AND FUNCTION OF THE OFFICE

I n this first chapter, we are going to ask you to think about words. Not just any words, but critical words found on the pages of Holy Scripture. Words have meaning. They have history. We are not at liberty to make a word mean whatever we want it to mean. Additionally, the meaning of a word is not determined solely by its definition. Usage is also important to our understanding of a word. Ultimately, as we note later, usage, not etymology, determines the meaning of a word. This is all the more true when they are biblical words. Biblical words are God's words, and their usage is intentional.

We will consider things like the meaning, history, usage, and the literal and figurative ideas contained in these words. We will look at the influence of both the Greek and Jewish cultures on their meaning. At times this may seem tedious. However, we believe that this examination and the information it yields is invaluable as we strive to understand the *nature and function* of the office of the deacon. As you work through the information in this chapter, it may seem like a box of puzzle pieces at first. However, each piece is necessary, and when connected, they create a biblical picture of the person and work of the deacon.

Whatever we understand about the office of the deacon, we must be sure that it is a biblical understanding. Therefore, the Scriptures will keep us from straying too far from *God's original intention for the office.*

As we begin our study, please read the following Scriptures to acquaint yourself with the relevant passages: Acts 6:1-7, Philippians 1:1, 1 Timothy 3:8-13.

DEFINITION OF TERMS

If you were to quickly look over the books written on the subject of the deacon, you would find that most of them have something to say about the *nature* of the office. There's a good reason for this. Our understanding of how a deacon ought to *function* is largely dependent on our understanding of the *nature* of the office. What this means is, if we're not clear in our understanding of the *nature* of the office, we cannot know with certainty what deacons are to *do*. God's Word gives us everything we need to know about the *nature* and *function* of the office in that one word: deacon.

In order to carry on an intelligent and profitable conversation on any subject, we must agree on the definition of the terms we use. Since the study of the *nature* of the office is critical to our understanding of how the office *functions*, it seems important that we begin by defining both of these terms. We'll not only define these terms, but we will also offer what we hope are some helpful illustrations.

We begin with the word *nature*. According to Webster, *nature* refers to the "[e]ssential qualities of a thing or person; that which makes it what it is."[1] For instance, the *nature* of a bird is very different from the *nature* of a fish. The bird has all the "essential qualities" for flight. These qualities distinguish the bird from other animals. A fish, on the other hand, has a *nature* suitable for living in water. The fish possesses all the "essential qualities" for aquatic life but not flight. Neither would live very long if they tried to function in a way that is not agreeable to their *nature*. The point we're making is that *nature* determines how something or someone will *function* or behave.

Let's shift our attention to the word *function*. Webster defines *function* as "performing, doing, executing . . . anything." He also refers to *function* as a "discharge; performance; as the function of a calling or office."[2] Implied in the word *function,* then, is the notion that certain specific duties must be performed in order to faithfully carry out the responsibilities of a calling or office.

This relationship between *nature* and *function* is biblically illustrated in what is referred to as human *nature*. Take sin, for instance. Why does every human sin? We all sin because we have a sinful *nature*. No one has to be taught to sin; it is in our *nature* to do so. Meaning that, one of the "essential qualities" of being human is that our sinful *nature* causes us to behave as rebels against God and serve ourselves. Only God's grace can set us free from the bondage of our old corrupt *nature* and enable us to behave, or *function*, with a new *nature* that takes on the image of God's Son.[3]

Thinking of the relationship between *nature* and behavior (function), one of our all-time favorite books is John Bunyan's *Pilgrim's Progress*.

---

1 Noah Webster, *American Dictionary of the English Language* (1828; repr. Foundation for American Christian Education), under "nature."

2 Ibid., under "function."

3 See 2 Pet. 1:4; Col. 3:12.

As you read this allegory of the Christian life, you soon discover Bunyan's keen insight into human *nature*. He insightfully illustrates the inseparable link between *nature* and *behavior* through the names he gives the leading characters.

Bunyan gives the characters names like "Christian," "Hopeful," "Talkative," "Pliable," and "Obstinate." These names were intentionally chosen to reveal the *nature* of the characters in his story. By naming a character "Pliable," we can be sure this person will cave in under pressure, which he does of course. The same is true when we read about "Obstinate." He is stubborn and unyielding even in the face of reason. Bunyan captures a character's most dominant trait (essential characteristic) in a single word—their name—and we not only understand their *behavior*, we could have predicted it as well. How? Experience! We know that an individual's *nature* (talkative, pliable, stubborn, hopeful, etc.) is a good predictor of *behavior*.

In case we've lost you, what does all of this discussion on birds, fish, human personality, and characters in Bunyan's story have in common with the office of the deacon? The bottom line is this: *nature determines function.*

This is a critical point. If we can determine the *nature* of the office or the *essential characteristic* of what it means to be a deacon, then we can also determine how a deacon is to *function,* those *specific duties that must be completed.*

Everything we need to know about the *nature* and *function* of the office is contained in that one word: *deacon.* And perhaps most importantly, if a deacon fails to *function* according to the *nature* of the office, he will fail to faithfully execute and fulfill God's intention for the office.

Having defined both *nature* and *function,* we are now ready to think about the term *deacon.* To provide a framework for our study, we will look at this word through four lenses. These lenses are just a tool to help us organize the material and focus on essential information.

Before we look through the lenses, we want to make it clear where this investigation is going. The goal is to emphasize a vital truth that can easily be overlooked, which is, *deacons are servants (nature), and God's original intention for the office is that of service (function).*

We hope the following lenses will make this truth clear.

🔍 FIRST LENS: THEIR NAME

Under this lens, we take a closer look at the word *deacon*. If we are to understand God's intention for the office of the deacon, it is essential that we focus our attention on the name God chose for both the office and the person who holds the office. Whatever conclusions we reach concerning this office, they must agree with the meaning of the word. In this case, it's the inspired word *deacon*.

God frequently chose names for the purpose of clarifying the essential characteristics (*nature*) and the resulting behavior (*function*) of the person holding the name. We'll offer a few examples.

First, consider the word *angel*. This name is given to the spirit beings created by God. In both Hebrew and Greek, the word means "a messenger."[4] God gave them a name that is translated "angel" to describe their essential characteristic (*nature*), which is manifested in their behavior (*function*). They are messengers of God.

Another example is found in the names God gave to one of the officers in the church: the Pastor. Several Greek words are used to describe both the office and the officer. The English word *bishop, episkopos* in the Greek,[5] conveys both the *nature* and necessary *function* of those who hold this office. This name tells us that he is to be "overseer, or superintendent."[6] W. E. Vine

---

4 Cf. James Strong, *Strong's Exhaustive Concordance of the English Bible* (Grand Rapids, MI: Zondervan Publishing, 2001), under "angel."

5 Ibid., under "deacon."

6 William E. Vine, *Vine's Expository Dictionary of Old and New Testament Words* (Grand

points out that *epi* means "over" and *skopeo* means to "look or watch."[7] This name identifies an "essential" trait of those who hold this office - they watch over the church. We won't take the time, but the same would be true of the words *elder* and *pastor*. The Spirit of God chose these names to describe both the *nature* and *function* of those who are placed in this office.

Of all the names given in the Bible, by far the most important are the various names for God. Each one is to be studied and reflected on if we are to have an appropriate sense of His nature and ways. A sense that leads to awe, wonder, and praise. Names like Yahweh, Adonai, El Elyon, El Shaddai and others. Collectively, they reveal who God is and what He is like. His names reveal His nature, attributes, characteristics, and help us to understand His actions. Not a complete understanding, but a beneficial understanding non the less. To the point, His names correspond to his necessary actions.

We use these examples to illustrate that the name *deacon* is a lens through which we gain insight and better understanding of the *nature* and *function* of the office.

As we will detail below, the *nature* and *function* of the office is *service*. That is what this word means: serve, servant, service. In fact, there is no other way for deacons to fulfill their appointment unless they serve. How do we know this? *It's found in their name!* Whatever comes to mind when you hear the word *deacon*, must be consistent with both the *nature and necessary behavior* of the office as God intended.

As we look at the name (deacon) that is given to the office, we need to focus our attention on the Greek word *diakonos*. Gathering, organizing, and researching all of the available information can be very tedious, but it is important if we are to have a working knowledge about the word that the Holy Spirit gave to the New Testament writers. A quick search reveals there

Rapids, MI: World Publishing, 1981), 128.
7 Ibid.

are various forms of this Greek word, and together they appear a total of 102 times in the New Testament. We will briefly look at these various forms.

First, the noun form: diakonos

This word is used a total of thirty-one times in the New Testament. It is translated twenty times as "minister," eight times as "servant," and three times as "deacon" (Phil. 1:1; 1 Tim. 3:8,12).[8] The basic meaning of this Greek word is translated in the words *minister* and *servant*. It literally means "an attendant, a waiter" and speaks of anyone who "waits on" or serves others. As for the translation *minister*, the definition of the English word may help us out here. *Webster's Dictionary* defines the primary meaning of *minister* in the following way: "an agent appointed to transact or manage business under the authority of another."[9] Perhaps this explains why the translators chose *minister* over *servant* so often. Regardless, the Greek word *diakonos* is a noun that refers to a servant, one who serves or ministers to others.

But what about the three times it is transliterated *deacons*? For that, we will have to focus our lens a little. Referring to its use in Philippians 1:1 and 1 Timothy 3:8, 12, Wesley Perschbacher states, "[T]here is, however, a strict application of the term to a specified class of officers in the church, who, in distinction from all others, bear this name."[10] Alexander Strauch agrees by saying, "[T]he word diakonos is plainly used three times in the New Testament to refer to the holder of a specific office" (Phil. 1:1; 1 Tim. 3:8, 12).[11]

---

8 George V. Wigram, *Englishman's Greek Concordance to the New Testament* (Peabody, MA: Hendrickson Publishers, 1996), 145.

9 Webster, *American Dictionary of the English Language* (1828), under "minister."

10 Wesley J. Perschbacher, *The New Analytical Greek Lexicon* (Peabody, MA: Hendrickson Publishers, 1996), 92.

11 Alexander Strauch, *Minister of Mercy: The New Testament Deacon* (Lewis and Roth Publishers, 1992), 48.

It is clear this noun form refers to *the person* who is appointed to the office of a servant. *Diakonos* in these references focuses primarily on the person in their capacity as a deacon, yet at the same time, it implies what must be their necessary activity. They are called deacons because it is the nature of the office to *function* as servants.

Second, the noun form: diakonia

This Greek word is found thirty-four times in the New Testament. It is translated "minister" twenty-eight times, "serve" four times, "relief" one time, and one more time as "office."[12] Thayer says this word refers to "those who execute the commands of others."[13] In these references, the focus is once again on the *person* doing the work: a servant who ministers to others.

Third, the verb form: diakoneo

This word is used a total of thirty-seven times in the New Testament. It is translated "minister" twenty-four times and "serve" ten times. Two times it is translated "the office of the deacon" (1 Tim. 3:10, 13) and one time "serve tables" in Acts 6:2.[14] Thayer defines this verb, "to provide, take care of, distribute, the things necessary to sustain life."[15] The verb *diakoneo* in these references focuses on both the activity of the *office* and the activity of the *person* who is placed in the office. Concerning 1 Timothy 3:10, George Knight writes,

> [T]his context most likely means [to] "serve as a [*diakonos*]," i.e., enter into the church office for which they have been tested (so also BAGD s.v. 5). This use of the verb helps us to

---

12 *The New Strong's Expanded Exhaustive Concordance of the Bible* (Nashville: Thomas Nelson Publishers, 2001), 1037.

13 Joseph H. Thayer, *Greek-English Lexicon of the New Testament* (Grand Rapids, MI: Zondervan Publishing, 1974), 137-138.

14 Perschbacher, *The New Analytical Greek Lexicon*, 92.

15 Thayer, *Greek-English Lexicon of the New Testament*, 137-138.

understand how a group of church officers received as their title the noun [*diakonos*], which states in a substantive the task that the verb [*diakoneo*] says they are to engage in. The relationship of noun and verb may well indicate a semantic link with the Seven of Acts 6.[16]

Let's bring this information concerning the *name* together. Looking at the various forms of the Greek word *diakonos*, we discover something very important. The name reveals the "essential characteristic" (*nature*) of the office and, therefore, should be the characteristic behavior (*function*) of every person who is placed in the office. All three Greek words say the same thing: deacons "serve," "minister," "provide relief," "attend to the needs of others." This is who they are (*nature*) and what they must do (*function*). Deacons exist to serve!

For some who already hold this office, or those who are being considered for the office, this may sound a little intimidating—"You exist to serve!" But we would encourage you with this thought: the Apostle Paul wore the title "servant" as a badge of honor. He uses these same three Greek words to describe his life and work as an apostle. He uses the word *diakonos* to characterize his own "ministry" in 2 Corinthians 3:6, Ephesians 3:7, and Colossians 1:23. He uses *diakoneo* to describe his "work" in Romans 15:25 and 2 Corinthians 3:3. And he uses the word *diakonia* to portray his life as "a servant" in 2 Corinthians 4:1 and 1 Timothy 1:12.[17] Paul had no reservations about characterizing himself as a "minister." It might be intimidating, but you will be rubbing shoulders with perhaps one of the greatest servants of the church after Christ Himself.

As further encouragement, we think it is very likely that Paul was ministered to by deacons and their families as he and his companions

---

16 George Knight, *The New International Greek Testament Commentary: The Pastoral Epistles* (Grand Rapids: W. B. Eerdmans, 1992), 170.

17 *The New Strong's Expanded Dictionary of Bible Words*, 1037.

labored in church planting (1 Cor. 16:15; Rom. 16:1-2). Perhaps the reason for their service to Paul was that Paul himself was so attentive to the practical needs of churches and personally led efforts to raise support to help those with needs.

While our focus is on the servant nature of the deacon, which is so evident in Paul's life, it should also be found in every spiritual leader (Titus 1:8), those who are called to be spiritual overseers of God's flock.

Only God knows how many times pastors have led the relief effort to help those who lacked basic necessities or have taken money out of their own pocket and put it into the hands of someone in need. It's hard for us to envision a shepherd who does not possess a servant nature, a nature that was so evident in both Christ and the apostle Paul. Both use the word *diakonos* to describe their work.

This picture of a compassionate servant pastor was etched on our minds as young boys. Our dad was a truck driver for thirty years, and the company he drove for was conveniently located across the street from our church. After Sunday evening services, he would walk across the street to the terminal and begin his overnight runs to the "Twin Cities," Minneapolis-St. Paul. We can still see our mom loading up her four sons and one daughter into an older, and often unreliable, car and making that long trip home across town.

The pastor of our church was a man by the name of Harold Roland. He was a very simple but tenderhearted man. We have vivid memories of him following Mom home because he was concerned about our old car breaking down along the way.

There was a special act of kindness he occasionally showed, one which we as young boys could only hope he would soon do again. A few blocks from our home, there was a new McDonald's restaurant. Occasionally, about ten minutes after we arrived home, Pastor Roland and his wife would pull into our driveway with a bag full of hamburgers and fries. Finances were very tight for our growing family, so this generous and rare treat left a deep impression on us. The impact of his kindness was even more amazing to our parents because they knew something we didn't—Harold and his wife had very little money themselves. Yet, we can still see his brimming smile as he plopped the bags on the dining room table. We didn't have to be called! All that was left was for Pastor Roland to give thanks.

Growing up, we heard many sermons from Pastor Roland, but none of them remain in our memories. Yet the impact of this servant left an indelible imprint on our lives. While we may not remember any of the sermons he preached, we do remember the message of his life. The message is that humble spiritual leaders, like Paul and Harold Roland, are ever ready and willing to serve their flock. As soon as they see or hear of a need, whether spiritual or physical, they jump into action, either personally or through the ministry of the deacons.

We vividly remember the day our mom received the phone call informing her that Pastor Roland passed away. She wept for several days. It may not have been clear to us then, but it is now. She wept because she lost both a beloved pastor and a dear friend, someone who watched over us, ever ready to help, someone the entire family loved and someone she knew loved and served her entire family. That's what servants do—they serve.

As we look through the lens of this name, deacon, we get a clearer picture of the *nature* and *function* of the office. The various forms of the word all reflect the same thing: deacons serve! In Acts 6:1, the noun form *diakonia* is used to describe the kind of care that was missing. In Acts 6:2, the emphasis is on a particular *function*, and therefore, the verb form *diakonao* is used. They (the Grecian widows) needed caregivers who could provide aid or help. The other Greek word *diakonos* is not found in Acts 6 but is used in Philippians 1:1 and 1 Timothy 3. This noun form refers to the person who is serving, the servant or minister, who is now called a *deacon* in these references. Generally speaking, *diakonos* refers to the *person* who serves, *diakonia* refers to the *nature* of serving, and *diakonao* is the *action* or *activity* of a servant.

As was said earlier, when we think of the *nature* of the deacon, we must think of that which is their "essential characteristic," that which "makes it what it is." All deacons are to have a *servant's nature*. Serving is to be their most distinguishing trait. Their *name* demands it!

 SECOND LENS: TRANSLITERATION

Under this lens, we will take a closer look at the English word *deacon*, which appears only five times in the New Testament: once in Philippians 1:1, and once in each of the following four verses: 1 Timothy 3:8,10,12,13.[18] However, we know the Greek word from which we get our English word *deacon* is found 102 times in the Greek New Testament. So why does the same Greek word get transliterated "deacon" only five times? Unfortunately, the translators did not leave a written explanation. However, the answer may lie in the context of these two references.

In the five references just mentioned, almost all English versions deliberately *transliterate* the Greek word instead of *translating* it, as they did in the other ninety-seven references. So, what's the difference between a translation and a transliteration? Keeping it simple, a transliteration is when we move a word from one language into another by simply applying or assigning letters that best match the sounds of the original language. In other words, it means to spell the word in English like it sounds in the original language.

The English Bible has many words transliterated from biblical Greek, words like angel, apostle, and Christ. An example worth looking at is the Greek word *baptizo*. Given the command from King James to retain "the old ecclesiastical words," the translators of the KJV chose not to translate but transliterate this Greek word. Had they translated *baptizo* into English,

---

18 Wigram, *Englishman's Greek Concordance to the New Testament*, 144-145.

they would have written "to plunge or immerse." Instead, they transliterated the word into English, and we have the word *baptize*.[19]

In the five verses under consideration, the word *deacon* arrived in our English Bibles the same way: *diakonos* became "deacon." The obvious question is, why? Why did this Greek word get transliterated into English instead of translated?

The deciding factor in these five references seems to be a simple matter of context. It appears the translators wanted to stress the fact that an *office* is being referred to, not an activity. That is, these five references are referring to something other than the general responsibility of all believers to serve one another. Rather, they point to the *office* of the deacon. A quick look at Philippians 1:1 makes this clear. Here we find three distinct groups in the church. First, there are "saints." This speaks of all believers in the church and naturally includes both deacons and elders as well. The other two groups, deacons and elders, are the officers of the church and, as such, make up the two offices of the New Testament church. Strauch recognizes this intentional transliteration in order to designate the office when he writes, "The word diakonos is plainly used three times in the New Testament to refer to the holder of a specific office" (Philippians 1:1; 1 Timothy 3:8,10,12,13).[20] Commenting on the 1 Timothy passage, William Mounce states, "'[T]o serve' here and in v. 13, means 'to serve as deacons,' since the passage does not discuss serving in general."[21]

---

19 *The New Strong's Expanded Dictionary of Bible Words*, 1037. Note: King James I instructed the translators to retain certain "old ecclesiastical words" such as church, and not to follow Tyndale's translation in these respects. This practice is still followed in all of the more modern Bible versions as well. This is not to say that the words *baptize* and *baptism* are not good words, for they are, and like many other words they convey nuances in the Greek not evident in a direct English translation.

20 Strauch, *Minister of Mercy: The New Testament Deacon*, 48.

21 William H. Mounce, *Word Biblical Commentary* (Nashville: Thomas Nelson, 2000), Vol. 46, Pastoral Epistles, 202.

So, what is the value of looking at the office through the lens of transliteration? Out of the 102 occurrences of this word in the New Testament, 97 times it is translated and 5 times it is transliterated. There was a very specific reason for this. While all of us are called to serve one another, these verses point to the *office* of the deacon. The *nature* and *function* of the servant are magnified when we recognize that an *office* was established in the church for a special class of qualified servant leaders. It was God's intention that certain qualified servants be entrusted with the responsibility to see that the needs of God's people are effectively met in the church. This noble office is specifically set apart in these five transliterated references.

THIRD LENS: THE INFLUENCE OF CULTURE

Under this lens, we will consider the influence that both the Greek and Jewish cultures had on the word that is used to identify the function and office of the deacon.

So, what is *culture*, and how does it influence the meaning of words? Generally speaking, *culture* has been defined as "the sum of attitudes, customs, and benefits that distinguishes one group of people."[22] Linguists (people who spend their lives pondering things like language and the etymology of words) confirm for us that culture plays a major role in both the meaning and understanding of words.

Words do not just appear in a vacuum. Their meanings are shaped by both historical and *cultural influences.* If you use an older English translation of the Bible, you will understand how words used in the sixteenth and seventeenth centuries have changed. How many know without looking it up that a *besom* is a broom? (Isa. 14:23). Searching out the Hebrew and Greek meaning of the original words is helpful not only for clarity, but also to preserve the original intent of the author.

---

22 From an online article on Greek culture.

The Holy Spirit inspired the apostles and others to write letters, and letters consist of words that are addressed to various people and assemblies. These recipients lived in various parts of the world, each with their own unique culture. These letters addressed various subjects they were dealing with at a specific time and place in history. The words they chose were familiar to both the writer and the reader. Most of the words were part of their everyday vocabulary. The exact meaning of these words was influenced by the culture in which they lived. In the Greco-Roman culture of the first century the word *diakonos* had a particular meaning.

Every generation of believers face the challenge of understanding biblical words in a way that is faithful to their historical, literal, grammatical, and cultural context. When it comes to the meaning of the Greek word *diakonos* and understanding it in light of ancient Greek culture, with a little research a clear picture begins to develop.

During the time frame in which the New Testament was written, *diakonos* was a common word whose meaning developed in the context of national and world events. Historically, when one nation conquered another nation, many of the educated and skilled servants were placed into the king's court to serve his needs and interests. Other skilled servants were given to some of the political and military leaders as a kind of reward for loyalty to the regime. Eventually, the rest were sold to the wealthier business leaders and citizens. The primary duty of these skilled servants was to attend to the needs of the household they served. Daniel, for instance, along with other gifted and highly trained captives, was given a special position in the court of King Nebuchadnezzar.

In the world in which the New Testament was written, *diakonos* was used to describe "such varied people as messengers, stewards, bakers, assistant helmsman, home-school educators, and even statesmen."[23] Some of the more gifted women would even be entrusted with caring for the

---

23 Thayer, *Greek-English Lexicon of the New Testament*, 137-138.

master's wife and children. Many were loved by, and loved in return, their master and his family.

Those in this category of "service" were given both material benefits and honor for their faithful service. In exchange, the master rightfully expected his servants to use their skills willingly, cheerfully, swiftly, and thoroughly. In *Greek culture* they were still "just servants," but were also recognized as a special kind of servant and were treated accordingly.

It's worth noting that Jesus used two different Greek words to represent the *nature* (essential trait) of His work on earth. In Matthew 20:28, He describes His actions as those of a servant when He said, "[T]he Son of man came not to be ministered unto, but to minister." In this text, He chose to use the culturally sensitive and contemporary verb form of the word that was used by people of His own day: *diakoneo*. He was teaching them that if they want to achieve true greatness, they too must become a "minister" (v. 26), a *diakonos* (the noun form). They must be willing to become a servant like Him, in order to do His work like Him.

Jesus did not "invent" this word. He borrowed it from the *Greek culture* of His day. What made this so unusual was that He chose a word that describes a person and a behavior the Greeks regarded as demeaning. No Greek wanted to be called a *diakonos*. The Greek philosopher Plato (d. 347 B.C.) said, "How can a man be happy when he has to serve someone."[24] Three centuries later, Jesus used the same word that Plato used. The apostles would use this word in Acts 6, Philippians 1, and 1 Timothy 3 to describe the person and the work (*nature* and *function*) of the deacon.

Not only did Greek *culture* impact the meaning of this word, but let's consider the influence of *Jewish culture* on *diakonos*. The Jews were very familiar with the concept of serving one another. Through the teaching of the Old Testament the Jews had been thoroughly indoctrinated in the

---

24 George C. Fuller, "The High Calling of Deacon," in *The Presbyterian Guardian*, Nov. 1978: 5-9.

idea of helping those in need, especially their ethnic brethren. In fact, God intended for them to become a "nation of servants" who served Him and one another. The very idea of serving Him meant serving others. To the spiritually minded Jew, this was a high and noble calling. Everything in their history and upbringing pointed in the direction of being servants. Even those special functions that God gave to their prophets, priests, and kings came with the title "servant."[25] Ultimately, all of this was intended to point to the work of the promised Messiah, who would be God's faithful servant and establish a kingdom of servants.

The converted Jews in the book of Acts seemed to understand the teachings of the Old Testament on this matter of serving those among them who had needs. For examples, see Acts 2:44-45 and 4:32-35. In these references, they were demonstrating *diakoneo*. It was a natural response of the leaders in the church to say, "We are in need of skilled servants who can oversee the necessary servant work and eliminate the problem of neglect." They needed a special class of servants who would care for those with needs in the Master's house.

The events that take place in this passage (Acts 6)—the choosing and installation of servants and their understanding of what a servant is—was influenced by the entire history and culture of Israel. It's just what they did.

This third lens, the lens of *culture*, has shown how the Greek word *diakonos* was understood two thousand years ago. Knowing how it was understood then sheds light on our understanding of the *nature* and *function* of the "office of the deacon" today. From the Greeks to the Jews, the word name "deacon" was understood to mean servant, someone who ministers to others like Jesus. This is the word the Spirit chose for those who are appointed to the office. This is what God intended for them to do.

---

25 See 1 Kings 11:13; Ex. 32:13; Neh. 1:6; Jer. 25:4.

Intellectually, those who hold the office are aware that they are to serve. It almost goes without saying—deacons serve. But in practice, is that what deacons and the church think of when they think of deacons? Is this actually what deacons are known for? Is it their reputation? At the time of Christ and the apostles, everyone—Jews and Gentiles alike—knew what it meant to be called a *deaconos*: someone who ministers to the needs of others.

THE FOURTH LENS: THE ORIGIN OF THE OFFICE

Webster defines the word *origin* as "the first existence or beginning of any thing" and "the [f]ountain; source; cause; that from which any thing primarily proceeds." He further states, "In history it is necessary, if practicable, to trace all events to their *origin*."[26]

What is the *origin*, "the first existence," of the New Testament office of the deacon? The answer matters. Because when it comes to God, He doesn't "cause" or bring anything into existence without an intention, a purpose. Nothing is incidental with God. The *origin* of the office and the context surrounding it, whenever it happened, will say much about God's intention for the office.

We believe the office originates in the narrative of Acts 6. If this is true, then the context of the passage reveals the intention. And what is the context of the *origin* of the office? Clearly, overcoming the neglect of the needy. So, the office comes into existence, has its source, in the context of the neglected widows. God's intention for the office, then, is fulfilled in serving the needy among us.

We realize that some do not accept the events in Acts 6 as the origin of the office. Our response is - if not, then when? If not these events, then what events? If not in Acts 6, then where does the office begin? We humbly

---

26 Webster, *American Dictionary of the English Language* (1828), under "origin." Italics in the original.

submit that the best answer to these questions is to recognize the *origin* of the office of the deacon as found in this inspired narrative.

And we are not alone. Recognizing the *origin* of the office in Acts 6 has a long and storied history. We offer the following witnesses for your consideration.

John Gill, the 18th-century Particular Baptist pastor and scholar, the man whose ministry followed Benjamin Keach and preceded Charles Spurgeon, had this to say on Acts 6:3:

> Wherefore brethren look ye out among you . . . or choose out among you, as the Syriac version adds, or as the Arabic and Ethiopic versions render it; which shows that this sort of offi-cers, deacon, must be members of the church, and of the same church to which they are ordained deacons.[27]

Gill sees the choosing of the seven as the choosing of officers, whom he also calls deacons. Clearly, he is pointing out the *origin* of the office.

A. T. Robertson, whom many consider to be the premier Greek scholar of the early twentieth century, said this on Acts 6:3:

> This word is the same root as *diakonia* (ministration) in verse 1 and deacon in Phil. 1:1 and 1Tim. 3:8-13. It is more frequently used in the N.T. of ministers (preachers) than of deacons, but it is quite possible, even probable, that the office of the deacon as separate from bishop or elder grew out of this incident in Acts 6:1-7.[28]

To say that the office "grew out of this incident" points us back to Webster's definition of *origin*: "the first existence or beginning of any

---

27 John Gill, *An Exposition of the Old and New Testaments* (Grand Rapids, MI: Baker Book House, 1980), 5: 840.

28 Robertson, *Word Pictures in the New Testament*, 3: 73.

thing" and "the [f]ountain; source; cause; that from which any thing primarily proceeds."

We add to our witness list William Arnot, a Scottish pastor, author, and Greek scholar. In his commentary on Acts, he titles the section on Acts 6:1-7, "The Deacons." In his summary of the events, he said this:

> As soon as the apostles heard of the complaint, they took effective measures to satisfy, and so resolve it. They surveyed the case, and promptly formed their resolution. At a glance they perceived that if the same methods should be continued, they must personally attend more minutely to the details of the distribution. But this would distract their attention, and occupy their time with secondary affairs, to the manifest detriment of their chief work, the ministry of the word. A new order of officials must be appointed to superintend this business.[29] The words, "a new order of officials" plainly speaks of the *origin* of the office.

The venerable Matthew Henry refers to these seven men as deacons in his comments on Acts 6:1-7. He writes, "The deacons are blessed by the apostles," and at the same time, he repeatedly speaks of them as officers of the church. Here are a few passages: "Those that are employed in any office in the church ought to be men of honest report," and "Philip . . . having used this office of a deacon well," and finally, concerning the laying on of hands by the apostles he writes, "[A]nd this was giving them authority to execute that office."[30]

---

29 Wm. Arnot, *The Church in the House* (New York, Robert Carter & Bros), 1883, 133.

30 Matthew Henry, *A Commentary on the Whole Bible* (Old Tappan, NJ: Fleming H. Revell), 6: 73.

By calling them deacons and speaking of them as officers, Henry obviously sees the beginning, or *origin*, of a new office and officer in Christ's church.

Although concise, Calvin's comment is particularly interesting as we think about the importance of knowing the *origin* of the office. On this text he wrote, "Now we see to what end deacons were made. The word itself is indeed general, yet [it] is properly taken for those which are stewards for the poor."[31]

This is doubly helpful in that he calls the newly appointed "deacons" and tells us the purpose for which they "were made," which is to be "stewards for the poor."

R. B. C. Howell, a Baptist pastor, author and noted journalist, in his classic book, *The Deaconship*, had this to say about the actions of the apostles:

> They determined, therefore, without delay, to change the existing condition of things, and to provide for these newly developed necessities of the church. The measure devised, resulted, under the guidance of the Holy Spirit, in the institution of the Deaconship.[32]

Like the others, Howell sees the narrative of Acts 6 to be a report concerning the "institution" or *origin* of the office.

The point we are making with the above quotes is that Acts 6 is *the starting point* for the office of the deacon. This is where diaconal ministry *originates*. Why is the *origin* of the office of the deacon important to our understanding of the *nature* and *function* of the office? Because the origin

---

31 John Calvin, *Commentaries* (Grand Rapids: Baker Book House, 2003), 18: 234, under no. 3.

32 Robert B. C. Howell, *The Deaconship: Its Nature, Qualifications, Relations, and Duties* (Philadelphia: American Baptist Publication Society, 1846), 20-22.

of something speaks to its purpose; it tells us why it exists. To say the same thing another way, *origin* points to intention. If this narrative is describing the *origin* of the office of the deacon, which we believe it is, then we actually know what *God's original intention was for the office*. Simply put, *to serve*.

It is an undeniable fact that the primary purpose for which God gave this office was to ensure that the church cared for the needy. And the appointed means for doing so is the servant ministry of the deacon. Whatever directives the church gives to her deacons, they must not conflict with *God's original intention*. This needs to be written on a sticky note in the mind. Whatever we ask our deacons to do, the work must not conflict with, hinder, or prevent the deacons from fulfilling *God's original intention* for the office. Deacons must serve the needy among us. This is both the *nature* and the *function* of the office.

As we close this lens on the importance of *the origin of the office*, we offer another fitting quote from Howell:

> When we look around us we see, almost everywhere, other and unauthorized officers introduced into the church to do their work; the deacons, where they exist at all, diverted from it; and engaged in other duties than those they were originally appointed to perform. I cannot but lament this perversion, so generally prevalent, since it must inevitably result in deep and lasting injury to the cause it is designed to subserve. What God appoints is always best for his people. To devise a plan of our own, and to substitute it for his, is to commit the folly of assuming to be more wise and to understand better the wants of the church than Christ himself! . . . Let us, beloved brethren, understand ourselves upon this subject; adhere unwaveringly to the word of God; maintain the Deaconship in *its original form and with its primitive purposes* [emphasis added]; and

we may confidently anticipate upon "our works of faith, and labors of love," the rich blessing of our Heavenly Father.[33]

CHAPTER SUMMARY

Our goal in this first chapter has been to build a broad foundation for the rest of the book. Simply put, if those who serve in the office are to *function* as God intends, then they must be clear on the *nature* of the office.

As we look through the *four lenses*, no matter which lens we look through, what angle we look from, everything points in the same direction and to the same purpose. We see an office in the church in which all those appointed serve the needy. We see *servants* who *serve*. This is who deacons are. This is what makes them deacons. They serve! It's the very *nature* of the office. In Webster's words, it's "that which makes it what it is." To do otherwise is to fail to *function* according to *God's original intention* for the office.

We stated at the beginning of this chapter that all of this information may seem like a box of miscellaneous pieces of a puzzle, but when it all comes together, it creates an amazing picture. What do we see? In language that John Bunyan might have used, we see 'Mr. Servant'! This is who deacons are by divine design. Theirs is a commission from God that will be carried out in and through the church. And their God-given commission is not fulfilled unless they serve! This is both the *nature* and the *function* of their office.

Unto Him be glory in the church by Christ Jesus throughout all ages, world without end. Amen. (Eph. 3:21).

---

33 Ibid., 32.

CHAPTER 2

THE VALUE OF THE OFFICE

Over the years, we have had many conversations with pastors and congregations on *the value of the office* of the deacon. We have thought about the evolution of our own beliefs and teachings on the office and of those who hold the office. The combination of peer conversations, member inquiries, and personal reflections have led to this observation: deacons are often grossly undervalued.

We've thought about this, quite a bit, actually. While this is a multifaceted problem, we believe there is a fairly simple explanation for how this happens. Basically, it boils down to this: deacons are undervalued when we do not have a biblical understanding of *the value of service in general*. If we do not highly esteem serving, then we will never highly esteem those who serve.

Our goal in this chapter is to heighten everyone's awareness of the *value of serving* in the church. Only when we have an intense appreciation for serving in general will we have an intense appreciation for the one who is set apart to serve—the deacon.

The corrective to a low estimation of the man and the office is to search the Scriptures to discover what they teach concerning the importance of serving others. As we dig into the Word, we learn of the value of serving in general and of the office and work of the deacon in particular.

Our search of the Word for *the value of serving* others begins with the Holy Trinity, specifically the relationship between the three Persons of the Godhead: Father, Son, and Spirit. The Son voluntarily offers Himself in service to the Father and becomes the suffering servant of God (Isa. 42:1-9; John 10:18). He comes to earth in the incarnation not to do His own will but the will of the Father who sent Him (John 6:38; 8:28). In return, the Father highly values the servant work of His Son (Matt.3:17; 17:50) and exalts Him for His humble service (Phil. 2:9-11). As for the Spirit, he serves not His own interests but only the interests of the Son, always pointing to Him (John 16:8, 14). At the same time, the Son always points to the Father. These Trinitarian truths stir our souls as we meditate on *the value of "serving others."*

Clearly, God highly values the work of a servant! If we do not fully grasp that foundational truth, then how will we ever highly value the office and work of the deacon? Serving others is the very nature of the office! Serving must be valued, treasured, admired. Why? Because God Himself *values serving.* Serving is not a peripheral issue; it is the heart of the issue.

As we search the Scriptures together to discover *the value of serving,* we hope that every member of the church, not just deacons, will catch a passion for serving. Out of this shared passion, the church will be made stronger, and Christ made more visible, in an evil age.

We divide our search on *the value of serving* into three sections. Each section will stress the importance of serving in general, and help us reach a proper estimation of its *value.*

- *Serving is a universal call.*

- *Serving is a necessary call.*

- *Serving is a noble call.*

FIRST SECTION:
Serving is a Universal Call

Anything that God deems to be universally applicable to every believer must have value. Would God require something of every single person of faith without first judging that behavior to be of value to His kingdom and His glory? And should we not also judge that it must be for our good as well?

The word *universal* means "extending to or comprehending the whole number."[34] When we say serving is a "universal call," we mean that everyone in the church, the "whole number," is called and responsible before God to carry out the command to serve. No one is exempt. It is essential that every member of the church knows and accepts this responsibility.

There is a tendency for church members to diminish their own responsibility when they know that others are chosen specifically to watch over the work of serving. However, watching *over* the work is not the same as *doing* all the work. *Serving is for everyone*, not just deacons. While deacons are chosen to lead the way for the church, serving others is not limited to deacons.

To buttress the value of serving by seeing the *universal* nature of the call, we turn to God's Word and make the following six observations.

---

34 Noah Webster, *American Dictionary of the English Language* (1828; re-printed San Francisco: Foundation for American Christian Education, 1987), under "universal."

FIRST OBSERVATION- The universal call to serve is a binding duty for all disciples of Jesus Christ.

> For, brethren, ye have been called unto liberty; only use not liberty for an occasion to the flesh, but by love serve one another. (Galatians 5:13).

In the above verse, the words "serve one another" are in the imperative mood, meaning they are a command. That all believers are to serve one another is not a suggestion, or a recommendation, or in any way optional for the follower of Christ. Paul is not simply saying it would be good for you to serve one another. No, this is a *binding universal Christian duty*. All believers must be actively serving one another.

Let's notice a few things concerning this mandate. First, the mandate to "serve one another" is a binding *ordinance*. In Matthew 28:18-20, Jesus is quoted as saying:

> 18 And Jesus came and spoke unto them, saying, All power is given unto me in heaven and in earth. 19 Go ye therefore, and teach all nations, baptizing them in the name of the Father, and of the Son, and of the Holy Ghost: 20 Teaching them to observe all things whatsoever I have commanded you: and, lo, I am with you always, even unto the end of the world. Amen.

With these words, Jesus is establishing a *Christian ordinance* for the entire church. Perhaps you find this language shocking. "What? An ordinance alongside baptism and the Lord's Supper?" No. Not that kind of ordinance, but an ordinance nonetheless. The word *ordinance* means "an authoritative order." It comes from the Latin word *ordinare*: "put in order."[35] Is the risen Christ using authoritative language here? That this is a *Christian ordinance*, or an authoritative order, is as simple as answering the

---

35 oxforddictionaries.com, Oxford University Press, 2019.

question, "Did Jesus command his disciples to serve one another, even as He served?" Obviously, yes. Jesus is saying, "It is your duty to teach them to do all that I have commanded. As I have given you the order to serve one another, give the same order to all my disciples." Jesus is not establishing a suggestion or hinting at something that we might consider doing. He is giving an *ordinance*, an authoritative order, a binding duty. The command to serve is not the only *ordinance*, or commandment that Jesus gave, not by a long shot. But it must certainly be among the chief *ordinances* that our Savior left us: serve one another!

This is Jesus' mandate to his disciples: go, teach, and baptize the nations. The words "Teaching them to observe all things" suggest complete indoctrination in all that Jesus taught. And not only indoctrinate, but teach them to do, carry out, obey—every commandment. To fail to insist on obedience by the new disciples is to fail to completely carry out the "commission" given by Christ.

Returning to Galatians 5:13, we notice a second important point. Paul states this binding duty (ordinance) as a *paradox*, the *paradox* that liberty brings servitude. Use your liberty to serve. Free to serve? *Paradoxical indeed!* Hendriksen wrote, "Surely no loftier description of the essence of true freedom has ever been offered than the one given in the words: but through love be serving one another."[36]

Third, we must pay attention to that which *activates* this voluntary spirit of service: "by *love serve one another*." Liberty is the condition, love is the motivation, and "serving one another" is the result. Christian love *activates* service. John Eadie stated it well: "Mutual service in their spiritual freedom was to be the result of mutual love, each serving and being served

---

36 William Hendriksen, *New Testament Commentary* (Grand Rapids, MI: Baker Books, 1995), 210.

in turn, a result which could not be obtained if they remained apart in cold and haughty isolation."[37]

In other words, *serving one another* flows out of *loving one another*. To back this up one step, loving others flows out of the fountain of God's love for us (1 John 4:7-16). The connection between God, love, and serving others is clear in Jesus' Words:

> 37 Thou shalt love the Lord thy God with all thy heart, and with all thy soul, and with all thy mind. 38 This is the first and great commandment. 39 And the second is like unto it, Thou shalt love thy neighbor as thyself (Matt. 22:37-39).

Paul's admonition to the church in Corinth adheres to this rule of love. In one of the most beloved and oft-quoted passages of the Scripture, Paul explains that, unless our actions are motivated by love, they are empty and worthless:

> 1 Though I speak with the tongues of men and of angels, and have not charity, I am become as sounding brass, or a tinkling cymbal. 2 And though I have the gift of prophecy, and under-stand all mysteries, and all knowledge; and though I have all faith, so that I could remove mountains, and have not charity, I am nothing. 3 And though I bestow all my goods to feed the poor, and though I give my body to be burned, and have not charity, it profiteth me nothing (1 Corinthians 13:1-3).

Pay close attention to the words "I am nothing" and "profiteth me noth-ing." Paul insists that he, personally, is worthless, and his deeds are worthless *if not motivated by love*. That's a stunning revelation! We, ourselves, amount

---

37 John Eadie, *Commentary on the Epistle of Paul To The Galatians* (Minneapolis, MN: James and Klock, 1977), 402.

to nothing unless we love one another. Out of love, and love only, flows every good deed. Our actions must overflow from *genuine affection* for one another.

It's important to notice the form of the Greek word *agape* that is translated as "charity" or "love" in 1 Corinthians 13 and Galatians 5:13. Over the years, we've heard a strong emphasis on love being a verb, a word that calls us to demonstrate our love through actions. We've been told that love is not about feelings but a decision that we make in our relationships. While the verb form of *agape* promotes these worthy observations, it must be noted that there is also a feminine noun form of *agape*. What does this form express? It focuses on the disposition or attitude of the heart when we show our love to another. This is at the heart of Paul's argument in 1 Corinthians 13:1-3, where he employs the feminine noun. Loving one another in action only is not enough. Biblical acts of love toward one another must be done with the right attitude or disposition of heart (feminine noun form of *agape*). This is the same form used in Galatians 5:13 where we are commanded "by love serve one another."

In Romans 12:9, Paul makes the heart attitude an issue when he writes, "Let love be without dissimulation," or, without hypocrisy; let it be genuine, authentic affection. The words of John Murray are apropos:

> In view of the primacy of love it is of particular interest to note how it is characterized. It is to be unfeigned. We find this emphasis elsewhere (2 Cor. 6:6; 1 Pet. 1:22). No vice is more reprehensible than hypocrisy. No vice is more destructive of integrity because it is the contradiction of truth. Our Lord exposed its diabolical character when he said to Judas, "Betrayest thou the Son of man with a kiss?" (Luke 22:48). If love is the sum of virtue and hypocrisy the epitome of vice, what a contradiction to bring these together! Dissembling affection![38]

---

38 John Murray, *The Epistle to The Romans* (Grand Rapids: Eerdmans, 1997), 128.

Fourth, as we finish up our thoughts from Galatians 5:13 on the *binding duty* to "by love serve one another," notice to whom Paul addresses this exhortation: "Brethren." To paraphrase, "Now that you, my brothers and sisters in Christ, have been set free from the bondage of sin, a bondage which leads to self-love and self-serving, use your new found liberty and 'by love serve one another.'" The term "Brethren" is all inclusive; it speaks of all who are in Christ. If we went no further than this one passage, it is obvious that God calls all believers to serve one another. *The universal call to serve is a* binding duty *for all disciples of Jesus Christ.*

SECOND OBSERVATION - The universal call to serve is modeled after the pattern of the Lord Jesus Christ Himself.

> 25 But Jesus called them unto him, and said, Ye know that the princes of the Gentiles exercise dominion over them, and they that are great exercise authority upon them. 26 But it shall not be so among you: but whosoever will be great among you, let him be your minister; 27 And whosoever will be chief among you, let him be your servant: 28 Even as the Son of man came not to be ministered unto, but to minister, and to give his life a ransom for many. (Matthew 20:25-28).

In this pericope, Jesus is dealing with sinful ambition. Ambition itself is not necessarily evil, but when it leads to quarreling and selfish posturing over positions of leadership, then it has become a sinful ambition. It is this self-serving attitude that Jesus is decrying.

As He often did, Jesus seizes the moment to teach His disciples a very important lesson. On this occasion, He's teaching them what His kingdom looks like, not in theory, but in practice. His disciples were guilty of posturing according to a very worldly and ungodly "me first" value system. In response, Christ teaches them, "This is not how we do things in my kingdom. In my kingdom we sacrifice ourselves in the service of others. In word and deed, we *value serving others* more than we value ourselves."

With the words "even as the Son of man" (v. 28), Jesus is establishing a *pattern* for all of his disciples to follow, namely, Himself. His values, His attitudes, and His actions are to shape our own. The words "ministered" and "minister" found in v. 28 come from the Greek word *diakoneo*.[39] It speaks of a very particular action: to *serve*. In context, it means to give up yourself and seek only the good of others in thought, word, and deed: "Even as the Son of man." He makes it clear that leaders are to set themselves apart by a spirit of self-sacrificial service. Though His disciples stumbled out of the gate, through the power of the risen Christ and the coming of the Holy Spirit at Pentecost, they did in fact lay down their lives in service for Christ and His church.

While it is true that Jesus is addressing the twelve, ten of whom were offended by the grandstanding of the two and their mother, clearly the application is for all who follow Christ. The point that Jesus is making here is; "If I, your Lord and Master have dedicated *my* life to serve others, then you who are my followers, and I mean all of you, must also be ready and willing to dedicate your lives to the service of others as well. You must *value serving* as much as I value serving. You must serve others as I have demonstrated." All disciples are called to serve in His kingdom. All disciples are commissioned to do diaconal work. By His life and teaching our Lord made serving a *universal call*. He also made His life the standard by which we are to *pattern* our lives after. It would be a mistake for the members of the church to leave this work for the deacons, as if they are the only ones who are called to follow the pattern established by Christ. The *universal call* is to be heard and obeyed by all true disciples.

---

39 James Strong, *Strong's Exhaustive Concordance of the English Bible* (Grand Rapids, MI: Zondervan Publishing, 2001), under 'deacon.'

Is this valuable work? Does not the life and death of "the Son of man" prove the value of a self-sacrificing spirit? Hear the words of the Father at Jesus' baptism, "This is my beloved Son in whom I am well pleased." One of the wonders of it all is that the Father calls on all disciples, sinful as we are, *to follow in the servant steps* of His Son and know the fellowship of His sufferings through the fellowship of serving. *Valuable?* Indeed!

THIRD OBSERVATION- The universal call to serve is why all disciples are given gifts.

> 10 As every man hath received the gift, even so minister the same one to another, as good stewards of the manifold grace of God. 11 If any man speak, let him speak as the oracles of God; if any man minister, let him do it as of the ability which God giveth; that God in all things may be glorified through Jesus Christ, to whom be praise and dominion for ever and ever. Amen. (1 Peter 4:10-11).

Peter is addressing the wrong notion that some have the "gift of service," while others have gifts that are somehow unrelated to serving others. They incorrectly perceive that the call to serve is for some only, not for everyone. Some, like those in the church at Corinth, seemed to think that serving is somehow meant for the lower tier believer and not as important as the more visible gifts, perhaps like leadership gifts. Peter, however, corrects the error in that kind of thinking by teaching us that the call to serve is not only a *universal call,* but it's *the only reason the Spirit has given gifts in the first place.* He writes, "As every man hath received the gift, even so minister the same one to another."

While there are different views regarding "the gift" in verse 10, the function of the gift is clear. All *gifts* are designed to serve the body of Christ.

The Greek word *minister* in both verses is *diakoneo*,[40] which means serve. If every member has received a *gift*, which they have, and all *gifts* are given to serve others, which they are, then all members of Christ's church are to use their *gifts* in the service of others. No one is exempt. Some indeed will be called to more visible service, like leading in diaconal work as an officer in the church, yet all of us are called to mold our lives and use our individual giftedness after the *pattern* of Jesus Christ, who came to serve, not to be served.

A secular idea that has infiltrated the church is the trend to focus attention on individual, personal giftedness. In other words, "It's all about me!" When we focus on individual giftedness, we can be so preoccupied with trying to "discover" our gift that we forget the mandate—serve! We can't find anything in Scripture that excuses church members from serving others while they wait to somehow discover their giftedness. And even more disturbing is the habit of some to insist that they cannot serve outside of their perceived area of giftedness. Christians who want to be obedient to the command to serve are not as preoccupied with "finding their gift" as they are with finding a way to serve. Servants serve others however, wherever, and whenever they can. And we are all called to be servants!

While there may be a warrant in some cases for giving attention to individual gifts, it must not come at the expense of neglecting what is clear: the *universal call* to serve includes the use of your *gifts*. *Gifts* tend to manifest themselves naturally in a church body where people are living under the authority of God's Word. And whatever those gifts are, they are all designed to accomplish the same thing: to "minister" or to *serve* the saints.

Furthermore, a careful reading of the New Testament shows that *gifts* are given in the context of "body life" (see I Cor. 12-14). Why is that important? "Gifts" are distributed by God primarily to serve the church where we worship and serve. While God has given unusual spiritual

---

40 Ibid.

giftedness to some that prove to be a blessing to the entire body of believers everywhere, and some gifted people are a blessing to others locally regardless of church affiliation, these prove to be the exception, not the rule. And even in those cases, they cannot neglect the duty to serve their own church first. Normally, God gives *gifts* to men and women to serve either in or through their local assemblies. As pastors, it grieves us when church members serve everywhere except in their own church. We'll leave the various explanations as to why this happens for you to work out. But when this occurs, you can be sure something is amiss. God gives *gifts* to be exercised first in the context of the local church.

The Scriptures tell us to serve one another. The point being, find someone to serve. Or serve everyone. Everyone has a need of some kind or another. It's your job to find that need and fill it. Even in a small church, if that is where God has placed you, there are many opportunities to serve; you just need to look for them. Here's the point: *servants serve*! They don't wait for an assignment from the pastors or deacons, and they don't think in terms of cubby holes or neat little boxes where they can put their service. Servants have a way of finding ways to serve. You can't stop them. It's in their spiritual DNA. The *opportunities* are limited only by our *unwillingness* to serve others.

Before we close out our comments on Peter's exhortation to serve one another in this passage, we have to point out that it teaches us the purpose for everything, including the use of our *gifts*. Peter writes, "[T]hat God may be glorified through Jesus Christ." *The universal call to serve must be highly valued* because it helps us accomplish the ultimate purpose for everything: "that God in all things may be glorified through Jesus Christ, to whom be praise and dominion for ever and ever. Amen."

Is the call to serve one another *valuable*? If glorifying God through Jesus Christ is valuable, then yes! God Himself highly values serving and is glorified when we serve others. This is a *universal call* to all believers to use their *gifts* to serve the body of Christ.

FOURTH OBSERVATION- The universal call to serve is a fruit of salvation and will inspire and edify others.

> 9 But, beloved, we are persuaded better things of you, and things that accompany salvation, though we thus speak. 10 For God is not unrighteous to forget your work and labour of love, which ye have shewed toward his name, in that ye have ministered to the saints, and do minister. 11 And we desire that every one of you do shew the same diligence to the full assurance of hope unto the end: 12 That ye be not slothful, but followers of them who through faith and patience inherit the promises. (Hebrews 6:9-12).

In the midst of a warning against falling away from the faith, the writer has confidence in the readers because they have manifested *the fruit of genuine salvation* (v.9). In verse 10, he states what this fruit is, namely, out of love (feminine noun *agape*) they *have ministered* and *continue to minister* to the saints. As O'Brien so succinctly put it, "They have a proven track record of Christian service."[41] Concerning the implications of the word *shewed*, O'Brien writes, "Their love has not simply been a matter of the heart but has been shown in concrete ways."[42] Although it may not be O'Brien's point, he is acknowledging what we stated earlier, that the *action* of love must be accompanied by the right *disposition* of heart: genuine affection.

Moving to the second aspect of this observation, acts of love will *inspire* others to perform their own acts of charity, which, in turn, *edifies* the body of Christ. Verse 12 reads, "That ye be not slothful, but followers of them who through faith and patience inherit the promises." He is telling us to look to those who persevered in ministering to the needs of others, that

---

41 Peter O'Brien, *The Letter to the Hebrews* (Grand Rapids, MI: Eerdmans, 2010, 231) 231.
42 Ibid.

we too might "inherit the promises" as they did. The connection between serving others, the assurance of hope, and inheriting the promises is worth looking into but beyond the scope of the point in hand. We are simply pointing out the obvious when we say that a testimony of diligence in serving others inspires and edifies the entire church to be doing the same kinds of things: things that ought to "accompany salvation" (v.9). Regarding the exhortation in verse 12, Haldane wrote, "In opposition to slothfulness, he urges them to be followers of them who through faith and patience are now inheriting the promises."[43] Commenting on the same passage, Puritan William Gouge wrote, "Precedents and examples do put a kind of life into men," and "It will therefore be a good means for our quickening . . . to observe the patterns of such as have been forward in the way of godliness."[44] On verse 12 he states, "The *following* here intended is a diligent endeavor to be like unto them, and in our time to do as they did."[45] He goes on to refer to those who have gone before us as "patterns and precedents" that serve as "a motive to incite the living to follow those who attained heaven[.]"

The point we are making here is that, beyond the personal benefits enjoyed by the faithful saints spoken of in the text, their faithful service to others edifies and inspires the church to follow in their footsteps.

This passage also reminds us that their commitment to serve others was a *lifestyle*, not an event. Notice words like "ye have," "ye do," "do shew," and "be not slothful." Some have been serving others all along; it's their habit to do so. Others have become slothful. The slothful, or those who have become dull, lazy, negligent, must *follow the example* of those who have been diligent in ministering to others. This is a fruit of those who have obtained salvation (v. 9), have a lively hope (v. 11), and persevere in the

---

43 J.A. Haldane, *An Exposition of the Epistle to the Hebrews* (Springfield, MO: Particular Baptist Press, 2010) 172-173.

44 W. Gouge, *Commentary on Hebrews, Exegetical and Expository*, Vol.1 (Birmingham, AL, USA, Solid Ground Christian Books, 2006) 427.

45 Ibid.

faith (v. 12). This passage clearly teaches that all believers are to be in the habit of serving the needs of others. We are either *inspiring* others to serve by our example, or we should be *following* those who are.

Besides being a matter of fruitful obedience, there are practical reasons for always being ready to serve others. First, opportunities to serve often come unexpectedly, without notice. They just seem to show up. In fact, the call to serve others often comes at what we might call, "the worst possible moment." Someone might say, "I can't help today; I'm not prepared!" Or, "My day is already scheduled. I can't fit it in." Unless ministering to others is a *lifestyle* decision made in the past and practiced in the present—in other words, a *habit*—we might not know how, or be willing, to deal with unexpected needs.

Not only do opportunities come unexpectedly, they also come randomly. Needs don't run according to a set schedule. Sometimes they show up in bunches, and sometimes they are few and far between. Even if we are in the habit of serving the needs of others, we simply don't know when the Lord will give us another opportunity to serve someone in need. We not only need to keep our wick trimmed, but we need a full supply of oil on hand at all times. It would be better for a servant to always be prepared.

This has practical application to deacons. As those who watch over this ministry of the church, are you always ready? Watching and listening for opportunities are one thing; being both *ready* and *able* to help when the opportunity is presented is another thing.

In this text, the words *minister* and *ministered* come from the Greek word *diakoneo*.[46] The writer challenges his readers in v. 11, when he says, "[E]veryone . . . show the same diligence." While we might rightfully expect the servant officers in the church to be models of service described here, yet all are responsible to be diligent in their efforts to serve others. We

---

46 Strong, *Strong's Exhaustive Concordance of the English Bible*, under "minister."

should look for those who best exemplify *diaconal* work in our churches and *follow them*, whether they are deacons or not. *Following the diligent* is one way that God raises up servants in general and future servant leaders in particular. Being always ready to serve is both *edifying* and *inspiring* to the church.

While the epistle known as *Hebrews* was written to Jewish converts to Christianity during a time of persecution, its message is for all of us. This is a *universal call* to serve. All of us should pattern our lives after those who demonstrate their salvation and perseverance in the faith by faithfully serving their brothers and sisters in need. *It's a lifestyle, not an event.* As O'Brien said of them, "[T]hey had a proven track record." Do we?

FIFTH OBSERVATION- The universal call to serve should be the goal of every family.

15 "I beseech you, brethren, (ye know the house of Stephanas, that it is the first-fruits of Achaia, and that they have addicted themselves to the ministry of the saints,) 16 That ye submit yourselves unto such, and to everyone that helpeth with us, and laboureth" (1 Corinthians 16:15-16).

As we continue pressing the point that the call to serve is a *universal call*, these two verses paint an amazing picture: the picture of a man who made serving a priority. That man was Stephanas. However, it was not only Stephanas but his *entire household*. The word *house* implies more than himself, and the words *first-fruits* and *they* are plural. There had to be more than just Stephanas living in his house. It includes his wife if he had one, children if he had any, relatives who may have been living with him, and even household servants if he employed any. *His entire household is serving.*

Under the leadership of Stephanas, everyone living under his roof banded together as one *diaconal family*. Paul tells us that everyone living there was "addicted" to serving the saints or, as the ESV reads, "devoted."

The word *addicted* is rich in meaning. The Greek verb *tasso* means to appoint, designate, or to set one's self to a particular task. And because they appointed or designated themselves, it speaks of volunteering, making a choice, placing themselves in this service. No one had to force this household into service. They took it upon themselves and were devoted to the task. Perhaps it was the influence of the life and teaching ministry of Paul that led Stephanas to understand that serving others was intrinsic to Christian living. Whatever it was, when they became aware that believers were in need, they stepped forward and said, "We'll do it. We will see to it that our brothers and sisters in Christ are taken care of." As David Garland put it, "[T]hey set themselves aside for duty."[47] John MacArthur points out, "He did not wait for an appointment, assignment, an office, they appointed themselves." *Tasso* means they were addicted, devoted, and even "predisposed"[48] through continuous action.

Once again, we find the word *diakonia*.[49] Stephanas and his household distinguished themselves through humble service to others. The point is that Stephanas did not see this as the work of a few church-chosen individuals. He saw it as a *universal call* for all who would be obedient to Christ. It is possible, of course, that this man was a deacon in the early church at Corinth. But the fact that his entire family served and were addicted to service shows they all understood this to be a *universal call*. It wasn't just for the head of the household.

The important lessons from this example do not end there. Paul knew the work and labor of Stephanas well enough to direct *the entire church* at Corinth to "submit" to his leadership in diaconal work. The word *submit* here has the usual meaning of voluntarily lining up under the authority of

---

47 David E. Garland, *I Corinthians* (Grand Rapids: Baker Academic, 2003), 768.

48 John MacArthur, *I Corinthians* (Chicago: Moody Press, 1984), 480.

49 Strong, *Strong's Exhaustive Concordance of the English Bible*, under "diakonia."

another.[50] They were to get in line of their own accord and follow his example. It appears that his entire household accepted the universal mandate to "by love serve one another."

We can only speculate as to how Paul came to know him. From 1 Cor. 1:16, we gather that Paul not only baptized him, but also was his father in the faith. Perhaps, as a result, he ministered to Paul as Paul ministered the Word to the church. We don't know for sure. What is sure is that Stephanas distinguished himself in the eyes of Paul for his work of service, a work that reached beyond Corinth and was to be emulated by the entire church.

What a wonderful example! Here is a man, Stephanas by name, who understood that serving is a *universal* Christian mandate, and he made sure everyone under his leadership understood this as well. He trained them all to serve others and together they dedicated themselves to the work. The word *helpeth*[51] (v.16) indicates that Stephanas and his entire household was recognized by Paul as helping hands, partners in his ministry.

They are also numbered among those who are willing to pull their own weight in the exhausting work of serving others. The word *laboureth*[52] (v.16) speaks of working to the point of exhaustion. Each member of his household volunteered to put their shoulders under the weight of the work until they were physically drained. Devoted indeed! To turn a phrase, "Many are called, but few are exhausted."

These are the kind of servants the entire church is to not only follow, but also hold in high regard. As was previously pointed out, deacons, as servants on behalf of the church, are to be respected and honored for their work's sake (see Phil. 2:29). Stephanas is mentioned again in verse 18, where Paul writes, "For they have refreshed my spirit and your's: therefore acknowledge ye them that are such." To acknowledge is more than

---

50 Ibid., under "submit."
51 Ibid., under "helpeth."
52 Ibid., under "laboureth."

giving mental assent. Thiselton's comments are helpful: "It is churlish not to give special respect to those who welcomed newer [Christians] into the church and offered support and nurture while they found their feet as newly baptized Christians and church members."[53] Concerning the ministry of Stephanas, Fortunatus, and Achaicus (v.17), Thiselton avers, "Now Paul can catch up with all the news from trusted fellow Christians who knew the church in Corinth inside out. This prompts him again to remind the church how lucky they are to have three such people among them, and to urge a second time that they show them due recognition and *respect*." (emphasis original).

SIXTH OBSERVATION- The universal call to serve includes churches serving churches.

> Am I not an apostle? am I not free? have I not seen Jesus Christ our Lord? are not ye my work in the Lord? (1 Cor. 9:1).

> 1 Now concerning the collection for the saints, as I have given order to the churches of Galatia, even so do ye. 2 Upon the first day of the week let every one of you lay by him in store, as God hath prospered him, that there be no gatherings when I come. 3 And when I come, whomsoever ye shall approve by your letters, them will I send to bring your liberality unto Jerusalem? (1 Cor. 16:1-3).

> 1 Moreover, brethren, we do you to wit of the grace of God bestowed on the churches of Macedonia; 2 How that in a great trial of affliction the abundance of their joy and their deep poverty abounded unto the riches of their liberality. 3 For to their power, I bear record, yea, and beyond their power they

---

53 Anthony C. Thiselton, *I Corinthians, A Shorter Exegetical and Pastoral Commentary* (Eerdmans Publishing Co., 2006), 299-300.

were willing of themselves; 4 Praying us with much entreaty that we would receive the gift, and take upon us the fellowship of the ministering to the saints...24 Wherefore shew ye to them, and before the churches, the proof of your love, and of our boasting on your behalf (2 Cor. 8:1-4; 24).

Diaconal work, the work of serving, is to be a characteristic trait of every follower of Christ. These verses show us that diaconal work calls out to local churches to be ministering to other local churches in need.

In the preceding verses, the church in Corinth is instructed, by no one less than the apostle Paul, to commit themselves to ministering to the needs of another church, the church in Jerusalem. With apostolic authority Paul calls upon them, as he did the churches in Galatia, to help the Jerusalem church in their time of suffering. He continues his plea in the second letter and points to the church in Macedonia as an example of one church helping another church in need.

This picture of a struggling church is far more common in other parts of the world than it is here in the United States. Churches in countries that are ravaged by war, famine, and religious persecution understand what it is to be in need far better than we do. Although persecution and suffering seem so far removed from us, because of technology the world is becoming a smaller place and we see and hear of the needs of suffering people almost immediately. As church leaders, we are constantly made aware of the suffering church of Christ (Smyrna churches).

In his letters to the Corinthian church, Paul is not afraid to impose on their collective conscience the responsibility to respond to a distant church in need. He intensifies the imposition in several ways:

- apostolic authority (1 Cor.1:1; 9:1; 2 Cor. 1:1)
- a prescribed pattern for giving (1 Cor. 16:2a)

- a reminder that everything they have has been given by God and therefore not their own (1 Cor. 16:2b)

- an expectation of generous giving (1 Cor. 16:3)

- the selfless example of a poor and afflicted church helping others (2 Cor. 8:1-6)

- an appeal to prove their love for God and his people (2 Cor. 8:8, 24)

- the example of Jesus Christ (2 Cor. 8:9), an example he expects them to copy

All of this is to motivate them to give generously to relieve the needs of the saints in Jerusalem. The work he is calling them to, as a church, is the work of "ministering" (*diakonia*), *serving the needs of another church.* (8:4; 9:1).[54]

We're sure that some struggled with Paul's pressure to contribute to a church that was primarily Jewish. This was the same church that was reluctant at first to invite the Gentiles into the grace of the Gospel. The believers at Corinth must now accept the Jewish believers as their brothers and sisters in Christ. They must also be willing to accept the responsibility to help them in their need.

Think of it. This needy church was well beyond their local church community, outside their cultural context, far removed from them geographically, and it was a body of people whom they may never meet in this life. However, we don't find Paul pausing to discuss these potential bones of contention. He simply presents the need and exhorts them to do the right thing, which is to give to help relieve their brothers and sisters in Christ. For Paul, it was both a privilege and a responsibility to help the family of God in crisis, no matter their location, their language, culture, history, or color of skin. The family of God has no borders.

---

54 Strong, *Strong's Exhaustive Concordance of the English Bible*, under 'diakonia.'

Paul understood that no one church could possibly supply every-thing or solve every problem the church in Jerusalem was facing. That is why he encourages them *to partner with other churches*, with each church doing their part.

We realize that much wisdom must be used in determining who your church should help, along with the questions of when, how, and with whom you should partner. These decisions are not made without much research and prayer. At the same time, while being careful, we do not want an opportunity to slip away simply because we are not ready or willing to respond. All decisions must follow biblical order and any oversight that has been established in your church. However, the teaching of the New Testament is clear. We ought to be practicing *church-to-church diaco-nal ministry* on behalf of our brothers and sisters in need. Wisdom, yes. Indifference, no.

SUMMARY

In this first section, we focused on the value of serving by recognizing that it is a *universal call*. First, *every believer* is called to embrace the role of a servant as a *binding duty*, an *ordinance* to be obeyed. Second, we are to *follow in Our Master's footsteps*, the greatest servant of all. Third, God gives *gifts* for the specific purpose of serving others. Fourth, serving is to be *a lifestyle* that inspires others to join the workforce. Fifth, we see the example of an *entire family* habitually serving others. And sixth, churches are called to *serve other churches*.

We cannot have a right estimate of the *value of the office* of the dea-con until we understand, and have a right estimate of, the *value of serving* in general. The fact that God has made serving others a *universal calling* is proof enough that it is *a valuable calling*.

SECOND SECTION:
Serving is a Necessary Call

In this section, we want to highlight the *value* of serving others by pointing to the *necessity* of serving others. There is an understood relationship between *necessary* and *value*. Webster defines *necessary* as "what must be, cannot be otherwise, indispensable"[55] and *valuable* as "having value or worth; having some good qualities which are useful and esteemed; precious; deserving esteem."[56] Anything that is deemed to be necessary must have a measure of value. Water, food, and social interaction are necessary for physical and mental health and are therefore indispensable or valuable for human existence. The fact that we might not like a particular food or the company of a particular person is beside the point; food and interaction with others are *necessary* and therefore *valuable*. *Necessity* points to *value*!

In the same way, if serving others is a biblical necessity, then it has value. But more to the point of this chapter in general and this section in particular, we are highlighting the fact that the work of the deacon is necessary and therefore valuable.

We trust Chapter 1 left everyone fully persuaded that the meaning of the word *deacon* is "servant." Based on the meaning of the word, their job description is pretty well set in stone! They are to function according to their name, and we cannot change their function without changing their name. When a deacon checks his "to do" list, serving is not just one thing among many things; it's the main thing. He cannot fulfill his calling unless he's serving. Just as it is the calling and duty of the pastor to care *primarily* for the spiritual needs of the flock, so it is the calling and duty of the deacon to care *primarily* for the physical and material needs of the flock. Both

---

55 Webster, *American Dictionary of the English Language* (1828), under "necessary."
56 Ibid., under "valuable."

offices are *necessary*, and therefore both offices are *valuable* as the church strives to honor Christ in all she does. *Necessity* points to *value*!

Think about your own church. Are the deacons excited, thriving, and accomplishing much in the arena of service? If so, they no doubt sense how valuable their work is to God, their church, and those they serve. In other words, they know their work is necessary. Having a sense of the necessity of an activity, that it is absolutely indispensable, gives a sense of the value of the activity. If deacons are to be effective, and properly valued, every-one—pastors, deacons, and the entire church—must first understand that *the work is absolutely necessary.*

In order to stress the *value* of this office, we are going to give you *five reasons* why it is *necessary* for deacons to function as servant leaders in the church. While these may initially stretch your thinking, we believe they will prove to be important as you evaluate the *necessity* of serving in general and the importance (value) of designated servant leaders in particular.

First Reason the Office is Necessary: The Ascension of Christ

The Great Servant, Jesus Christ, has ascended into heaven. The One who came to serve, not be served, left earth and is now seated at the right hand of the Father. At the risk of stating the obvious, he's no longer here. Who then will pick up the robe of the servant and lay down his life for others? Who will deny himself, take up his cross, and follow in His footsteps to serve and not be served? While it is a universal call, the Father, in His wisdom and mercy, created a specific office in the church to make sure that someone is there to tie on the apron of a servant after the departure of Jesus. The office that carries on the ministry of mercy in the stead of Jesus is the office of the deacon.

That Christ came to minister primarily on a spiritual plane is beyond question. But that does not diminish the equally true fact that He was concerned about our physical well-being as well. How often did Jesus show a genuine concern for people's physical needs, like food and water? How often did He show sympathy for the sick and grieving? His own disciples carried a purse of money to care for the poor. Even at the cross in a time of personal crisis, He tasked John with looking after Mary.

A unique relationship exists between the servant work of the deacons and the servant work that Jesus Christ performed while He walked on the earth. Christ put into motion a standard for all servants and then entrusted it to His church, specifically deacons. Deacons have the unique privilege of being called to follow Christ and the standard He set. Is it possible to have a church without deacons? Yes, under certain situations, a church may find itself without qualified or willing candidates. However, eventually the church will be hindered by their absence (Acts 6:1-7). When something is necessary, it is "indispensable," "cannot be otherwise," and "must be." The servant ministry of the deacon is necessary if the work of *the ascended Lord* is to carry on as He planned.

Additionally, the *necessity* of this office is clearly expressed in Paul's letter to Timothy regarding church order and structure (1 Tim. 3:8-13). The church is to appoint two officers and two only: elders and deacons. The elders care primarily for the spiritual needs of the body, while deacons care primarily for the physical needs of the body. Are we to think that God would require the church to have both offices if they were not absolutely necessary? If God in His wisdom and mercy created a separate office to carry on the servant ministry of *the ascended Lord*, He must consider that work *necessary*, or, "what must be."

Jesus Himself stressed that His own work was diaconal in nature. In Mark 10:42-45, Jesus used the word *minister* twice in verses 43 and 45, and the word *ministered* in verse 45. These are the Greek words *diakonos* and *diakoneo*.[57] We mentioned earlier that Peter summarized the life of

---

57 Strong, *Strong's Exhaustive Concordance of the English Bible*, under 'diakonos' and 'dia-

Christ in Acts 10:38-39. Peter tells us that Jesus of Nazareth "went about doing good, and healing all that were oppressed of the devil" (v. 38). Joseph Alexander explains, "not merely doing right, but doing favors, showing mercy."[58] The Gospels make it clear that Jesus Christ was actively showing grace and mercy to those around Him, and no doubt some of the good deeds involved meeting physical and emotional needs. Wherever He went during His days on the earth, He "went about doing good." The words "went about" are literally "went through." Calvin comments on Christ's going about:

> The going of Christ is taken for the course of his calling, as if he should say that he fulfilled his function until the time appointed before. The similitude is taken from travelers which go forward in their journey until they come unto the appointed place; although he showeth therewithal that he walked through Judea in three years, so that no corner was without his good deeds.[59]

TWO BRIEF OBSERVATIONS

First, this shows that doing good was not an occasional event for Jesus. Doing good was something He always did as He "went through" His earthly journey. Although it seems trite to say, doing good was His "lifestyle." Secondly, it demonstrates how often Jesus was moved with compassion by the damages of sin on the physical body. He took genuine interest in the whole man. Whether it was hunger (feeding thousands), thirst (a cup of water in His name), despair (the madman of the tombs), or physical

58 Joseph A. Alexander, *Commentary on the Acts of the Apostles* (Minneapolis, MN: Klock and Klock, 1980), 411.

59 *Calvin's Commentary upon the Acts of the Apostles* (Edinburgh: Calvin Translation Society, 1844), 444.

disability (the man at the pool of Siloam), these and similar deeds of mercy so impacted Peter that he summarizes Jesus' activities by saying, "[H]e went about doing good."

It seems like a good time to ask, "Who will fill the vacuum left by the Great Deacon, Jesus Christ?" Everyone in the church should be ready with the answer, "It's a *universal call* to serve and everyone must fill the vacuum He left *when he ascended into heaven.*" However, we also know from the events that took place in Acts 6 and Paul's letters to Timothy that Jesus Christ made sure this *indispensable* work would get done by appointing deacons to watch over "this business." (Acts 6:3).

What we see, then, is that *when Christ ascended* to the right hand of the father, He did not abandon the needy among us. The appointed means of demonstrating His compassion for the sick, poor, widows, orphans, and others is the church, His body. We are His hands, His feet, His voice, His heart. The church is to carry on His work until He returns to claim His bride. And this work is to be overseen by the two offices of the church. As the two officers of Christ's church effectively manage their respective spheres of responsibility, they demonstrate Christ to the church and the world.

No, Christ did not abandon this *necessary* work when *He ascended to heaven.* He lovingly delegated it to others. He delegated it to all disciples generally but then deacons specifically. It is important for the church to see their deacons fulfilling a ministry that Christ Himself performed first and then entrusted the oversight to them. As long as the risen and *ascended Christ* remains in heaven, the work of the deacon remains *necessary.*

Therefore, as a church grows in their understanding of the *value of serving* generally, the more they will *value* the office of the deacon and hopefully see it as *necessary* (indispensable) for the general health, spiritual development, and overall effectiveness of their local church.

Second Reason the Office is Necessary: The Power of the Ascended Lord

It is an undeniable fact that God conquered His enemies through the work of His servant. He openly displayed to heaven and earth His power to overcome evil through the work of the servant lamb (Rom. 8:31-36; 2 Cor. 12:9-10). The world cannot understand how *power* and *servant* can come together in one person. *A powerful servant?* Yet that is exactly what we find in the person and work of Christ.

In the forty days between the resurrection and ascension, Jesus met with His disciples and told them, "[A]ll power has been given unto me in heaven and earth." As the risen Christ speaks, this *power* is ready to be unleashed on behalf of his church. He then tells them, "[G]o ye therefore." Christ is saying, "Having finished the work the Father gave me, and having received all authority and *power* on the completion of my mission, I am now authorized to empower you to go to the world in my name and in my power." He then instructs them to wait in Jerusalem until they receive power from the Holy Spirit. But in order for the Holy Spirit to come with power, something had to happen first. That's right—He must go away (John 16:7). What does that mean? He's referring to His ascension into heaven, the great coronation day of the victorious Son, when He is seated at the right hand of the Father (Acts 2:33; 7:55; Col. 3:1; Heb. 8:1).

That Christ is presently in a position of *exalted authority and power* is one of the most comforting truths in the New Testament. And praise be to God, he is not stingy with that power. All that the church does in obedience to the Lord is the result of His *power* at work in us. *This is ascension power!*

This is expressly taught in Ephesians 1:22, where Paul states concerning Christ, "And gave him to be the head over all things to the church." Eadie writes, "He is its head in a near, tender, necessary, and indissoluble relation. His intelligence, his love, his power, therefore, secure to the church that all things will 'work together for good.'" He goes on to say, "The history of the church is a proof extending through eighteen centuries; a proof so often tested, and by such opposite processes, is to gather irresistible strength with its age; a proof varied, ramified, prolonged, and unique, that the exalted Jesus is head over all things to the church."[60] Amen!

His *authority and power* were on display in the apostolic period and on into the following ages. As the Gospel spread and sinners were converted, baptized, transformed, and preserved from falling, a witness was given to *the power of the ascended Christ*. We can rest assured that *the power of the ascended Christ* was not for an earlier age only but for every age. Jesus concludes his final words to the disciples by promising, "[L]o, I am with you always, even unto the end of the world." And He punctuates the promise with a final "Amen."

It was, and is, Christ's intention that the church should continue to experience results similar to the former days. What kind of results? Sinners converted, baptized, discipled, and obedient to all of His commands. But how? By ourselves, we are powerless. The answer is, by His power! We are His servants, and He has given us a small measure of His power through the work of His Spirit (Eph. 1:19-23). He went so far as to promise that His disciples would do "greater works" than even He had done (John 14:12).

When Jesus informed them that it was necessary for Him to go away, perhaps they panicked. How could they possibly do what He did, and even more, without Him by their side? The answer lies in the words "because I go unto my Father." The only explanation as to how it would be possible for them to do "greater works" is the promise of His Holy Spirit. By faith we can do greater things *because* Christ has ascended to His ordained position of authority at the right hand of His Father to exercise his power throughout the ages.

---

60 John Eadie, *Commentary on the Epistle to the Ephesians* (Minneapolis: James and Klock Christian Publishing Co., 1977), 107.

Unpacking the full meaning of this, and why the disciples are able to do "greater works," is beyond the pale of this chapter. However, we understand this promise—we must not limit the "greater works" to the spiritual victories and the progress of the church triumphant. Surely, the "greater works" also include a variety of servant ministries that follow in the footsteps of Christ. Christ himself went about "doing good." To quote Alexander again, "[N]ot merely doing right, but doing favors, showing mercy." As already discussed, Jesus spent much of His time helping people with various kinds of needs. Furthermore, He revealed that caring for the physical needs of people along the "journey" is in perfect harmony with His Father's will (e.g., the good Samaritan). There was never a time that the Father was disappointed with the Son. There was never a time that Jesus did anything that did not glorify the Father. Therefore, this must have included His compassionate acts of kindness. In fact, these compassionate, practical acts of Jesus were frequently used to advance His mission in the world, never hinder it.

We strongly suggest that the diaconal ministry of the first disciples, and later of the entire church, is included in the "greater works." Through serving one another in general, and through the servant ministry of deacons particularly, the church manifests *the power of the ascended Christ*. The resurrection and ascension mark the dawning of a new day in God's plan of redemption.

Surely, every church desires the power of God to rest on them more fully. The incarnate Son revealed the power of God in His own life through becoming a humble servant. That's exactly what diaconal ministry is all about, and that's why the servant work of the deacon is so *necessary*. Diaconal work is a channel for *the power of the ascended Christ* to rest on the church as it serves in a fallen world. The Gospel compels us to look out over the broken and shattered lives around us and follow the example of Christ's compassion toward those who are in the church, the community, and beyond.

Third Reason the Office is Necessary: The Benevolent Nature of God

What do we mean when we say that God is *benevolent,* and what exactly does it have to do with the work of a deacon? First, some of the older theologians made a distinction between *benevolence* and *beneficence.* J. L. Dagg, a 19th-century Baptist theologian, when explaining the Goodness of God stated, "Benevolence is love in intention, or disposition; beneficence is love in action, or conferring its benefits."[61] So, benevolence has to do with one's internal attitude, or disposition, whereas beneficence has to do with outward, observable actions. When God acts in love, the action flows from a heart of love. Together, the heart and the action point to the attribute of goodness. Webster seems to combine the two notions when he defines *benevolence* as "active kindness."[62]

Getting back to God, He has both a disposition to do what is good for us and actually does what is good, showering us with goodness and kindness (Matt. 7:11; Luke 12:32; 1 John 4:9). Why does God load us with these benefits? Because He loves us (Eph. 2:4). It is impossible to separate His *benevolent* intention and disposition toward the objects of His love, from His *beneficent* acts of kindness, mercy, and grace (Eph. 2:4-7; Titus 3:4, 5). While these two terms are often used as synonyms, the bottom line is, *God has a benevolent nature!*

This attribute of God is without question a key to understanding who God is and what He is like. As we grow in our understanding of this generous quality of God's nature, our hearts will grow correspondingly in joyful gratitude toward God and tender mercy toward the afflicted; "Blessed are the merciful for they shall obtain mercy" (Matt. 5:7).

---

61 John L. Dagg, *A Treatise on Church Order* (1858; repr. Harrisonburg, VA: Sprinkle Publications, 1982), 76.

62 Webster, *American Dictionary of the English Language* (1828), under 'benevolence.'

Additionally, a fuller apprehension of God's *benevolence* tends to purify our motives as we serve Him. When we meditate on God's loving disposition toward us, we learn to serve more out of disinterested selfless love and less out of self-serving interests (Eph. 4:32). One of the accusations God pinpoints against rebellious Israel was their disobedience in caring for the poor, orphans, and widows. Why was this so egregious? Their behavior, fueled by a lack of concern, failed to accurately represent the goodness, love, and kindness of their God—in other words, His benevolent nature.

The active kindness of God is manifest in its full glory when He gave His Son for us. Paul wrote to Titus, "But when the *goodness* and *loving kindness* of God our Savior appeared, he saved us, not because of works done by us in righteousness, but according to his own mercy, by the washing of regeneration and renewal of the Holy Spirit, whom he poured out on us richly through Jesus Christ our Savior" (Titus 3:4-6, ESV, emphasis added). As we think about the great gift of His Son, we are meant to be moved not just in our love for God, but in our love for one another. John wrote, "Beloved, if God so loved us, we ought also to love one another," (1 John 4:11) and Paul exhorts, "And be ye kind one to another, tenderhearted, forgiving one another, even as God for Christ's sake hath forgiven you" (Eph. 4:32). We are meant to be vessels of the *benevolent nature of God* to others.

Jesus himself demonstrated *the benevolent nature of God* throughout His earthly ministry. How could he do otherwise? He was God incarnate. That being said, Jesus made it clear He came to reveal His Father. Jesus was saying, "Look at me, my life, my actions, and you will see the Father" (John 14:9-10). It may be said that, when we see Jesus in the four Gospels, we see the clearest revelation of the nature of God that mortal men have ever seen (John 1:14; Heb. 1:3; Col. 1:15-19). Therefore, when we look at Jesus, it is no surprise that a leading characteristic of his public ministry was his "active kindness," (Acts 10:38) and in that kindness we see *the benevolent nature of the Father.*

Additionally, we find Jesus commending benevolence, or kindness in action, in Matthew 25. Speaking of the coming judgment when "the Son of man shall come in his glory," Jesus warns "he shall set the sheep on his right hand, but the goats on the left" (vv. 31, 33). As He describes that day in figurative language, He is very clear about what distinguishes the sheep from the goats. The distinguishing quality found in the sheep is their *benevolent nature* (love in intention) coupled with beneficence (love in action). They (believers) fed Him, gave Him drink, took Him in, clothed Him, brought Him medicine, and visited Him in prison. In short, they showed *Him* kindness through actively serving *others*, those whom he calls "my brethren" (v. 40).

Serving others is how the active kindness of God is both demonstrated and funneled to the church and the world. Jesus revealed through His own life of sacrificial service and plain teaching that *benevolence is not optional—it is necessary!*

This brings us to the primary point: the *necessity* of diaconal work. Jesus, the kindest person who ever graced this earth, ascended and left the work of manifesting the kindness of God to us. While all of us are responsible to display this quality of God to one another, the office of the deacon was established to make sure that *God's benevolent nature* continues in the church and through the church until Christ, the ascended Head of the church, is revealed from heaven. The office of the deacon in general, and each deacon individually, is called to manifest the *benevolence of God*, in Christ's stead!

Fourth Reason the Office is Necessary: The Wisdom of God

Before we attempt to connect *the wisdom of God to the value of serving,* and of those who serve, we want to give a simple definition of the *wisdom of God*. There is always a risk in giving a simple definition of anything relating to God, especially when it comes to His nature and attributes. Given that there are many, many layers to the *wisdom of God*, think of this as merely a "top layer" definition. Here it is: *the wisdom of God* is God using His infinite knowledge to skillfully work out His eternal plans throughout creation and through all ages. (Stephen Charnock would cringe if he read this brief definition![63])

A special manifestation of *His wisdom* is His eternal plan of redemption (1 Cor. 1:21-24). Wisely and intricately interwoven with the plan of redemption is God's plan and intended function of His visible body on earth, the local church. These two eternal plans are beautifully woven together and unquestionably reveal the manifold *wisdom of God.*

Paul brings these two eternal plans together in his letter to the Ephesians in Chapter 3. In words that are both breathtaking and mind-numbing, he writes:

And to make all men see what is the fellowship of the mystery, which from the beginning of the world hath been hid in God, who created all things by Jesus Christ: To the intent that now unto the principalities and powers in heavenly places might be known by the church the manifold wisdom of God. According to the eternal purpose which he purposed in Christ Jesus our Lord (9-11).

This is not the place to fully exposit this text, but we must point out that the "manifold" or the multifaceted, multidimensional, illustrious, and brilliant *wisdom of God* is on display. As a many faceted diamond acts as a prism to refract light into the full spectrum of colors, so the manifold *wisdom of God* breaks out across the universe like a cosmic rainbow to the glory of the One who planned it all. To what end or intent has He done this? That the angels gathered in heavenly places might behold His wisdom! And how will His infinite, eternal, and immutable wisdom be displayed? By the church! Oh, if His Word was not true, we would scarcely dare to

---

63 Stephen Charnock (1628-1660), Puritan author of *The Existence and Attributes of God*, a classic work.

think it. By the church! Behold the wisdom of weaving the plan of redemption with His plan for the church. The way that God designed the church and gave His Son to be the Head, the Cornerstone, the Bridegroom of the church, and gave His Spirit to the church for enlightenment and empowerment, and ordained the church to be the pillar and ground of truth, and that the evil serpent himself can do nothing to prevent the church from kicking down the dark gates of hell does without question point wholly to the omniscient *wisdom of God* (Eph. 2:19-22; 3:10; 4:1-32; 1 Tim. 3:15-16). According to our simple definition above, God is using His infinite knowledge to skillfully work out His eternal plans throughout His creation. Behold it. Admire it. Adore the One who planned it all.

Now, to the point: the indelible thumbprint of God is on *every* part of the church and displays *His wisdom*. And this obviously includes the office and function of the deacon. The office itself, and the calling of God on those who serve in the office, should cause every member of the church to pause and admire the genius of the One who designed it all. *What inscrutable wisdom* is on display in the structure of the church! Every part of his temple (1 Cor. 3:16) is to reflect *the wisdom* of its architect. The flaws of the visible church on earth are due to our ongoing struggles with our sinful natures. The design, however, truly displays *the wisdom of God*. Oh, that we longed to reveal Him more fully and reflect *His wisdom* more clearly.

In our hometown, there is a house designed by the celebrated architect Frank Lloyd Wright. It sits on the western bank of the Rock River. If you take a scenic ride on the city-owned paddle boat, *The Spirit of the Rock*, the captain will proudly point out this architectural landmark. As you view the house he called "my little gem" along the riverfront, a brief history of Wright's work, distinguishing characteristics, and some thoughts on his genius are offered. This information is very important. What would be the point of drawing our attention to this historical landmark but say nothing about the architect? "Look over there, folks; isn't that a really cool house?" The whole point of calling our attention to the house is to consider the brilliance of the designer. IT'S A HOUSE THAT FRANK LLOYD WRIGHT BUILT!

In an infinitely more significant vein, Jesus said, "I will build my church" (Matt. 16:18). Not only will He build it, but He will be the Cornerstone of the structure (Eph. 2:20). As the Builder and Cornerstone of the church, our Lord has left the thumb print of *God's Wisdom* on every part. Every line on the blueprint of this beautiful institution is significant. Nothing was left out. Nothing was left to chance. Nothing was unimportant. And everything fits together perfectly (Eph. 2:21; 4:16). That being true, when a church is planted and follows His blueprint, one of the distinguishing features that points to the unmatchable *genius and wisdom of the designer* is the office and work of the deacon. The very fact that the *all-wise* God gave the office and work of the deacon to the church is proof enough that the work is *necessary*. Hopefully, the work of the deacon causes both the church and the world to admire the builder of the church (Matt. 5:16) and to exclaim, "LOOK! IT'S THE HOUSE THAT CHRIST BUILT!"

Fifth Reason the Office is Necessary: The Need for Servant Role Models

Christ Himself modeled servanthood when He washed His disciples' feet (John 13:1-17). Reading between the lines, if Christ's followers ever needed a pattern to follow, an example to point the way, it's in the arena of service. It doesn't come naturally. Therefore, it has to be *modeled*. It is for this reason the church needs men and women to exemplify Christ-like servanthood, examples the church can look up to and follow, those who are willing and humbly say, "Look at me. Walk where I walk. Go where I go. Do what I do." Thank God there are some. But the truth is, there are not many. It is in the office of the deacon, however, when functioning according to the design of God, where *role models* for serving others are to be found.

If any man ever understood the importance of godly examples to the life of the church, it was the apostle Paul. He did not just suggest it; he shouted it!

- Wherefore I beseech you, be a follower of me (1 Cor. 4:16).

- Be ye followers of me, even as I am of Christ (1 Cor. 11:1).

- Be followers together of me (Phil. 3:17).

- For yourselves know how ye ought to follow us (2 Thess. 3:7).

- To make ourselves an ensample unto you to follow us (2 Thess. 3:9).

The word *follow* as seen in the above verses means to "mimic" or "imitate."[64] Paul was not satisfied with just putting his own life out in front for others to follow; he challenged others to do the same. Paul wrote to Timothy and exhorted him, "Be thou an example of the believers" (1 Tim. 4:12). He told Titus, "In all things showing thyself a pattern of good works" (Titus 2:7). With the word *pattern*, Paul was calling upon Titus to "model . . . a visual form to be copied."[65]

The responsibility to be an *example* is not limited to the apostles and first century church leaders. While all are called to be good role *models* of Christian behavior, it must be true of the officers of the church. Truly there is a desperate need today for men and women who are so devoted to Christ that they challenge others to "imitate" their servant lifestyle. Both the pastors and deacons are meant to be the standard by which the members measure their development in Christ-like virtue. In fact, church members have a right to expect their officers to set an *example* for them to follow. Anyone who is unwilling to be an *example* should never be promoted to a position in any office. The servant ministry of the deacon is therefore *necessary* because all the members of the church *need role models* for serving others.

---

64 Strong, *Strong's Exhaustive Concordance of the English Bible*, under "follow."
65 Ibid., under "pattern."

May God help us to never diminish *the value of the deacons* in our churches, but rather foster a deep appreciation for their "indispensable" work. Like Paul did with Stephanas, hold them in high regard, lift them up, and exhort others to *follow* in their footsteps (1 Cor. 16:15-18).

In this section, we offered *five reasons* why the work of the deacon is necessary:

- The *ascension of Christ* left a vacuum, and the church *needs* leaders to step up and serve the physical needs of others in His place.

- The office is *necessary* as a channel for *the power of the ascended Lord* to manifest itself to the church and the watching world.

- The work of a deacon is kindness in action and as such reveals *the benevolent nature of God.*

- The *wisdom of God* is seen in the intricate design of the church, requiring us to see that every part is absolutely *necessary.*

- The church *needs role models* to serve as a pattern for others to follow.

Our hope is that these five reasons for *the necessity of the office* will, in some measure, cause every church to appreciate more fully the office that is given to oversee the work of service.

THIRD SECTION:
Serving is a Noble Call

Up to this point, we have tried to impress upon you *the value of serving* by seeing it as both a *universal* and a *necessary* call. Finally, we want to consider the *nobility of the call.* By *noble* we mean "elevated, dignified, great."[66] But, you might ask, how can serving others be considered dignified or

---

66 Ibid., under "noble."

noble? It is a *noble* work because none other than Christ Himself took the form of a servant and became the Suffering Servant of God. That is both amazing and humbling! He who "thought it not robbery to be equal with God" (Phil. 2:6) nevertheless "made himself of no reputation, and took upon him the form of a servant" (v. 7). In fact, everything that Christ came to do He did as the servant of God. The King of Heaven, having a glory equal to the glory of the Father, became a servant! Think of it. God incarnate came to serve others to the glory of the Father. And then to realize that we are called to model our lives after Christ, to serve as He served—oh, what an elevated, dignified, and noble calling indeed! The deacon's work in particular, a work of service, is *noble* because it is patterned after the entire life and work of Christ.

The *nobility* of serving others has been misunderstood by both the world and the church. The world's view of greatness is measured by having power over others, personal recognition, or the accumulation of earthly things. This reminds us again of Plato's question, "How can a man be happy when he has to serve someone?" He couldn't conceive of a happy servant nor can the world around us. Serving? That's menial, demeaning, and depressing work.

Sadly, all too often the church's understanding of greatness is influenced by the "me first" world in which we live. Leadership in the church is often confused with having the authority to Lord over the flock and *be* served rather than *to* serve. Yet, God's standard of greatness is in direct conflict with this self-serving attitude. In Christ's church, everything is to be different. When the disciples of Christ argued over who would be the greatest in His kingdom, He said, "[I]f any man desires to be first the same shall be last of all, and servant of all" (Mark 9:35). George C. Fuller acknowledged this conflict of values in an article he wrote on the office of the deacon. In response to Plato's question, "How can a man be happy when he has to serve someone," Fuller writes, "For the Greeks, menial service was not dignified, surely not to be sought as a way of life. But Jesus changed all that, radically reversing the world's standards. He did not make some changes or adjustments in a well-entrenched system. He turned the whole thing upside down, making as it were, the first last and the last first. That kind of change does not allow for compromise."[67]

Here we are in the 21st-century, and Plato's skewed values are as alive as ever. Happy through serving? This is a perplexing paradox to the world. The world screams, "Me first." However, in the church, we "live by dying," "gain by giving," and become "great by serving."

This radical others-oriented commitment is rapidly fading from the landscape of the modern church. A by-product of living in the world is the constant danger of being of the world. It's a sad fact of history that cultural influences inevitably find their way into the church. While looking through the lens of "man-centeredness," an optical illusion occurs. We think the way to happiness is through promoting and exalting ourselves. This lens dupes us into believing a lie. In reality, at the end of this path is sorrow and the ultimate loneliness. True happiness comes through serving others: first God and then our fellow man.

The problem with Plato, the world, and even many within the church is they are looking at serving through the wrong lens. The only way we can have a clear picture of the *nobility* of service is to look through the lens of the Scripture. And what do we see? We see Christ, the living embodiment of what it means to grow in favor with both God and man, serving others! There is no better way to understand the *nobility* of serving others than focusing our vision on the life of Christ (Phil. 2:5). He dignified this humble role and made service something to be honored and even something to be sought after by God's people.

At the beginning of this section, we posed the question, "How can serving others be considered dignified or *noble?*" Our answer is, how can

67 George C. Fuller, "The High Calling of Deacon," *The Presbyterian Guardian*, November 1978, 5-9.

serving others *not* be considered *noble* when we are "looking unto Jesus the author and finisher of our faith" (Heb. 12:2). The warp and woof of Christ's incarnation was to serve others (Matt. 20:28).[68] Since Jesus Christ dignified and exalted the work of serving others, and we are to see the *nobility of diaconal ministry* in the church, it seems appropriate that we examine this aspect of his life a little closer.

The Old Testament declares that the coming Messiah would be a servant, while the New Testament clarifies what this means. The Old Testament predicted that he would come as a humble servant. The New Testament clarifies this prediction when He humbled Himself and became "a servant" (Phil. 2:8). The prediction and the fulfillment regarding Christ's ministry make it clear this was not a last-minute adjustment based on unexpected circumstances. This was God's plan for His Son from the beginning.

To deepen our appreciation for the predictions that the "Christ of God" (Luke 9:20) would be "God's servant," let's look at a couple of Old Testament passages. Our hope is that, by looking at these servant predictions concerning Christ, it will deepen our appreciation for the *nobility of serving.*

Christ, the Servant of God, Isaiah 42:1-7

Behold my servant, whom I uphold; mine elect, in whom my soul delighteth; I have put my spirit upon him: he shall bring forth judgment to the Gentiles. 2 He shall not cry, nor lift up, nor cause his voice to be heard in the street. 3 A bruised reed shall he not break, and the smoking flax shall he not quench: he shall bring forth judgment unto truth. 4 He shall not fail nor be discouraged, till he have set judgment in the earth: and the isles shall wait for his law. 5 Thus saith God the Lord,

---

68 In weaving, the threads that run lengthways are the warp, and the treads that run cross-ways are the woof. Together they make up the fabric and give the garment its strength and stability. Here it speaks of that which makes up the fabric of Christ's incarnation.

he that created the heavens, and stretched them out; he that spread forth the earth, and that which cometh out of it; he that giveth breath unto the people upon it, and spirit to them that walk therein: 6 I The Lord have called thee in righteousness, and will hold thine hand, and will keep thee, and give thee for a covenant of the people, for a light of the Gentiles; 7 To open the blind eyes, to bring out the prisoners from the prison, and them that sit in darkness out of the prison house.

This prediction concerning Christ begins with the word *behold*. It is a call to all who hear these words to sit up and take notice, to pay attention to what follows. The prophet is drawing our attention to something unusual and worthy of our consideration. So, what is it? What are we to behold? It is the *servant of God*. God's servant will distinguish himself from all other servants. From the passage, we draw out a list of facts concerning God's servant:

- God's servant gives his life to serve the will of God.
- God's servant is sustained and empowered by God.
- God's servant delights the soul of God.
- God's servant will succeed in his mission for God.

These prophetic words predict the success of God's Son, the Servant above all servants, in whom God's "soul delighteth." Oh, the exalted, *noble* privilege of humbling one's self and being a servant of God!

Christ, the Servant of God, Isaiah 52:13-14

13 Behold, my servant shall deal prudently, he shall be exalted and extolled, and be very high. 14 As many were astonied at thee; his visage was so marred more than any man, and his form more than the sons of men.

Once again, we read the word *behold*. What does the prophet want us to see about the Servant in this text?

- God's Servant will exercise wisdom in fulfilling his calling.

- God's Servant will be exalted through service.

- God's Servant will sacrifice his own life.

These two Old Testament Scriptures declare the nature of Christ's calling. He was destined to be a Servant. Not just any servant, but God's "Special Servant"! As such, serving would be the nature and function of His earthly ministry.

When we turn to the New Testament, the Old Testament predictions concerning His calling are clarified. Every step, every word, every action of Christ brings Isaiah's prophecies to life. The Servant of God has arrived.

We want to draw your attention to two obvious things concerning the life of Jesus Christ. First, we find that Jesus willingly embraced His Father's will for His life: to be His Servant. Second, He calls upon His followers to imitate His life of service. By His actions, God's Servant has made serving a *noble* calling.

25 Ye know that the princes of the Gentiles exercise dominion over them, and they that are great exercise authority upon them. 26 But it shall not be so among you: but whosoever will be great among you, let him be your minister; 27 Even as the Son of Man came not to be ministered unto, but to minister, and to give his life a ransom for many (Matthew 20:25-28).

Notice seven very important words: "it shall not be so among you." Jesus rewrote the book on greatness. *Greatness, honor, and nobility* are not found in the word *dominion*. They are not found in the word *authority*.

Behold! They are found in the word *minister, diakonos.*[69] Interestingly, this is the first time this Greek word is used in Matthew's Gospel. It seems significant that its first use is in connection with Christ calling His disciples to be servants even as the Son of Man, the Servant of God, came "not to be ministered unto, but to minister."

Here in Matthew 20, and throughout his earthly ministry, Jesus Christ paints a verbal "self-portrait" of His life. He intentionally paints Himself as a willing *diakonos* or minister. Now that's an accurate picture of Jesus—an intentional servant. It is imperative we see that Jesus fulfilled His mission by willingly becoming the Servant of God. If we don't understand this, then we don't understand His calling. And if we don't understand His calling, then how can we ever understand ours?

All disciples generally, and deacons specifically, are called to the same ministry: to give their lives in the service of others. It is only as we look at His life through the lens of God's Word that we discover the nobility of being a servant. The words of Charles H. Spurgeon concerning our Lord's disciples in Matthew 20 are worth repeating. He wrote:

> They were confounding his kingdom with the ordinary government of men, and therefore they dreamed of being great, and exercising dominion in his name; but he wished them to correct their ideas, and turn their thoughts another way. It was true, that to be his followers was a highly honorable thing, and made them partakers of a kingdom; but it was not like earthly kingdoms. In the great Gentile monarchies, princes ruled by authority, force, and pomp; but in his kingdom the rule would be one of love, and the dignity would be that of service. He who could serve most would be the greatest. The lowliest would be the most honoured: the most self-sacrificing would have the most power. Whenever we see the nobles of earth contending

---

69 Strong, *Strong's Exhaustive Concordance of the English Bible,* under "minister."

for precedence, we should hear our Master say, *'But it shall not be so among you.'* We must forever quit hunting after honour, office, power, and influence. If we aim at greatness at all, it must be by being great in service, becoming the *minister* or servant of our brethren.[70]

Another New Testament reference that shows us the *nobility* of serving is John 13:12-17:

12 So after he had washed their feet, and had taken his garments, and was set down again, he said unto them, "Know ye what I have done to you? 13 Ye call me Master and Lord: and ye say well; for so I am. 14 If I then, your Lord and Master, have washed your feet; ye also ought to wash one another's feet. 15 For I have given you an example, that ye should do as I have done to you. 16 Verily, verily, I say unto you, The servant is not greater than his lord; neither he that is sent greater than he that sent him. 17 If ye know these things, happy are ye if ye do them.

In this text, Jesus gives us a visible demonstration of what the role of a servant looks like in practice. It might be good to remember: *the nature of a person will be reflected in their behavior.*

Following the puzzling action of washing their feet, He proceeds to explain that His behavior has been an object lesson. He's teaching His followers the nature of the work that He, and they, are called to do. He begins with the question, "Know ye what I have done to you?" In other words, "Do you understand? Do you get it? I, the Christ of God, just washed your feet! Do you realize what this means for you as my disciples?"

---

70 Charles H. Spurgeon, *An Exposition of the Gospel According to Matthew: The Gospel of the Kingdom* (London: Passmore and Alabaster, 1893; facsimile reprint with additional material and illustrations, Springfield, MO: Particular Baptist Press, 2015), 172-173.

Notice the terms that Jesus uses to describe Himself. First, in verse 13 He said "ye call me Master" and again in verse 14 "If I then, your...Master." This word *Master* means "instructor or teacher."[71] Jesus is acknowledging that He is what they themselves have called Him. He is their Teacher, and they are His students. The purpose of a "Master" was to disciple His students so they would learn their lessons and put into practice what He taught them. From there, they were expected to go out and teach others to do the same. So, the Teacher is questioning them, "Are you learning what I'm teaching you in these actions?"

The second term by which Jesus self-identifies is Lord. "Ye called me . . . Lord: if I then your Lord." "Lord" means "supreme in authority."[72] With these words, Jesus is acknowledging the true relationship between Himself, the supreme owner, and the servants of His realm. This is made clear in verse 16: "[T]he servant is not greater than his lord." Why would the subjects of His realm not be willing and ready to do what their Lord was willing and ready to do? Do they think more highly of themselves than their Lord does of Himself? Are they greater than He? (Perhaps we shouldn't go on until we're forced to answer that question about our own lives).

Jesus also speaks to them as their example. In verse 15, He says, "[F]or I have given you an example that ye should do as I have done to you." The word *example* means "an exhibit for imitation."[73] It is obvious that in every way Jesus exhibited the life of a servant, even before this scene. They had been with Him long enough to know that He served others in everything He did. That's who He was, a servant of others. And that's what He expects from his followers. Having demonstrated by example what a servant does, He now expects this kind of behavior to be imitated by His students.

---

71 Strong, *Strong's Exhaustive Concordance of the English Bible*, under "master."
72 Ibid., under "Lord."
73 Ibid., under "example."

In verse 17, the word *know*[74] points to the possibility of not understanding the importance of this example, and the word *if* recognizes the possibility of neglecting the practice once it is understood. If, however, they both understood and practiced what He did, Christ gives this promise: "[H]appy are ye if ye do them."

There is much unhappiness in the lives of many who profess Christ as the Lord and Master. Is it possible that one of the reasons for so much discontent is that we are too preoccupied with self instead of imitating Christ? "If ye do them," that is, if you imitate His example, then "happy are ye." In the Scripture, happiness is the result of obedience. Here, happiness is connected to imitating Him in His humble role of a servant. "Blessed are the merciful: for they shall receive mercy" (Matt. 5:7). We personally do not believe that Jesus was instructing us to practice literal foot washing but rather the humble act of ministering to the needs of others. This is what Jesus came to do as God's Servant. Among many other things, He expects us to imitate His life of service.

In verse 14, He told His disciples that they "ought" to do this for one another. This word speaks of being under an obligation to repay, such as a debt.[75] Why are His disciples under obligation? Why ought they do as He did? The obligation arises from the fact that the object lesson is taught by their Master and Lord. It is expected that His followers, students, and the subjects of His realm will do as their Lord has done. That's what disciples and subjects do! Therefore they "ought'" to do as He has done and serve others as He has served them.

---

74 Ibid., under "know."
75 Ibid., under "ought."

What He did by example should forever establish in our minds that serving is *noble* work. If He wore the servant's garment, let us not only do the same, but be honored to do so.

We cannot conclude our thoughts on the *nobility* of serving without briefly returning to Philippians 2:5-8:

> 5 Let this mind be in you, which was also in Christ Jesus: 6 Who, being in the form of God, thought it not robbery to be equal with God: 7 But made himself of no reputation, and took upon him the form of a servant, and was made in the likeness of men: 8 And being found in fashion as a man, he humbled himself, and became obedient unto death, even the death of the cross.

Here we are once again confronted with the humble attitude of Christ. He was both ready and willing to be the Servant of God. He set no limitations as to how far He would go to serve His Father's will. So, He went all the way, even to death on a cross.

When we contemplate that Christ exchanged the form of God for that of a servant, surely, we must "pour contempt on all our pride."[76] For a fallen sinful man, humility is a reasonable thing. But for the God of heaven to come into His created realm and humble Himself to serve us is incomprehensible! And according to the text, all servants must have this same mindset, this same commitment, if they are to effectively imitate their Savior's life.

Proverbs 23:7 tells us, "[A]s a man thinketh . . . so is he." From Christ's actions we know what He thought of Himself. He thought of Himself as a servant, the Servant of God. How can we be so proud as to think more

---

76 From the famous hymn by Isaac Watts, "When I Survey the Wondrous Cross."

highly of ourselves than He thought of Himself? In fact, that's what Paul exhorts all believers to think about themselves, to think of themselves as humble servants of God: "Let this mind be in you, which was also in Christ Jesus" (Phil. 2:5).

CHAPTER SUMMARY

Before reading this chapter, if we had asked you to rate the importance of the servant ministry of the deacon, which of the following boxes would you have checked?

[ ] Not important

[ ] Somewhat important

[ ] Important

[ ] Very important

[ ] Extremely valuable

We are persuaded that when every church member is fully convinced that the call to serve is a *universal* call, a *necessary* call, and a *noble* call, then the servant ministry of the deacon will be seen as not just *very important*, but *extremely valuable* to the church.

To deacons, we would add this: every member who understands this call biblically should be able to look to you, their deacons, to model the life of service and help them fulfill their own call to serve.

"It is the wonderful privilege and awesome responsibility of the church to acknowledge the activity of Christ by recognizing and receiving those men who are the gifts of Christ to his church."[77]

---

77 *Diaconal Manual* (Montville, N.J.: Trinity Baptist Church, 1995), 5.

CHAPTER 3

THE BIBLICAL QUALIFICATIONS FOR THE OFFICE

And in those days, when the number of the disciples was multiplied, there arose a murmuring of the Grecians against the Hebrews, because their widows were neglected in the daily ministration. 2 Then the twelve called the multitude of the disciples unto them, and said, It is not reason that we should leave the word of God, and serve tables. 3 Wherefore, brethren, look ye out among you seven men of honest report, full of the Holy Ghost and wisdom, whom we may appoint over this business. 4 But we will give ourselves continually to prayer, and to the ministry of the word. 5 And the saying pleased the whole multitude: and they chose Stephen, a man full of faith and of the Holy Ghost, and Philip, and Prochorus, and Nicanor, and

Timon, and Parmenas, and Nicolas a proselyte of Antioch; 6
Whom they set before the apostles: and when they had prayed,
they laid their hands on them (Acts 6:1-7).

Likewise must the deacons be grave, not double-tongued, not
given to much wine, not greedy of filthy lucre; 9 Holding the
mystery of the faith in a pure conscience. 10 And let these also
first be proved; then let them use the office of a deacon, being
found blameless. 11 Even so must their wives be grave, not
slanderers, sober, faithful in all things. 12 Let the deacons be
the husbands of one wife, ruling their children and their own
houses well. 13 For they that have used the office of a deacon
well purchase to themselves a good degree, and great boldness
in the faith which is in Christ Jesus. (1 Timothy 3: 8-13).

It seems odd to talk about the qualifications for a job that most people in the world will never want. The sad reality is that many in the church
have the same attitude toward this office as the world: "Who wants it!"
Because of this attitude, if a church has someone who is willing to hold
the office and might be somewhat effective in serving in certain areas, that
person is likely to hear, "Congratulations, you're elected!"

God, however, is never so desperate as to accept just anyone. While
talents, gifts, leadership skills, and the willingness to serve are all good
attributes, those who would serve as deacons in the church must meet
God's requirements.

With God, character is the most important *qualification*. The definitions of "character" and "qualifications" are like two intersecting lines. A
qualification is defined as "a quality, accomplishment, etc., that fits a person for some function, office, or the like."[78] Character, when speaking of a
person, means "the peculiar qualities, impressed by nature or habit on a

---

78 dictionary.com

person, which distinguish him from others; these constitute real character, and the qualities which he is supposed to possess, constitute his estimated character, or reputation." Character can also mean "to cut or to engrave."[79] Used metaphorically, character speaks of the qualities that are "cut" or "engraved" into a person. Think of character as "chisel marks" engraved into the life of an individual. These "chisel marks" are character *qualities* that distinguish and suit the person for a particular calling.

When it comes to choosing men for an office in the church, biblical churches first look to God's Word to discover the required *qualifications* and then look for those who have the required "chisel marks" etched into their lives. These required markings must be visible to the church before they are even considered, let alone chosen. Yes, there will be varying degrees to which these marks are engraved into a life, but they will be there in some measure and visible to the church.

The *qualifications* mentioned in Acts 6 and 1 Timothy 3 have been thoroughly discussed in books, commentaries, conferences, and public squares for centuries. There seems to be little left to say on the subject. But since this is a book on the office of the deacon, we would be remiss if we failed to address the *qualifications*, so we will attempt to make a small contribution to the discussion.

Having read, studied, and taught these passages numerous times over the years, we will begin with *five general observations* before briefly digging into the texts themselves. Think of these as "fly-over" observations from thirty thousand feet, in other words, big picture observations that everyone on the plane can see.

---

79 *Noah Webster 1828.*

First general observation

These two lists of *qualifications* (Acts, 1 Timothy) are not in conflict with each other. One list is brief and general, yet proves to be very comprehensive when thoroughly evaluated. The other, while longer and more specific, still requires effort to squeeze out the meaning of each *qualification*. Although the general requirements in Acts are not specifically mentioned in 1 Timothy, what they embody is there, so that what Luke records is expanded on by Paul.

Second general observation

These *qualities* (or character traits) should be of interest to every believer for they are not for deacons only. Each of these *qualities* are *Christian* qualities, not just diaconal qualities. The difference, however, is that, while every member *should* be living out these *qualities*, a servant leader (deacon) *must* have some measure of these qualities already evident in their life before they are chosen for the office.

Third general observation

As already pointed out, God puts more emphasis on character than personality, abilities, education, popularity, or leadership experience. Even unbelievers may possess these *qualities*. But there is a difference between personality traits and godly character. While all these traits would prove to be beneficial in the life of a servant leader, they do not necessarily translate into the character traits that God requires.

Fourth general observation

While the necessary qualities are clear, the quantity is not. This begs the question: how much, or to what degree, are these *qualities* to be found in your servant leaders? We believe the quantity (amount, measure) of a *quality* will vary from one leader to the next. Additionally, as a man grows in grace and experience, both the quantity and quality of a trait are bound to grow accordingly.

If you think about it a minute, you know there are many factors that influence how deeply and how quickly a particular "chisel mark" is etched into a life. Here are several factors that we've observed over our years of ministry:

1. Age is a factor. Age does not necessarily make a better servant leader, but it does provide more opportunities for growth. Sometimes the quantity of a particular *quality* is simply a matter of age and life experience.

2. Years in the faith can be a factor. How long someone has walked with God should influence their maturity. This is not always true, but generally, it is a reason why some are more advanced than others.

3. Church experience can also be a factor. Not all churches provide the same kind of discipleship and overall spiritual leadership that promote spiritual growth.

4. Wisdom is a factor. Growth in wisdom and discernment is the fruit of a submissive life that endeavors to live obediently under the authority of God's Word (James 1:19-25; Heb. 13:17). While every deacon should be both born again and full of wisdom and the Holy Spirit (Acts 6:3), some, owing to a life of humble obedience, will walk in more wisdom than others. This doesn't disqualify others, but it does distinguish the development of wisdom in some.

Caution—We must be cautious about setting up standards of measurement that either fall short of God's requirements or exceed them. The reality is, the degree of a *spiritual quality* will vary among those who are *qualified*.

Fifth general observation

Meeting the necessary *qualifications* is only one side of the coin. The other side has to do with the nature of the office. A person with good character must also possess the nature of a servant to some recognizable degree. While these two passages (Acts 6, 1 Tim. 3) focus primarily on character, they do not diminish the fact that there ought to be some discernible interest in, and even evidence of, serving others before they are given the office of the deacon. We must always remember that we are choosing *qualified* servant leaders.

With these five general observations in mind, let's take a closer look at the two "*qualification*" passages.

ACTS 6:1-7

As we look at the first list of *qualifications*, it's reasonable to assume the apostles met together and discussed the necessary qualities for those who would assume the oversight of this very important function. Under the guidance of the Holy Spirit, they set the parameters for the congregation in choosing servant leaders. The *qualifications* in v. 3 limit their options, or "narrow the field," you might say.

Furthermore, they were instructed to choose men who already possessed these necessary qualities. They were not told to look among themselves and find seven with the potential to someday have these qualities but those who already possessed these *qualities*. They are requisite to being nominated for the work, let alone chosen for it.

First qualification: honest report

These were to be men who were already in possession of a "good report." The Greek word for *report* means to "testify" or "give evidence as a witness."[80]

---

80 James Strong, *Strong's Exhaustive Concordance of the English Bible* (Grand Rapids, MI:

G. Campbell Morgan, commenting on the phrase "men of honest report," writes, "The root of the word 'report' is the same root for the word 'witness'[:] martyrs, men of good witness." He goes on to say, "They are men to be well reported of, and they are to be men who have borne such witness as to create a good report . . . men of whom other men spoke excellent things." He then summarizes with these words: "This suggests the absolute necessity for the choice of men of character in the eyes of the world, for the carrying out of the function of the church."[81]

The prospective deacon's testimony, that he is a good man, would include such things as how his family, church, workplace, and the world view him. This does not mean that everyone always agrees with him. Nor does it mean that everyone always likes him. But what it does mean is that his moral character is sound. We recognize there may be failures in his past. But in such cases, time has proven that there is real change and the report on him is a "good report." There are no unsettled accusations hanging over his character.

Second qualification: full of the Spirit

This focuses on the evidence of the Holy Spirit's work in every major area of his life. Whether public field or private chamber, every area will be under the influence of the Spirit. The Greek word for *full*[82] can refer to being "filled to the top," or it can mean "abounding in, wholly occupied with, completely under the influence." Those who are chosen must give ample evidence of the Spirit's continuing work in all areas of life. However, those with whom critical areas of the Christian life have been, for one reason or another, neglected or are totally absent are to be deemed unqualified for the office. They may, in time, prove to be qualified as they submit to

---

Zondervan Publishing, 2001), under "report" (Acts 6:3).

81 G. Campbell Morgan, *Acts* (New York: Fleming H. Revell, 1924), 173.

82 Strong, *Strong's Exhaustive Concordance of the English Bible*, under "full" (Acts 6:3).

and learn to "walk in the Spirit," but this requirement has to do with their current submission to the Spirit. This protects not only the church, but also the person who needs more time to mature in areas of weakness, areas not wholly submitted to the Spirit's leading.

This *qualification* is similar to the directive given in Ephesians 5:18, where every Christian is admonished to be "filled with the Spirit." The word "filled"[83] is a form of the word *full* in Acts 6:3. We know that we cannot have more or less of the Spirit. Quantitatively speaking, we have all of the Spirit in us at the moment of our salvation. The command to be "filled with the Spirit" is not telling us to get more of Him because we only have some of Him, but rather, we are being commanded to submit or yield more fully to Him. We are being told to humbly give Him more access to every area of our lives until all areas are under His influence to a greater degree. Every one of us should have a sign hanging over the doorway of our soul that reads: "Pardon the mess while I remodel," not "Coming Soon." This is especially true of the officers of the church. We should see evidence of the transforming work of the Spirit in his life before he is chosen as a leader in the assembly.

Here in Ephesians 5:18, the apostle is contrasting drunkenness to the Spirit's control, which is the exact opposite of the state of drunkenness. While "drunkenness" produces "excess" or excessive and extreme behavior,[84] the filling work of the Spirit produces just the opposite. Areas that were once out of control and exhibited unbecoming excessive behaviors are now managed and under the control of the Spirit. This is a *qualification* for anyone whom the church would choose for service.

To be "full of the Spirit" does not suggest that a person is without sin but rather speaks of someone who is dealing with the weaknesses of his life with some degree of effectiveness through the empowerment of the Spirit.

---

83 Ibid., under "filled" (Eph. 5:18).
84 Ibid., under "drunk" (Eph. 5:18).

Struggling with a particular area does not necessarily disqualify someone from this office. It might, but not necessarily. However, the neglect of an area of life in which the Holy Spirit is not evident, where there is no conviction, correction, or change, should be a matter of concern as you consider the individual for office.

Third qualification: full of wisdom

This requirement focuses on the ability to apply truth to their life. The apostles' understanding of wisdom was no doubt formed by the Old Testament teaching on wisdom. That teaching is exemplified in Proverbs. The Hebrew word for *wisdom*, *hokma*, means "skill, expertise, to master something."[85] But not just anything; Solomon equates wisdom, *hokma*, with mastering life in "the fear of the Lord" (Prov. 1:7; 9:10). Thus, wisdom is to live life well, which means in reverent obedience to the Lord.

The Greek word used in Acts 6:3, *sophia*, was largely associated with both philosophy and practical knowledge. J. A. Alexander writes, "[N]ot merely practical skill or professional experience, but heavenly prudence, teaching how to act in all emergencies."[86] The English word *wisdom* refers to "the right use or exercise of knowledge . . . It is the knowledge of what is best, most just, most proper, most conducive to prosperity or happiness."[87]

The word *full* relates to wisdom in the same way it relates to the Spirit. Every area is to be "under the influence" of wisdom. Wisdom implies a skill that is gained through knowledge and enlightenment. Wisdom is more than knowledge of the truth, yet it is never without the knowledge of the truth. Our contribution to growing in wisdom is to gather all the knowledge we can from God's Word. We can gain this knowledge by listening

---

85 Bruce Waltke, *The Book of Proverbs, New International Commentary on the Old Testament* (Grand Rapids, MI: Eerdmans, 2004), 76.

86 Joseph A. Alexander, *A Commentary on the Acts of the Apostles* (New York, 1857; repr. Minneapolis, MN: Klock and Klock, 1980), 244.

87 Webster, *American Dictionary of the English Language* (1828 ed.), under "wisdom."

to those who teach us His Word and by studying the Word for ourselves. Wisdom can also be gained through the good counsel of those who have gained wisdom themselves through life experiences and the knowledge of God as revealed through his Word. However, listening and reading is only the beginning. We must also meditate on those things until our understanding apprehends or grasps the truth.

Yet, while these avenues of growth are to be pursued, we must at the same time confess that wisdom will not come unless God enlightens us by His Spirit and empowers our efforts to live out the truth we have seen and heard (James 1:1-5, 22-25; Heb. 5:11-14).

This process of learning and applying truth to our life reflects the measure of wisdom that we have. To be "full of wisdom" speaks of a man who has been effective, in some measure, in the application of the truth to all areas of his life. This does not imply that he is without failures or that he does not struggle in some areas more than others. To be "full of wisdom" is inextricably related to being "full of the Spirit." Wisdom at work in our life reflects the degree of the influence of the Holy Spirit within. The measure of one will always reflect the measure of the other. Some areas may be more advanced, but all areas of life must reflect the ability to take the truth of God's Word and "stretch it out" (Prov. 2:1-7) or "work it out" (Phil. 2:12-13).

The man "full of wisdom," then, will demonstrate that he is a "doer" of the Word and not a "hearer" only (Luke 6:46-49; James 1:22-25). He is no novice in the application of truth. These are men who have taken personal responsibility to practice the truth with consistency. Moreover, he not only demonstrates wisdom in his own life, but he is able to help others do the same. Their wisdom is both spiritual and very practical. Concerning practical wisdom in a deacon, John Gill said the following:

> Wisdom is highly requisite in them, that they may be good economists of the church's stock, and dispose of it in the most

prudent manner, and conduct themselves agreeably to the different tempers and spirits of men they have to do with, and especially in composing differences among members.[88]

To conclude our comments on the *qualifications found in Acts 6*, we leave you with a quote from F. F. Bruce:

> These seven must be men of honorable reputation, so that their probity might command complete confidence; they must be wise men, competent in administration and also qualified to deal wisely with a situation in which there were such delicate human susceptibilities to consider; above all, they must be men filled with the Holy Spirit. It would be well if this precedent were observed in all church appointments. If such men were appointed to take charge of the distribution and see that no further cause for complaint arose, the apostles would be free to devote their own distracted attention to the regular worship of the church and to the preaching of the gospel.[89]

1 TIMOTHY 3:8-13

We will begin with some general observations before dealing with the specific *qualifications*.

First general observation

The list of *qualifications* found in Acts 6 is the "Shorter Catechism" on the requirements for holding the office of the deacon. Paul's list of *qualifications* in 1 Timothy 3:8-13 is a more comprehensive list. The second and

---

88 John Gill, *An Exposition of the Old and New Testaments* (London: William Hill, 1852-1854; reprinted Grand Rapids, MI: Baker Book House, 1980), 5: 840-841.

89 F. F. Bruce, *The Book of Acts*. The New International Commentary on the New Testament (Grand Rapids: William B. Eerdmans Publishing Co., 1975), 128.

larger list does not void the earlier and shorter list. The two lists comple-ment each other. Without much difficulty, you can place each of the *quali-fications* in the larger list, under one of the *qualifications* in the shorter list. Although different in length, through both we can know God's require-ments for those who would hold the office.

Second general observation

We are not given a reason why the Holy Spirit saw fit to expand on the qual-ifications in Acts 6 and give a more comprehensive list of requirements. But allow us to speculate. Over thirty years had passed since the apostles gave the original list as reported in Acts 6. The ever-growing challenges that faced the early church during those years are well documented. It was a time of persecution, dispersion, and expansion. Just as important, the ethnic and cultural makeup of the new church was ever-changing. And let's not forget the church was now full of new converts. Some, perhaps, desired to be officers in the church. Others might have been seeking out qualified officers to serve in the ever-expanding church. It might be for reasons like these the Holy Spirit compelled Paul to expand the list of qualifications. Not that the first list was faulty, but in the ever-changing landscape of the early church, it makes sense that the qualifications needed to be clarified with more precision, precision that meets the needs of the growing church.

Third general observation

Like the list in Acts 6, this list in 1 Timothy 3 focuses on the moral char-acter of the candidate. To use the metaphor again, each character qual-ity is "chiseled" into the individual candidate and should be clearly visible before he is nominated. Gill referred to these *necessary qualifications* as "the rules for choosing."[90] And the rules dictate that they must be people of high moral character.

---

90 Gill, *An Exposition of the Old and New Testaments*, 6: 603.

Because the *qualifications* have been thoroughly and accurately explained in other works, works that are readily available, we will keep our comments brief. At the same time, we cannot neglect the importance of this list to our study and therefore the importance of a few comments. While our contribution may be small, we trust it will be helpful.

First qualification: must be grave

The Greek word translated as "grave"[91] is complex and takes several English words to define it. It speaks of someone who is dignified, worthy of respect, noble, highly principled, honorable. This is a person who has been a guardian of his reputation, cautious and circumspect in his walk. Through living a dignified and highly principled life, they have distinguished themselves and gained an honorable reputation.

"Grave" is not the same as self-righteous, or worse, grumpy. A highly principled and careful Christian can be cheerful, pleasant to be around, and manifest all the fruit of the Spirit. They practice Ephesians 4:32 with ease, being kind and soft-hearted, forgiving others as they have been forgiven, exemplifying a gracious attitude toward everyone. They love others and are ready to "bear all things, believe all things, hope all things and endure all things" (1 Cor. 13:7). Yet, knowing they have earned a good reputation, they are careful to maintain it, not willing to give it up with a careless word or deed. While this is a quality that every believer ought to be pursuing, it is not optional for those who hold an office in the church. Whether at home, church, work, or in the world, they live a dignified and honorable life, respected by all.

---

91 Strong, *Strong's Exhaustive Concordance of the English Bible*, under "grave" (1 Tim. 3:11).

Second qualification: not double-tongued

This is the first of three negatively stated prohibitions that will either *qualify or disqualify* a person for this office. The Greek word[92] means "to tell a different story." Surely, we all recognize the significance of this requirement. Those elected to be servant leaders will be exposed to numerous issues and conditions in the lives of the church body. Matthew Henry's commentary says this requirement refers to saying "one thing to one and another thing to another, according as their interest leads them: a double tongue comes from a double heart; flatterers and slanderers are double-tongued."[93] Therefore, the deacon must not be known for distorting, exaggerating, or gossiping.

The positive side of this prohibition is that they will have a reputation for being discreet in their handling of sensitive information. Those under consideration for the office must demonstrate they can be trusted with the intimate details of another's life. If and when it's necessary for them to discuss the details with, say, their mate or the spiritual leaders of the church, the church must be confident that this officer will speak accurately about the situation. Deacons must be people who do not say what they shouldn't say and say only what is true when it is said.

Third qualification: not given to much wine

This is the second negatively stated *qualification*. This prohibition refers to someone who is preoccupied with the consumption of wine. We will leave the discussion on "to use or not to use alcoholic beverages" to others who have written on this subject. Our conclusions are that this is not about the use of wine but the *abuse*. We recognize that every church has its view on this subject. Gill refers to this abuse as that "which impairs the health,

92 Ibid., under "double-tongued" (1 Tim. 3:8).
93 Matthew Henry, *Commentary on the Whole Bible* (Old Tappan, NJ: Fleming H. Revell), 6: 816.

stupefies the mind, and so renders [one] unfit for any such office, as well as wastes the temporal estate."[94]

The flipside of a prohibition is the thing that ought to be done. In other words, there will be the trait of temperance, the evidence of self-discipline. This is a quality that is produced by the Holy Spirit. The point is, everything about their life should reflect moderation. Whether it's food or drink, nothing should be allowed to "impair the health or stupefy the mind." This includes not only the necessities of life, like food and drink, but would also include appropriate pleasures (1 Tim. 6:17). Even when "Christian liberty" is allowed, excessiveness is not (Eph. 5:18).

Fourth qualification: not greedy of filthy lucre

This is the third prohibition. It basically means "greedy for money." This requirement is intended to keep out of office those who have a mind for earthly things above eternal things.

Concerning this prohibition, Alfred Rowland, in a chapter entitled "The Ideal Deacon," writes this:

> Some gain is the fair and God appointed stimulus to toil. Success in business, when it is won by integrity and diligence, is a sign of fitness for service in the church rather than a disqualification from it. But when a man makes money the chief object of life, and will gain it by evil means, and holds with a tight hand what he wins, he is unfit for office as a Christian, for he is one of those who are lovers of money more than lovers of God.[95]

---

94 Gill, *An Exposition of the Old and New Testaments*, 6: 603.
95 Alfred Rowland, *Studies in I Timothy* (London: James Nisbet and Co., 1887; reprinted Minneapolis, MN: Klock and Klock Christian Publishers, Inc., 1985), 139.

The root problem behind this prohibition is a covetous or greedy nature. Covetousness is not limited to inappropriate gain of money. While we often limit the application of "dishonest gain" to being greedy for money, it can also apply to being greedy for other things as well. A person might have a sinful desire for reputation, recognition, or position and a willingness to take inappropriate and dishonest steps to advance his own selfish interests.

The flipside of this prohibition is a merciful and generous nature. It would seem a contradiction to appoint someone who has a greedy and covetous nature to oversee the care of those in need. So, while the words *filthy lucre* tell us Paul is mostly concerned with greediness for money, a greedy nature is the root problem, and greediness of any kind is likely to be a hindrance to the person chosen to care for the needs of others.

Fifth qualification: holding to the mystery of the faith in a good conscience

Concerning this *qualification* Homer Kent wrote this:

> Although the deacon is not required to have the gift of teaching, he does need to be settled in his faith. In Paul's use of the term "musterion," there is always the idea of something previously hidden but now revealed. The genitive "tes pisteos" (of the faith) is a descriptive or defining genitive which explains what this mystery is. The mystery is 'the body of truth which comprises Christian faith.' The great truths of the faith are not to be held as theological abstractions, but are to be properly employed in daily life. To hold the mystery of the faith in a pure conscience is to live in the light of Christian truth so that the enlightened conscience will have no cause to condemn. A pure conscience indicated a pure life. Although the primary task of the deacons is not to teach, his ministrations will

require him to bring spiritual comfort to others. Thus, his own spiritual life must be pure.[96]

The gist of this *qualification* is that the candidate must be demonstrating an active faith life. As Kent put it, "The great truths . . . are to be employed in daily life." They have what the older authors referred to as "experimental" or "experiential" religion. They have the ability to take truth into the mind and then put it into practice, thereby experiencing the truths they embrace in real life situations.

The words *holding to* speak of having a firm grasp, even to the point of possessing something. While some "concerning faith have made shipwreck" (1 Tim. 1:9), not this man. This language here suggests a person who has weathered more than one storm and has proven himself to be unwavering. Concerning his adherence to the tenets of the faith he professes, his conscience is clear. Robert Mounce writes this:

A deacon's possession of the mystery of the faith is to be accompanied, 'with a clean conscience.' It is not sufficient to have a grasp on the theological profession of the church; that knowledge must be accompanied with the appropriate behavior, in this case a conscience that is clear from any stain of sin. Once again Paul connects right belief with right behavior.[97]

This is not always about being able to completely grasp and effectively argue all Bible doctrines. In fact, their grasp of truth may be very simple. But when tested, they continue to "hold on," and putting their faith into practice, they do so with a clear conscience.

---

96 Homer A. Kent, *The Pastoral Epistles* (Chicago: Moody Press, 1958), 139.

97 Robert H. Mounce, *Word Biblical Commentary* (Nashville: Thomas Nelson, Inc., 2000), 46 (Pastoral Epistles): 200.

Sixth qualification: tested first

The church must not advance someone prematurely. This protects every-one! There is a sequential order that the church must not alter. The word *first* is telling the church that the candidate must be "proved" before they are entrusted with the office. "Then," next in sequence, they can "use the office." "Proven" must come before "using." This is the divine order and must not be altered. Some believe the word *proved* refers to the previous *qualifications.* Others believe this is referring to demonstrating a servant's nature before they are elected. We believe both are true. Before being cho-sen, the candidate must meet all the *qualifications* and at the same time demonstrate a servant's nature. Kent observes that the verb *proved* "is a present imperative which does not call for a formal test but a constant observing or testing, so that when deacons are needed, *qualified* ones may be nominated as candidates."[98] Rowland's comments on this phrase, "let these also be first proved," are worth repeating:

Their qualifications ought to be evidenced and recognized, in order that they may have the confidence of their brethren. When any citizen of Athens was appointed by lot, or chosen by suffrage, to hold public office, he was obliged, before entering on its duties, to submit to a scrutiny into his life and conduct, and it is the verb representing that noun which the apostle uses here. He means that if a man were chosen to office who was known to be unworthy, any member of the community might object to him, for it is of the first importance that confidence should be felt in those who lead the church.[99]

The church *must* wait until the individual first demonstrates the *nec-essary qualities/qualifications before* being chosen. The church does not have the liberty to change the order. All candidates must "*first* be proved; *then* let them use the office of a deacon." The word *proved* seems to be explained

---

98 Ibid.
99 Rowland, *Studies in I Timothy,* 139.

in the last phrase, "being found blameless," that is, nothing stands out that would potentially disqualify them from holding the office.

The next four *qualifications* have to do with women. We will deal with these qualifications now, in the order they're presented in the Scripture, and then pick up on the final *qualifications* for men that follow.

The gender in 1 Timothy 3:11 is not in question. However, who these women are has been debated for centuries. We will deal with this debate and her identity in a later chapter. For now, whoever she is, we all agree she must meet the following *qualifications*.

First qualification concerning women: must be grave

This is the same Greek word used in v. 8, only the feminine form.[100] She too must guard her reputation at all times. She may have a warm and vibrant nature, or she may be reserved and prefers to do things behind the scenes. In either case, she must live carefully, be aware of her demeanor, guard her reputation, and "not let her good be evil spoken of."

Second qualification concerning women: must not be a slanderer

The Greek word here is *diabolos*, the word for "false accuser, devil, slanderer."[101] Technically, it means to make a false accusation. Practically, however, it seems to include the idea of malicious gossip as well (NASB). George Knight thinks perhaps this word in this place "may be an indication of emphasis in terms of the besetting sins of the tongue."

Whether or not the word has such a broad meaning as Knight suggests, this *qualification* makes sense. She will interact with others, especially women, who have needs. How important it is that she not only keeps what

---

100 Strong, *Strong's Exhaustive Concordance of the English Bible*, under "grave" (1 Tim. 3:11).

101 Ibid., under "slanderers."

she hears and sees confidential, but guards her own words when she must talk these things over with others. We already have one foul accuser of the brethren (Rev. 12:10); we don't need church members running around "spreading their innuendos and criticisms in the church."[102]

Third qualification concerning women: must be sober

This is the same word in v. 2, translated as "vigilant." It means "self-controlled" and "has the sense of 'temperate'" in all things. It is very similar to the word *grave* or dignified. Mounce states, "The word carries the double nuance of being temperate in her use of alcohol and clear-minded in her judgments."[103] The sober woman lives a well-ordered life and is vigilant at keeping herself under control in all things. Any excessive tendencies would not only conflict with this requirement, but would also be contrary to a Spirit-filled life.

Fourth qualification concerning women: must be faithful in all things

"Faithful" expresses the idea of trustworthy, dependable, and reliable. She is a woman who has proven trustworthy in the things for which she is responsible. Whether it's her role as a wife, mother, church member, friend, or neighbor, she has earned the reputation as faithful in every way.

Returning now to the qualifications for the office, if you believe the four *qualifications* in verse 11 of our text are for deacons' wives, then collectively they serve as the seventh *qualification* for him.

---

102 *Vine's Expository Dictionary of Old and New Testament Words* (Nashville: World Publishing, 1981), 4: 39, under "slanderer."

103 Mounce, *Word Biblical Commentary*, 46 (Pastoral Epistles): 204.

Eighth qualification: a one-woman man

This obviously emphasizes his marriage fidelity. This would include everything from physical adultery to all kinds of fornication, body or mind. He is totally devoted to his wife. If you have questions about divorce and remarriage and whether this disqualifies a candidate for the office of a deacon, we suggest you discuss this with the spiritual leaders of your church.

Ninth qualification: ruling their children and houses well

There are two parts to the oversight of his home. The first part focuses on his parenting skills. The phrase "ruling their children" means that he is "residing over"[104] his children living under his care. This suggests he effectively maintains and manages all areas of watchcare over his children. There are a number of areas that fall under the oversight of a father. This would include their spiritual, emotional, intellectual, and material care.

It is important that we do not judge the quality of a man's child-rearing skills by either subjective or cultural standards. Nor should we leave it up to the officer of the church to determine for himself if he is *qualified* in this regard. Therefore, it is extremely important for the church to know what the Bible has to say on the subject of parenting. The Word of God alone is our objective standard, and if the church is to faithfully carry out its responsibility to evaluate and choose *qualified* candidates, then it must be familiar with what it teaches concerning the role of a father in the home.

The Greek word for *well*[105] means "with propriety, becomingly," meaning, in his dealings with his children, he is neither too harsh nor too lax and careless. Everything he does in regard to his children seems appropriate. Being a man with a good reputation, full of the Spirit and wisdom,

---

104 Strong, *Strong's Exhaustive Concordance of the English Bible*, under "ruling" (1 Tim. 3:12).

105 Ibid., under "well" (1 Tim. 3:12).

he leads and influences by both principle and example. He manages it all "well."

He is not a perfect parent, neither are his children perfect. Children are sinners and need his instruction, correction, and continuous warnings when they stray from those things they have been taught. The fact is that the struggles of his children will reveal the wisdom and dignity of his oversight. The kind of wisdom that he possesses will be seen in his handling of difficult matters as his children grow through the various stages of life. As always, we must not take liberty with God's Word in limiting its statements nor in exceeding its boundaries. A man doing a good job parenting has no guarantee that his children will ultimately embrace the instruction and leadership he has faithfully provided. While all parts are under his oversight, he trusts God with the outcome. The emphasis, however, is not primarily on the outcome but rather on the process. He brings principled, balanced, appropriate, godly leadership to the home.

The second part of this *qualification* focuses on "their own houses." The Greek word for *houses*[106] refers to the various facets of his household, and there are many. It would include everything presently under his management, from the care of his property and goods to his personal finances. It appears that the emphasis is on his ability to care for what has been entrusted to him. Is he careless or negligent with his God-given responsibilities? Does he demonstrate good judgment in the use of his resources? This is not to suggest that his judgment and discernment are perfect. For instance, this does not rule out the possibility of making investments that go bad or any number of other financial missteps. He may even be experiencing some financial difficulties due to some mistakes in the management of resources. Then there are things like changes in employment or lack thereof, unforeseen health-care expenses, and so on. However, he is a man who demonstrates an awareness of what's causing these problems and the

---

106 Ibid., under "houses" (1 Tim. 3:12).

ability to correct them. If, on the other hand, he is presently in the state of gross mismanagement or has not yet learned how to prevent or deal with these things biblically, then he would not meet the requirement of "presiding over his household well." These are often complex issues that require a great deal of prayer and open discussion to sort through.

Note—we will deal with the promised rewards for the deacon that are stated in I Tim. 3:13 in a later chapter.

CHAPTER SUMMARY

When looking for candidates to serve as deacons, we might be tempted to settle for the most gifted, the most successful, or the most willing. God is not; He requires proven moral character, individuals who have already distinguished themselves as having the necessary "chisel marks" engraved into their lives. All in all, they are people of "good report," "full of the Spirit," "full of wisdom," and meet the requirements as laid out by the apostle Paul.

It is a blessing from God to have candidates for the office of deacon in your church who are both *qualified* and ready to be servant leaders. We know that it matters to the Lord and Head of the church that we choose those who possess a good measure of these biblical requirements. Therefore, it should matter to the church.

CHAPTER 4

THE PROCESS OF SELECTING QUALIFIED INDIVIDUALS

n Chapter 3, we focused on what a qualified deacon looks like, not physically, of course, but their character profile. We looked at character as "chisel marks" cut into their life by God. It is very important for the church to understand that every candidate for the office must possess specific qualifications before they are chosen to be a servant leader. Each qualification may not be as pronounced in some as in others, but they will be there. They must be there. They are the marks of qualification.

In this chapter, we will shift our focus from the candidate to the duties of the church and their spiritual leaders. Specifically, how does a congregation of believers move from a need for deacons to actually having deacons? We will use Acts 6 as a model for answering that question.

In the early church at Jerusalem, moving from having a need to meeting the need involved a process. By *process* we mean there was a clear, identifiable procedure or a series of actions as the body met the need for servants. Some of the steps in the *process* are clearly stated. Others are only implied. Whether stated or implied, together they help the church meet the need for qualified servant leaders. It's this *process* that we'll now zero in on. In the directives of the apostles and the actions of the church, we see a *four-step process* to move from "need" to "need met."

Step 1—*Finding* qualified candidates.

Step 2—*Electing* qualified candidates.

Step 3—*Installing* qualified candidates.

Step 4—*Directing* qualified candidates.

Before getting into the details, we must first make a few general comments concerning the literary genre of the book of Acts. Like most of the Bible, Acts is a narrative. A narrative can be defined as "the recital of a story, or a continued account of the particulars of an event or transaction."[107] While caution is called for when interpreting and applying a biblical narrative, the stories of the Bible are not the same as made-up fiction. These are not Aesop's stories; these are God's stories. They are inspired, inerrant stories. They come from "The Book of God." As such, they are meant to convey truth, God's truth. 1 Corinthians 10:11 tells us that the events recorded in the Old Testament, most of which are narratives, were written for our instruction. There Paul writes, "Now all these things happened unto them for our ensamples: and they are written for our admonition, upon whom the ends of the world are come." To which we add another quote from Paul, "All scripture is given by inspiration of God, and is profitable for doctrine, for reproof, for correction, for instruction in righteousness" (2 Tim. 3:16).

---

107 Noah Webster, *American Dictionary of the English Language* (1828; reprinted San Francisco: Foundation for American Christian Education, 1987), under "narrative."

We cannot be afraid to draw out timeless truths from these books of the Bible. It's worth repeating David Wells' thoughts:

> The importance of the story form in the Bible does not lie in the story form itself. Its importance lies in the fact that as a narrative of God's acts in the external world, it has yielded truth that is as objective as the events to which it is wedded . . . The prophets of the Old Testament and the apostles of the New . . . were convinced that God's revelation, of which they were the vehicles and custodians, was not merely true *in their time;* it was not true *approximately.* What God had given was true universally, absolutely, and enduringly.[108]

This brings us to the narrative in the book of Acts. The events recorded in Chapter 6 contain timeless truths. These are truths that are meant to guide the church throughout the ages as it seeks to *find, elect, install,* and *direct* qualified servant leaders. Along the way, we will do our best to be respectful of the difference between explicit and implicit truth, as well as the difference between prescriptive and descriptive biblical history.[109]

As you work your way through the following steps, you might notice they tend to overlap in places, so that a point made under one step flows over into another step. We are not unaware of this. Let's just say we tried, but we couldn't help it. With that said, let's get into the steps. We've

---

108 David Wells, *No Place for Truth; or Whatever Happened to Evangelical Theology?* (Grand Rapids, MI: William B. Eerdmans, 1993), 259.

109 Our study and use of Acts 6 require us to consider the difference between, and value of, both the descriptive and the prescriptive portions of the Scripture. This is a necessary part of the observation component in the inductive study process. *Descriptive* refers to those historical narratives that describe events that happened. While we can and ought to gather principles and guidelines from these portions of the Scripture, we must guard against establishing imperatives or rules that conflict with the prescriptive portions of the Bible. *Prescriptive* refers to clearly defined commandments. These imperatives for the church are contained primarily in the New Testament Epistles.

rearranged the steps to simulate a staircase. We'll start at the bottom and work our way up.

Step 4—Directing qualified candidates.

Step 3—Installing qualified candidates.

Step 2—Electing qualified candidates.

Step 1—Finding qualified candidates.

"Wherefore, brethren, look ye out among you seven men of honest report, full of the Holy Ghost and wisdom, whom we may appoint over this business" (Acts 6:3).

As we begin the *process* of putting individuals into office, we focus our attention on the first step of *finding the qualified* with the words "look ye out among you." We will use the inductive study method to flesh out the meaning of the text. The inductive method includes three primary components: observation, interpretation, and application. We will focus most of our attention on the observation component, knowing that the interpretation and application of a text are drawn from the observation process. The process involves asking a series of questions of the text: who, what, where, when, why, and how do we find qualified candidates.

FIRST INDUCTIVE QUESTION: WHO IS RESPONSIBLE TO FIND THE QUALIFIED?

As per our study of the text, the responsibility *to find qualified candidates* is a privilege and responsibility that is given to a specific and clearly identifiable group of people: the "whole multitude" (Acts 6:5).

The first thing we notice is that the directive to "look" is given to them all, not just some. We will discuss what it means to "look" later, but for now, *who* is responsible for looking? Luke tells us that the apostles "called the *multitude*" (Acts 6:2) and told *them* to "look *ye* out *among you*" (v. 3). Verse

5 tells us, "And the saying pleased the *whole multitude* and *they* chose . . ." (italics added). Finally, the same group, referred to as "they" (v. 6), brought the candidates to the apostles. It's obvious *who* the "ye" are in verse 3 and what "they" are doing. "They" are the members *who* make up the "whole multitude" or the full number of believers. As soon as the apostles gave the instructions and authority to act, the whole assembly immediately began *the process of finding qualified candidates.*

Following the looking and choosing *process*, the apostles accept their choice and install these men into office. Is it any wonder the proposal pleased the *whole* church (v. 5)? They are choosing for themselves, with the full permission and authority of the apostles, those who will take care of their needy members. It no doubt gave them (the congregation) a sense of ownership over *the process of finding the qualified*. Not only were they involved in *the process of finding* or identifying the candidates, their choices would ultimately influence the outcome as well.

Secondly, there is something else embedded in the passage that is easy to overlook concerning *who* is responsible to *find the qualified*. The apostles called "the multitude of disciples" and addressed them as "brethren" (vv. 2-3). Implicit in this directive is that the apostles intentionally directed their instructions to saved members of the assembly. The apostles called, or invited, "disciples" to hear their proposal. It's reasonable to believe there were some unbelievers among them. Maybe they were still searching for answers, or maybe some were just curious about all the excitement the church was experiencing. This was the case even during the ministry of Jesus. It's also reasonable to assume there were some unbelievers who were looking to be cared for by the church. This was also true of the ministry of Jesus. Surely the twelve learned this firsthand as they followed and were taught by Christ. Knowing this and knowing the importance of what they were about to propose to the church, they intentionally invited and addressed their comments to only "the brethren" among them. It would be hard to believe the apostles would give this important responsibility to a mixed multitude without specifying that they had true believers in mind.

There is both an inclusion and exclusion in *the process* of *who* is allowed to *find the qualified*. The fact that one specific group is invited means that all others are not. The text states that only believers are given the right to "look ye out among you" or find qualified candidates. The danger of not following this prescription is that we allow unbelievers the right to look and make recommendations on the basis of their findings. Surely all manner of evil is possible if this is allowed. Why? Because unbelievers do what unbelievers do—they make carnal decisions. The church must do what the apostles did: invite only "disciples" or "brethren" to the *finding process*.

Furthermore, we think it is fair to say that those who were invited to join in the process of finding candidates were not only converted, they were most likely, if not most assuredly, baptized as well. Think it through. Our Lord directed these same apostles to "make disciples of all nations, baptizing them" (Matt. 28:19, ESV). Then, on the day of Pentecost, Peter declares, "Repent, and be baptized every one of you" (Acts 2:38). And what happened? "Then they that gladly received his word were baptized." This pattern of *first believe then be baptized* is consistently adhered to throughout the book of Acts.[110] *Only* believers were baptized, and *all* believers were baptized upon faith in Christ. The idea of an unbaptized believer was unheard of in the early church. This being true, throughout the early stages of the church, both the apostles and the entire multitude had various ways to distinguish between believers and unbelievers, and one very important distinguishing mark was baptism.

So, *who* is responsible for finding *the qualified candidates*? The narrative gives us the answer: "brethren, look ye out among you." By calling them "disciples" and "brethren," they were unquestionably believers in

---

110 See Acts 2:41; 8:12, 36-38; 9:1-18; 10:44-48; 16:14-15, 27-34; 19:1-5; 22:6-16.

Christ and baptized members of the congregation. They, and they alone, are assumed to be capable of *finding the qualified*.

We would like to draw out a few general observations regarding the first inductive question of *who* is charged with *finding the qualified*.

First Observation

It is apparent to us that no individual or group within the church has the right to usurp this congregational responsibility. The right to identify and select deacons resides with the assembly. If we allow either one person or a special interest group within the assembly to take over *the process of finding qualified deacons*, then we undermine the importance of this biblical narrative. We are simply making what we believe to be an obvious and biblical observation from the passage. The right to *find qualified candidates* for the office resides with "the multitude" or congregation of believers.

Second Observation

Individual members do not have the authority to appoint themselves to the office. It is the whole church's right and responsibility to *find qualified candidates*. The directive is not "look ye out and find yourself." Having a desire is one thing; being qualified is another.

On the other hand, there may be those who are qualified and have genuinely distinguished themselves by demonstrating a servant's heart. These same individuals might even look forward to using the office as a platform for developing a more effective servant ministry. However, even though they have a biblical desire for the office, even qualified candidates are dependent on the providence of God and the recognition of the entire body.

Third Observation

No member in the church has the right to be disinterested or disengaged in the process. Choosing any officer is a serious moment in the church, and the responsibility falls upon "the whole multitude." Any member who takes an I-don't-care attitude does not fully understand the importance of the office and their responsibility as a member of the church. We know this is a hard question to ask, but is it even possible for a true believer to not care about such an important event in the life of the church of Christ? Not care? Not interested? Not take their membership responsibilities seriously? This is a responsibility that no member of the church has the right to ignore.

In summary, we have the answer to the first inductive question of *who* is to *find qualified candidates*? It is both the right and responsibility of *every saved and baptized member of the church.*

SECOND INDUCTIVE QUESTION: WHAT SPECIFICALLY IS THE "WHOLE MULTITUDE" INSTRUCTED TO DO?

Verse 3 tells us: "Wherefore, brethren. look ye out among you seven men of honest report, full of the Holy Ghost and wisdom, whom we may appoint over this business." We dealt with the qualifications earlier, so we won't repeat them here. The important thing here is that the church was told exactly *what* to do. The members in Jerusalem were told to "look" for seven men and were given very clear instructions on *what* to "look" for. The congregation of believers was given a brief but nonnegotiable list of qualifications that must be true of every man that was to be set before the apostles for appointment.

In order to solve the problem of neglect, the apostles determined the whole church needed some guidelines. And the guidelines are simple: *find qualified men. Find* honest men, Spirit-led men, wise men, and we will appoint them! Read between the lines: "If you bring us unqualified men,

men who do not meet the requirements, they will not be appointed. Bring us only *qualified candidates*! If you want the problem solved and the church to be blessed, follow these instructions." The apostles themselves set the parameters for the searching-out process. If we alter the process, we put the whole assembly at risk.

When it comes to all matters of faith and practice, the Word of God is our standard. We acknowledge that God's Word is silent on many things relating to the specific activities of the officers of the church. However, when it comes to the qualifications for the individuals who will serve as officers, the Scriptures are very clear. We are not free to make up our own list, amend the list, selectively apply the list, or, worst of all, totally ignore the fact that God has given us a list of qualifications at all. The only acceptable response to the God-given qualifications is, "Yes, Lord." The church must find biblically *qualified* candidates or find no candidates at all. This is *what* the church is directed to do. "Look for" only the qualified.

First Observation

Every member must be thoroughly acquainted with the qualifications in order for the church to carry out its God-given responsibility to find only qualified candidates. How can we be effectively engaged in the process of *finding qualified candidates* if we do not know *what* the qualifications are?

Second Observation

In order for the assembly to know and submit to the qualifications, someone is responsible both to teach what the qualifications are and to insist that only qualified individuals are put before the assembly for consideration. Ultimately, the responsibility falls on the shoulders of the spiritual leaders of the church to make sure the church is biblically equipped to both know and submit to the qualifications.

In summary, *what* is the church instructed to do? Look for and find only *qualified* candidates. Given that the church has the right and responsibility to choose its own deacons, it is absolutely essential that the members know and follow exactly *what* the Bible actually directs them to do. Everyone, members and leaders alike, must be conscious of and committed to the biblical qualifications.

THIRD INDUCTIVE QUESTION: WHERE DOES THE CHURCH "LOOK" TO FIND QUALIFIED CANDIDATES?

The obvious answer, of course, is found in the words *among you*. In other words, find them *in the church*, not just any church, but the church *where* the deacons will be serving. The deacons chosen in Acts 6 for the church in Jerusalem did not serve the same function in every church. Every church is instructed to find their own deacons.

Observation relating to where the church looks to find qualified candidates

Finding qualified candidates from the assembly has a very practical upside. The best way, perhaps the only way, for the members to be certain they are choosing *qualified* candidates is by choosing from *among themselves* individuals they already know, those with whom they worship, serve, and fellowship. Is there a better way for a member of the church to be sure the candidate is indeed *qualified* and suitable for this office?

We're so thankful that God raises up *qualified* servants in the church where they are to serve: servant leaders who are then recognized and chosen by that church. G. Campbell Morgan said, "This is the first law of Christian service, that those employed in serving the disciples of the church should be of the number of the disciples."[111]

---

111 G. Campbell Morgan, *The Acts of the Apostles* (New York: Fleming H. Revell, 1924), 173.

In summary, *where* does the church look for qualified servant leaders? They look among the members of the church. The very important practical benefit of "looking out from among you" or from your church membership is the advantage of knowing the spiritual condition of a candidate beforehand.

FOURTH INDUCTIVE QUESTION: WHEN IS THE CHURCH TO LOOK FOR QUALIFIED CANDIDATES?

Luke simply reports, "[T]here arose a murmuring," that some of the church's widows were being neglected. In response to the murmuring, "the twelve called the multitude of the disciples unto them." We don't know how long the apostles were aware of the problem before they acted. It's quite possible, in fact even likely, that the twelve were already aware of the problem to some degree. It's also possible they had been discussing it among themselves and praying for wisdom. What we do know for sure is that they immediately met the situation with a Spirit-directed master plan to solve the crisis, a master plan for the ages to come.

Let's take a minute to think through the situation. First, the twelve in Acts 6 are not the slow-to-learn twelve of the early days with Jesus. There is a remarkable difference between the two groups. These are the post-Pentecost twelve. Those who were discipled by Jesus are now empowered for ministry by the promised Holy Spirit. While they were not perfect, it is hard to accept the idea that they were either clueless, which they sometimes were while being discipled by Christ, or, worse, thoughtless regarding the problem that was developing among the Grecian widows in the church. Pentecost changed these men, and we should acknowledge the impact this event had upon them. Pentecost, in fact, changed everything.

Second, their experiences with Jesus and then the church in the opening chapters of Acts tell us that the apostles weren't out-of-touch, "ivory tower" kind of leaders. Why should we automatically assume they had their heads and hearts so buried in spiritual duties that they were unaware of the whole unfortunate situation? Or that they were unwilling to roll up their sleeves and get their hands dirty to help the needy? You might say they were street-level leaders, out among the people. They were there when Jesus fed and healed the multitudes. They just spent over three years in the highways and byways with the one "who went about doing good." They themselves became hungry and tired trying to keep up with Him. Surely, they learned some situational awareness from these experiences, and now they have the Spirit Himself equipping and empowering them to continue the good works modeled by Christ.

In Acts 4:32, Luke reports, "[A]nd no one said that any of the things that belonged to him was his own, but they had everything in common" (ESV). And what did they do with those things? They "laid them down at the apostles' feet: and distribution was made unto every man according as he had need" (vv. 35-36).

Here's the point we're making: the apostles are no strangers to the collection and distribution of supplies for the needy. Supplies are "laid at the apostles' feet." Why? For starters, they are overseeing the collection and distribution of goods. These experiences following Pentecost, coupled with their time spent with Jesus, paint a picture of fully informed and fully engaged apostles.

By the time we get to Chapter 6 and the murmuring starts, the apostles already recognize their limitations. They can't continue to take care of the needy and keep up with their primary responsibilities of prayer and ministering the Word. As if to call a sanctified "time-out," they exclaim, "It is not right that we should give up preaching the word of God to serve tables" (6:2, ESV).

When they say "it is not reason that we should leave the word of God and serve tables," it sounds like a line-in-the-sand moment. It sounds like they had their prayer, study, and preaching time interrupted one too many times, and they couldn't allow the situation to continue. The word *reason* suggests the apostles believed God would not be pleased if they were so distracted with practical things that they ignored the spiritual things. It was not the "right" thing for them to do.[112]

This is the picture the text is painting. They have the insight to see that the demands for this work would eventually take them away from their nonnegotiable priorities of the Word and prayer.

So, *when* the "murmuring" arose (symptom) that some were being "neglected" (problem), they met with the whole assembly to resolve the situation (solution). The text seems to suggest, as soon as the murmuring started, they already had a solution in hand. That would explain how they so quickly called all the disciples together to give them the heaven-sent solution.

Back to the question at hand—*when* did the church receive the authority to *find qualified men*? Answer—*when* the need arose. Two observations follow.

First observation relating to when the church is to find qualified candidates

Using the book of Acts as our starting point for the office, it's worth noting that the office of deacon was born out of need. But not just one need, there were actually two. First, there was the need to care for the neglected and, secondly, the need to shield their spiritual leaders from unnecessary distractions. Both must be kept in mind. It wasn't just about the needy widows; it was about the apostles as well. The church needs to be alert to both concerns and ready to take action on behalf of both groups.

Think of the office of the Deacon as "The Office of Necessary Actions." This is the place where the membership goes *when* action is necessary. If

---

112 James Strong, *Strong's Exhaustive Concordance of the English Bible* (Grand Rapids, MI: Zondervan Publishing, 2001), under "reason."

there are people with physical or material needs, everyone knows where that office is. If the spiritual leaders are distracted with the physical/material needs, someone from that office is ready to step in and take care of it on their behalf. Whatever other functions the deacons may serve, if they do not look out for the needy and shield the spiritual leaders from unnecessary distractions, they run the risk of not fulfilling the dual function of the office. So, *when* is it time for a church to find more qualified candidates? *When* needs are not being effectively addressed and resolved.

Second observation relating to when the church is to find qualified candidates

The observation that we are about to make might appear to be in conflict with the previous observation, that the call to find qualified candidates was born out of need. However, in drawing lessons from a biblical narrative, we must make a distinction between what is being described and what is being prescribed. The fact that some were "murmuring" is descriptive of the historical events. But we cannot take that to be prescriptive in the sense that we must wait until murmuring begins before we should take action to find qualified candidates. As if to say, no one is complaining about not being served, so apparently, we don't need more deacons. It seems much wiser for both the spiritual and servant leaders to be anticipating future needs and preparing beforehand to meet them. Isn't this an important component of being prepared?

So how can a church get to the point that it is *always* ready to act, *always* having servant leaders ready to spring into action? We think the answer is in the word *always*. So, *when* should a church be *finding qualified candidates* for the office? *Always!*

Perhaps this is as good a time as ever to tackle two frequently asked questions. The first is, "You say we should *always* be looking for and *finding qualified candidates*, but what if we don't need any deacons right now? What's the point in looking for them if they're not needed?" The second question is similar, but the focus is different. "What if our church always has more qualified individuals than is currently needed? Finding a candidate is not the problem; we have a bunch of them. The problem is knowing what to do with those who are bypassed yet deserve to be chosen."

First, what if you don't need more deacons? We'll start with an illustration. Did you know the first automobile company Henry Ford was involved with went broke because they couldn't keep up with the demand? Ever heard of the Detroit Automobile Company? Probably not, and the company bearing his name would have suffered the same fate except for an idea he borrowed from his competitor, the Olds Motor Vehicle Company. That idea was the assembly line. By adding the assembly line, they would *always* have enough cars for every potential buyer. Ford's goal? *Always* be ready to meet the need.

What does this have to do with *always finding deacons*? When demand is greater than supply, failure is lurking around the corner—not a good way to run a business. But why is it a good way to run a church? More specifically, why is it a good way to manage the diaconal ministry of the church? Why is it a good idea to wait until we can't keep up with demand to place an order for another deacon? It doesn't seem right. If we wait until there's a crisis we can't handle or needs that we can't get to, we're always behind, always trying to catch up. It will come down to having to say, "Sorry, you'll have to get in line. We won't have another deacon until after our annual meeting."

We're not suggesting this happens all the time or in every church. It doesn't. But it happens. It can happen in small churches where the members expect the pastor to take care of these things. He too bears some blame for allowing himself to be distracted from his priorities. But it can happen in large churches where people and problems get lost in the crowd or fall between the cracks, all because of an inadequate number of watchful deacons. Regardless of how it happens, that it happens at all should be unacceptable. Instead of trying to catch up with the needs, or overworking the few, or distracting the spiritual leaders, wouldn't it be better to already have deacons in place to meet the need when it comes up? Instead of waiting to add more deacons when we can't keep up, why not *always* be finding deacons so that the needy aren't the ones left waiting? So, to the first question, "what" if we don't need more deacons? Being prepared is wiser than playing catch-up.

Second, what if you have more *qualified* servants than you currently need? You have one "opening" but several qualified candidates. We know of a small church (fifty to seventy-five in attendance) who recently took nominations for the office. Several men were nominated; all were biblically qualified and all had distinguished themselves as servants in the church. Furthermore, their wives were eager servant partners with them. When the members turned in their lists of potential candidates for the office, every list had the same names. When it came time for a vote, the elders instructed the church to vote for every candidate on the ballet that they would like to see serve as a deacon. Every ballot came back with a vote for every man on the list. Clearly, the church members were focused on both having qualified men and recognizing the men that God had already raised up in the church. They weren't obsessed with how many they *needed* but with how many were already *qualified*.

We realize this isn't the normal way for determining how many deacons a church has. But why not? Why not find and install all the qualified servants that God gives the church? He put them in the church. He planted the desire to serve others. He continues to grow them in grace. Why shouldn't the church then recognize them and give them the opportunity to serve in the office?

In summary, "*When* should the church be looking for *qualified candidates*?" We believe the answer is, "*Always!*"

FIFTH INDUCTIVE QUESTION: WHY IS THE CHURCH TO FIND QUALIFIED CANDIDATES?

Perhaps you're thinking this is a no-brainer. This inductive question hardly merits more than a few words, right? In a sense, that's true. Every Christian can come up with reasons as to *why* the church finds qualified candidates. However, there may be more to this question than first meets the eye. When we stop and think of what is at stake, suddenly this simple question starts to take on more significance. We can think of at least six reasons *why* the church must *find qualified candidates*. Keep in mind this is a selective list, not an exhaustive list.

1. Why find qualified candidates? For the glory of God.

The ultimate purpose for everything is the glory of God. God's chief end is His own glory. Therefore, everything God directs His church to do, whatever it is, He does so with an eye toward promoting His own glory. As the church humbly submits every detail of its existence to the All-Wise, All-Loving, All-Good God as revealed in His All-Sufficient Word, it promotes His glory, His honor, His supremacy in the world. Given the fact God has given only two offices to His church, this is a detail we cannot ignore without running the risk of distracting from His glory in the church and in the world. *Why?* Because God is glorified when the church finds biblically *qualified candidates* to serve as deacons.

2. Why? For the work of the Lord.

In Acts 6, we cannot miss what happened after the installation of servant leaders. Verse 7 reads, "And the word of God increased; and the number of the disciples multiplied in Jerusalem greatly; and a great company of the priests were obedient to the faith." Although it isn't explicitly stated, it seems to us there is an organic connection between the installation of the seven and the *continued advancement* of *the work of the Lord* in the world. The relationship seems undeniable. William Arnot writes this:

> Divisions impede the progress of the kingdom; but divisions wisely, generously, promptly healed, not only restore matters to their former condition, but carry the common cause further forward . . . Thus it often happens in Christian communities, that where faith and love are in exercise, incidental difficulties become the occasion of edification and progress, according to the promise that God will make all things work together for good to his own.[113]

When the neglect, the murmuring, the division, and the distractions were all dealt with, what happened? The work of the Lord advanced. And how, specifically, did they deal with both the causes and effects? By appointing deacons.

David Peterson observes that the first six chapters of Acts describe the remarkable growth of the Christian community in Jerusalem. More to the point, he writes, "The gospel is shown to prosper in spite of, and even because of, struggle and suffering. Most importantly, however, the present context suggests that, if decisive action had not been taken to deal with the social issue disturbing the church, 'growth' of the word may not have continued."[114] When problems within the assembly are not handled in a biblical manner, the work of the Lord is often hindered. When, on the other hand, problems are dealt with in a God-honoring way, the church is positioned to promote the work of the Lord.

---

113 Arnot, *Studies in Acts*, 133.

114 David Peterson, *Acts of the Apostles* (Grand Rapids, MI: William B. Eerdmans Publishing, 2009), 229.

This relationship between *finding qualified servant leaders* and the success of *the work of the Lord* is implicitly suggested in the apostles' explanation as to *why* this action was necessary. Listen to them:

- "It is not reason that we should leave the word of God and serve tables,"

- "whom we may appoint over this business,"

- "But we will give ourselves continually to prayer and the ministry of the word."

What are they fighting for? What are they protecting? Their God-given priorities! The spiritual leaders of the early church are fighting to keep first things first. They cannot get so deeply entangled with the practical affairs of the church (the needy) so as to be restrained from being fully engaged in Word and prayer. And *why* is that? Because the work of the Lord will suffer! Conversely, by disentangling themselves from the practical needs by appointing *qualified* leaders, they can devote themselves entirely and robustly to the spiritual oversight of the church, which in turn becomes a means of advancing *the work of the Lord*.

Why is finding qualified servants so important? Whether it's by lovingly taking care of the needy or by allowing the spiritual leaders to focus on priorities, when the church finds and appoints *qualified* servant leaders, *the work of the Lord* is advanced.

3. Why? For the benefit of the qualified.

Here we will pick up on one of the questions asked earlier, "What if there are more qualified than we currently need?" Ask yourself this question: what if the church fails in its responsibility to advance qualified candidates? What if they are never given the opportunity to serve in the office? Does it affect the believer who is in every way qualified but never acknowledged? We believe it does. If the church fails in its responsibility to find and install *qualified candidates, the qualified* themselves suffer loss. How? It robs them of the benefits that are associated with the office.

First, the office of the deacon can serve as a platform to do even greater works for God's kingdom and Christ's church. A man may go into office with biblical yet simple expectations: just serve the needy when called upon. Yet, as he serves, he gains more awareness, more wisdom, and more encouragement to do even greater things. Perhaps deeds of mercy that have lain heavy upon the heart are now able to become realities. Or opportunities never dreamed of are made possible. Now, recognized by the church and under the leadership of the spiritual overseers, he feels empowered to be bolder as he seeks to serve the needy in the church, the community, and beyond. Taking advantage of the privilege of serving in the office of the deacon, he is propelled on to greater acts of service. Not that he wouldn't serve anyway; it's in his "spiritual DNA." The office becomes a channel through which he demonstrates the active kindness (beneficence) of God to everyone around him. Surely, he has a right to enjoy these *benefits*.

Second, appointment to the office holds the promise of *personal gain* for the *qualified* servant. In 1 Timothy 3:13, Paul writes, "For they that have used the office of a deacon well purchase to themselves a good degree, and great boldness in the faith which is in Christ Jesus." Not only does the office provide a platform for faithful deacons, they are promised *special benefits* for themselves as they serve others in Christ's stead.

Paul uses the word *purchase* metaphorically to say that faithful deacons are buying/acquiring for themselves two special rewards: a good reputation in the community of faith and greater confidence in Christ that comes as a result of doing works of mercy. They are distinguishing themselves, rising up above others in their reputation, as obedient and trustworthy leaders in the church and the community. Not that they sinfully seek recognition or advancement for themselves. No, this is something God Himself has promised to those who serve well. Therefore, the church that fails to recognize *qualified* candidates runs the risk of standing in the way of God-appointed blessings for those who would use the office of the deacon to serve the needy.

While we are on the subject of the *promise of personal gain* for the deacon, we would like to comment on two groups of individuals in the church: those who will never be candidates and those who might be overlooked as candidates. First, church leaders should always give recognition to those members who willingly and joyfully serve others yet, for various reasons, may never be chosen to hold office. Not everyone is qualified, but that doesn't mean their service should not be appreciated and acknowledged or that their service will go unrewarded. God will surely bless them for their labors of love on His behalf. Furthermore, their humble service is often a powerful testimony to both the church and the community of the power of grace in a life once controlled by sin.

Now a word concerning the second group: those who are often overlooked as viable candidates. When assessing candidates, we must consider the whole person, not just this or that desirable personality trait. Yes, they must be qualified, and we want them to show a present interest in serving others. But a desire to serve others will manifest itself differently from person to person. Some will serve with a contagious enthusiasm that is obvious to everyone. Others, however, will serve quietly, preferring anonymity over recognition. Passion and zeal will not look the same in every candidate. That will vary. We have to be careful that we do not automatically rule out potential deacons because of preconceived notions. They are individuals with individual personalities, interests, areas of expertise, and different levels of spiritual maturity. But they all share a common interest: serving the needs of the body, whatever those needs might be. If we overlook someone simply because they don't show a lot of enthusiasm or swell with emotion at the mention of a needy family, we run the risk of neglecting *qualified candidates* and depriving them of the *blessings of serving* in the office.

In summary, another reason *why* the church must find *qualified candidates* is for the sake of the *qualified*. The church must not rob them of the promised *benefits* that are associated with the office and those who serve well.

4. Why? For the sake of the needy.

If the church does not find *qualified* individuals to serve as deacons, then the first to suffer are those who need them the most: the poor and needy among us. This gets us back to one of the primary reasons the office exists. Our beneficent God has designed an office to ensure that the physical needs of those around us are met. It is almost unthinkable that the body of Christ, for want of interest in, or obedience to the master plan of God, would allow those who need help to suffer without an adequate number of advocates who labor on their behalf. Surely, we all agree that serving the needy is another reason *why* the church must *find qualified candidates* for the office.

5. Why? It is our duty.

As recorded in Acts 6, there were widows who were being neglected. So, what did the apostles do? They put the burden for solving the problem on the assembly. It was the responsibility of the whole multitude to choose men to make sure the neglected were cared for. In a word, it was their *duty*.

Beyond the *duty* embedded in the narrative of Acts 6 and the Old Testament Scriptures that stand behind it, there are clear commands in the New Testament to care for the physical needs of the body of Christ. To quote just two,

- Galatians 6:10, "As we therefore have opportunity, let us do good unto all men, especially unto them who are of the household of faith."

- 1 John 3:17, "But whoso hath this world's good, and seeth his brother have need, and shutteth up his bowels of compassion from him, how dwelleth the love of God in him?"

These passages, and others like them, teach us it is our God-given *duty* to care for the material needs of those around us, especially the needs of our brothers and sisters in Christ. *Why* must the church find *qualified servants?* Because it is the *duty* of the church to do so. And let us quickly add—it is also our privilege to do so.

6. Why? For the good of the church.

Every church seeks not only to please God, but we long to be blessed by God. God has made His will clear in the matter of church officers and their qualifications. To disregard His revealed will for the church is to disregard *His* favor and *our* good. Any church that wants to be a blessed church must, among other things, be *finding* individuals to love and care for the needy among us. Surely this is a good reason *why qualified* deacons must be found and appointed by the church. *It is for the good of the church.*

SIXTH INDUCTIVE QUESTION: HOW IS THE CHURCH TO FIND QUALIFIED CANDIDATES?

The word *how* speaks of the way, manner, or means by which something is done. It often refers to *the process* by which something is accomplished. In Acts 6, the apostles begin the process by calling the multitude of disciples together. They complete *the process* by setting the seven apart for service. In between, the assembly was told *how* to *find qualified candidates. How?* As stated earlier in this chapter, they were to "look" for them. This was the way, manner, or means by which the church was to deal with the problem of the neglected widows.

But what exactly does it mean to "look"? This is not a simple glance of the eyes or a mental visualization exercise that the apostles have in mind. They are not suggesting the church members casually "look" around at their fellow church members or take a few minutes to "look" through the membership directory and choose the first seven able bodied men they see. J. A. Alexander points out the word *look* literally means to "*look at*, visit, or inspect, for the purpose of discovering the necessary qualifications."[115] Often the church "looks" no further than the most popular, or most attractive, or most educated, or the most successful, or just anyone who is willing. It is as though no serious thought even goes into the nomination process.

The word *look* suggests a *process* that is much more intentional, purposeful, and deliberate. To use a more contemporary word, the candidates are to be "vetted." Their lives need to be carefully and intentionally inspected for any significant disqualifying issue according to the required biblical qualifications. We're not suggesting the church hire a detective to sift through someone's garbage or snoop around for a week or two to see where they go and what they do. This "vetting process," in most cases, will be done ahead of time. The true candidates for the office will have already distinguished themselves as trusted servants of the church. But even when a good man comes to mind, his life is to be inspected, revisited as it were, to make sure he meets the necessary qualifications as prescribed in 1 Timothy 3:8-13. This is the first thing the church must do: engage in a serious, careful, and intentional process of choosing its candidates. This is what it means to "look." Looking is *how* the church is to *find the qualified.*

To get a better handle on what it means to "look," we point out four important details concerning this word.

- First, it's a verb. Verbs speak of action. *How* was the problem to be solved? By performing a specific action. Here, the action is

---

115 Joseph A. Alexander, *A Commentary on the Acts of the Apostles* (New York, 1857; repr. Minneapolis, MN: Klock and Klock, 1980), 243.

"look ye out." This is the first action involved in finding deacons. You look.

- Second, it's in the imperative mood. Imperatives are commands. The required action, "look," was not optional. It wasn't a suggestion. It was a directive, a command, something they must do. Solving the problem God's way meant obeying the imperative.

- Third, it has a specific purpose in mind: "look ye out." This speaks of making distinctions between people: this person, not that person, someone, not everyone. The problem would be solved when they carefully identified the seven *qualified* members of the assembly.

- Fourth, it's inclusive, not exclusive. That is, the directive was to be carried out by "the whole multitude." We see no room for either nonparticipation or exclusion. Everyone was expected to follow the apostolic directive. While not everyone will come up with their own list of candidates, every member is expected to honestly evaluate the nominated candidates and make a choice.

The *process* required action, obedience, purpose, and full corporate participation. This is *how*, generally speaking, the assembly was to *find qualified candidates*.

Let's move now from general details to specific details. *How* specifically did they *find the qualified*? Have you ever wondered how news of the apostles' decision to include the whole church in solving the problem spread among the believers? By the time we get to Acts 6, the church had thousands of members. In Chapter 2, three thousand are saved, and another five thousand in Chapter 4. Many scholars estimate the number of new believers in and around Jerusalem to be around twenty thousand. *How* in the world do you let that many people know they must now choose their own servant leaders? And not just any leaders, they are to look for leaders who meet specific qualifications. How would they carry out the vetting process, the collection of nominations, the deadline for turning in the list of candidates, and so forth? And all of this information had to spread through the "whole multitude" and conclude with them bringing the seven to the apostles.

Just think about any one of these details: the vetting of candidates for example. *How* did they do that? Who collected the information? Who verified the results? *How* long did it take? And we're just thinking about one step in the process: making sure they were *qualified*. Barring a miracle, which doesn't seem to have happened, this must have been a huge organizational challenge. Although Luke does not give us the details, it is fair to infer from the challenge before them that certain steps had to be followed. There had to be a *process* for accomplishing such an important service to the body of Christ. But *how* would they actually do this without cell phones, tweeting, texting, or Facebook? Fast donkeys?

As one of us was teaching this lesson on a Sunday evening to our church, one of our men raised his hand. He is a retired Air Force Master Sergeant working on base as a civilian. His area of expertise is "supply," meaning he is responsible for everything that goes in or out of the base, both military and civilian, and making sure that every contractor working on base meets Department of Defense standards. Thinking about the enormity of the task, he queried, "How in the world did they do this? This is something I know a lot about. I do this kind of work for a living. And when you add the collection and distribution of funds and other supplies for the needy into the equation, it gets a lot more complicated. If I was responsible for managing these details for an estimated twenty thousand people, it would be a logistical nightmare! I've never thought about this before, but the fact they were able to organize both the vote and the relief effort in a short amount of time is simply amazing!"

The truth is, we simply do not know the details of *how* this was accomplished. But if you would allow us to speculate, perhaps something like the following took place:

136

- Step one—they divided the entire assembly into manageable groups, perhaps according to where they lived in the city.

- Step two—every group began to earnestly pray.

- Step three—they assigned a qualified teacher, perhaps an apostle or New Testament prophet, to every group.

- Step four—they made sure that every member of the expanding church understood the qualifications, and that every voting member must submit his or her own personal feelings to the authoritative instructions given by the apostles.

- Step five—the names of candidates were submitted for consideration.

- Step six—they began the process of evaluating the recommendations to determine who was qualified. Every individual whose name came up had to be carefully, yet discreetly, vetted.

- Step seven—they narrowed the list of potential candidates to a much narrower list of qualified candidates from which the church will choose the seven, as directed by the apostles.

- Step eight—they devised a system to allow every member of the "whole multitude" to say (vote) whom they had chosen to oversee the care of the needy.

- Step nine—they gathered and tabulated thousands of votes.

- Step ten—they notified the entire assembly of the outcome of the vote.

- Step eleven—they planned a church-wide public gathering so that the whole multitude could bring the seven to the apostles to set them apart for service.

All of this was just to choose seven servants! Then, after having been chosen, the seven had to make sure the concerns of the many who were underserved were resolved to everyone's satisfaction. Wow!

Was the selection of the original seven anything like we described? We don't know. Regardless of *how* they did it, and however long it took, they did it. We know that much. It is possible, of course, that the Spirit of the Lord swept over the entire church and the whole process took just a few minutes. Possible, but we don't think so. At no point do the apostles say anything like, "Now all of you go to your own homes and wait for the Holy Spirit to come upon you and reveal seven names to you." If for no other reason, just the directive "look ye out among you" suggests a process that involves both human activity and human responsibility. They, themselves, were directed to "look." Furthermore, the very fact that the apostles gave a list of qualifications means that the multitude must take those qualifications into account as they choose the seven.

Regardless of the steps the early church took or the *process* that any church follows today, it is absolutely essential that the members both know and follow the known biblical directives. Every individual member is responsible to know what the biblical requirements are and to always be on the lookout for *qualified candidates*. While the specifics will vary from church to church, every assembly must have a process that sticks closely to the biblical text.

We began this section by pointing out that the word *how* speaks of the way, manner, or means by which something is done, the process by which it is accomplished. The sixth inductive question we've been answering is, "*How* does the church *find qualified candidates*?" The way the church does this is by following the biblical pattern.

Before moving on to the next step, let's quickly review step one. It's been a long step, and we don't want you to lose track of where we are. The first step in appointing qualified candidates to oversee the care of the needy is found in the imperative to *find qualified* candidates. We've examined this step using the inductive study approach. Following are the inductive questions and their answers:

1. *Who* is responsible to find the qualified? All members of the assembly are to be involved in the process.

2. *What* are the members to find? All members are responsible to find only qualified candidates.

3. *Where* do the members find the qualified? The assembly looks among its members to find those who are biblically qualified.

4. *When* should members be looking for the qualified? Always!

5. *Why* must the church be looking for qualified servants?

   - For God's glory

   - For the work of the Lord

   - For the benefit of the qualified

   - For the sake of the needy

   - For obedience to the duty

   - For the good of the church

6. *How* does the church go about this process of finding the qualified? By "looking."

We now turn our attention to the second step -

Step 4—Directing qualified candidates.

Step 3—Installing qualified candidates.

Step 2—Electing qualified candidates.

Step 1—Finding qualified candidates.

And the saying pleased the whole multitude: and they chose Stephen, a man full of faith and of the Holy Ghost, and Philip, and Prochorus, and Nicanor, and Timon, and Parmenas, and Nicolas, a proselyte of Antioch. (Acts 6:5).

Once the church goes through *the process of finding qualified candidates*, there has to be a *process* of choosing or *electing qualified* individuals to serve. If everything is done as God has directed, then ideally this will not be a vote between good and bad candidates, but a vote to confirm the *qualified*.

Working from our text in Acts 6, the two most basic questions are, *who* chose, and *how* did they choose? The first question is, "*Who* gets to vote?" The answer is simple. The same group who *finds* them has the right and responsibility to *choose* them. *Who?* The "whole multitude." Specifically, the members of the congregation chose these seven men to serve and oversee the care of the needy on their behalf.

In following the passage, we find the apostles in verse 3 telling the assembly to "look ye out among you." Verse 4 states the reason for the directive: to prevent them from being distracted from devoting themselves to prayer and the Word. Immediately following the directive, we find the word *and* used twice in verse 5. "*And* what they said pleased the whole multitude: *and they* chose . . ." (italics added). The sequence is clear. Those who were told to "look," then "chose."

Clearly the believers understood exactly what the apostles were commissioning them to do. Make a choice. *Choose* seven men. And they did! This is a case where the results make the directive clear. If we weren't sure what "look ye out" meant before, it becomes clear by their actions: "they chose."

Although the narrative does not explicitly divide so neatly into two phases—the *qualifying* phase and the *voting phase*—it is implied. First, they "looked" among the brethren for *qualified candidates*. The very act of "looking" suggests that something is to follow. They weren't told to look around for the sake of looking around, as if that was an end in itself. Secondly, after identifying those who were qualified to serve, the next thing was to choose. This would be the *voting phase* of the *process*. At some point, the assembly of believers had to make a choice. They had to *vote*. Verse 5 says, "[L]ook ye out," and verse 6 tells us, "[A]nd they chose." This word *chose* means to "select, make a choice, choose."[116] Interestingly, the word *look* in verse 5 is sometimes translated as "pick" (ESV). The primary meaning of the Greek word is as described above: "to inspect" and "look over."[117] However, picking is implied. This is the purpose for looking. They were to select the servant leaders who would solve the problem of the neglected widows and free up the apostles' work load.

As we step back and look at the whole picture described in the passage, we see the entire sequence of events unfolding in a very orderly manner:

- The Grecians murmured against the Hebrews.

- The apostles gave their solution.

- The assembly was pleased.

- They looked for qualified candidates.

- They made a choice, seven choices to be exact.

- They brought the chosen to the apostles for confirmation.

- The apostles set the chosen apart for service.

Not only was the whole *process* done "decently and in order" (1 Cor. 14:33, 40), but it established a precedent that stands today. We can think of no better *process* than the one established by the apostles under the direction of the Holy Spirit. Exactly how the finding and choosing phases are

---

116 Strong, *Strong's Exhaustive Concordance of the English Bible*, under "chose," no. 1586.
117 Ibid., under "look," no. 1980.

carried out is up to each individual church. But that each church is to *find* and *elect qualified* candidates is nonnegotiable.

Now that we have established who chose, we move on to the second question: how did they choose? You might be wondering if there was a precedent for how the church members were to elect an officer. For that we turn to Acts 1 and the choice of Matthias to replace the fallen Judas. Concerning the setting forth of the two candidates in verse 23, something we would call the nomination phase, John Gill writes this:

> [A]nd this choice or ordination was moved to be made, and was made, not by the other eleven apostles, but by the whole company of a hundred and twenty, for these are the persons addressed by the apostle, and to whom he said, as the Arabic version renders it, *one of these men ye must choose*; and if the choice and ordination of such an extraordinary officer was made by the whole community, then much more ought the choice and ordination of inferior officers be by them.[118]

Setting the controversial method of choosing aside, Peter allowed the entire company of believers to choose an apostle. Our point in referring back to this selection is to highlight Gill's observation that, if they can choose an apostle, certainly they can choose a deacon. By the time the events of Acts 6 were completed, the precedent had been established: let the entire church *elect* its leaders. From that point on, we see the entire church making a variety of corporate decisions:

- Acts 11:22, the *church* sent Barnabas to Antioch
- Acts 14:23, the *church* "appointed" elders
- Acts 15:2-3, the *church* sent Paul and Barnabas to Jerusalem

---

118 John Gill, *An Exposition of the Old and New Testaments* (London, 1852-1854; reprinted Grand Rapids, MI: Baker Book House, 1980), 5: 806.

- Acts 15:22, the *church* joined the apostles and elders in sending messengers with Paul and Barnabas to Antioch

- 1 Cor. 5:5, the *church* is exhorted to discipline a member

- 2 Cor. 2:6, the discipline was carried out by the *church*

- 2 Cor. 8:18-19, the *church* chose a companion for Paul (the word translated chosen is *cheirotoneo*, which means to choose by the showing of hands[119])

In summary, when it comes time to *elect qualified candidates*, this is the right and responsibility of every eligible member of the church. The fact that the early church was given the right to choose its own servant leaders is in line with the precedent established in Acts 1 and agreeable to the voting practices of the church following Acts 6. This has been the practice of most churches from the earliest days of Christianity to the present.

Now, we turn our attention to step three -

Step 4—Directing qualified candidates.

Step 3—Installing the qualified.

Step 2—Electing qualified candidates.

Step 1—Finding qualified candidates.

Wherefore, brethren, look ye out among you seven men of honest report, full of the Holy Ghost and wisdom, whom we may appoint over this business. (Acts 6:3).

Steps one and two are the responsibility of the entire assembly. Let the church *find* and *elect* its officers. As we now move to consider *installing*

---

119 Strong, *Strong's Exhaustive Concordance of the English Bible*, under "chosen," no. 5500.

and *directing* the duly elected deacons, we shift from congregational rights and duties to pastoral rights and duties. Taking our cue from the events recorded in Acts 6, there is a difference between *finding* and *electing the qualified* and *installing* and *directing the qualified*. The fact that the membership has the responsibility to *find* and the right to *choose* candidates for the office does not mean that the spiritual leaders of the church are locked out of the *process*. Verse 3 tells us the whole congregation picked out seven men, but the apostles reserved the right to appoint them. They specifically said, "[W]hom *we* may appoint over this business" (emphasis added). To "appoint" is to place, designate, constitute.[120] The assembly *chose them*, but only the apostles could *designate them* for the special service for which they were chosen.

Furthermore, verse 6 tells us that the whole assembly "set before the apostles" those they chose. What exactly does that mean? To "set" means, to place, to cause to stand. As Alexander explains, "[I]t denotes the presentation of the persons found to possess the prescribed qualifications."[121] In other words, the members looked, assessed, chose, but then brought or presented the individuals to the apostles. Why? Recognizing the limitations of their granted responsibilities, they brought their candidates to the only body of men who could officially designate them for service.

Today, built upon the foundation laid by the apostles, the spiritual leaders *oversee* the affairs of the church of Christ. That's what overseers do: they watch over every aspect of the church (1 Tim. 3:1; Heb. 13:17). A previous observation bears repeating here. No individual church member or group of members has the authority to install deacons on their own. It is a collaboration between members and leaders. Following the model of the early church and biblical instruction concerning leadership in the church,

---

120 Ibid., under "appoint," no. 2525.
121 Alexander, *Commentary on the Acts of the Apostles*, 246.

the responsibility to install or place individuals into office rests with the spiritual overseers.

The public ceremony to acknowledge the individuals who have been chosen by the members and approved by the spiritual overseers is typically referred to as the installation service. While our English words *install* and *installation* are not in the Bible, they are perfectly suited to describe what took place in Jerusalem and what generally takes place in most churches when a new deacon is officially placed into office.

Webster defines *install* as "to set in a seat, to give place to, to establish in a place." He defines *installation* as "the act of installing, giving possession of an office, rank, or order, with the usual rites or ceremonies."[122] When we compare these definitions to the events that are described in Acts 6:6, Luke certainly seems to be describing an "installation" service as we understand this word today.

Seeing the events in Acts 6 as "The Inaugural Installation Service," we would like to make a few observations from the text that might be helpful as we think of installing deacons today.

First observation—the installation was a public event

This was not a private ceremony performed behind closed doors, nor was it limited to a few hand-chosen friends to serve as witnesses. The entire process was very public in nature. The public nature of this event reminds us of the ceremonial setting apart of Timothy, as when Paul wrote, "[A]bout which you made the good confession in the presence of many witnesses" (1 Tim. 6:12). The implication is that when we install officers today, both servant and spiritual leaders, it must be an open, public event, witnessed by all who will be served by the elected officer.

---

122 Webster, *American Dictionary of the English Language* (1828), under "install" and "installation."

Second observation—the installation was a corporate event

This is implied in the first observation, but it goes beyond being held in public view. It was not just *for* the entire church; it was *by* the entire church. In other words, it is a public event that includes the full engagement of the entire congregation. Verse 5 identifies the "whole multitude" or full number of the disciples who "chose," and verse 6 says, "[T]hey set." It was the whole church that brought the chosen servants to the apostles to be set apart (installed). Both the seriousness and the grandeur of the moment call for full corporate participation. It is a blessing to take part in an event that has the approval of God stamped all over it. It is both the right and the obligation of every member to be involved in the process.

Third observation—the installation was a solemn event

The solemnity of the event is suggested by the actions of the apostles: they prayed for and laid hands on the men (v. 6). First, think about those apostolic prayers on behalf of the seven men. Luke does not give us any details. Did one pray? Did they all pray? Did they pray for each man by name or for all of them as a group? We simply cannot say. While we don't know for sure, think of the obvious possibilities. Perhaps they prayed for such things as increased and continued wisdom, sanctification, and perseverance for the seven. Perhaps they prayed for their safety. They might have remembered the members of their families, some of whom might be called into service to assist their husband or father. Surely, they prayed that they would have success in alleviating the nagging problem that necessitated their service. Perhaps their prayers included the entire church and their response to the work they were to oversee. Surely, all of these concerns would be on the minds and hearts of the apostles. Again, we just don't know. However, whatever the content of their prayers, they must have been solemn, serious, and full of the Holy Spirit.

Second, it wasn't just the fervent prayers of the apostles that cauterized this moment in the minds of all who witnessed this event. As they called out to the Father in heaven, they also laid hands on the seven chosen leaders. Surely, this added to the solemnity of the installation. Verse 6 states, "[A]nd when they had prayed, they laid *their* hands on them."

This practice has roots in the Old Testament that reach into the New. The Hebrew word behind the physical action means "to lay the hands on heavily, even to lean upon the person or object."[123] The Greek word means to "lay upon, put or set on."[124] The physical action itself—putting the hands on heavily, even to the point of pressing down—seems to suggest a kind of gravitas, or serious, solemn, importance. When the Israelite laid his hands on the sacrificial animal (Lev. 1:4; 3:2; 4:15, 24, 29), it meant he was to lean upon, to transfer his weight upon, to press down upon the animal—a solemn moment indeed. Most importantly, the solemnity of the event came from the meaning behind the event. The physical action was meant to coincide with the symbolic meaning of the laying on of hands. For the Israelite, it was the symbolic transfer of guilt from the sinner to the sacrifice. He laid his hands heavily upon the animal, as heavily as he felt the guilt of his own transgressions.

When the apostles laid hands on the seven, they were publicly and solemnly identifying these seven, and these seven only, as having apostolic approval and support. It is a symbolic gesture in that they are identifying themselves and the full authority of the apostolic office with these men. It sets these seven apart from everyone else as having been chosen by the assembly and now publicly recognized by the spiritual leaders of the assembly: the apostles.

---

123 Strong, *Strong's Exhaustive Concordance of the English Bible*, under the Hebrew word çâmak (*saw-mak´*), no. 5564.

124 Ibid., under the Greek word ĕpitithēmi (*ep-ee-tith´-ay-mee*), no. 2007.

The "laying on of hands" in the New Testament, when associated with installation into office, always has the same basic meaning. It sets the individual apart for service. It conveys a number of things: the approval of both God and men, the authority to act within the bounds of the office, the responsibility to carry out the purpose of the office, and it identifies those who have been chosen to serve in the office. Robert Mounce writes, "Most significantly, the laying on of hands is a ritual identifying a person's call to a specific task, and as such is applied to Stephen and his colleagues."[125] As we think about the responsibility placed upon these seven men, the laying on of hands serves as a kind of sacred contract between the men who have been chosen, and those who chose them. They serve on their behalf, and must carry out their assignment with their best interests in mind.

When we imagine the fervency of apostolic prayers and visualize the laying on of apostolic hands, we see a very solemn installation service of the seven servant leaders. What impact would these actions have on the entire church? We answer that question in the next observation.

Fourth observation—the installation was a perception-enhancing event

This being a *public, corporate,* and *solemn event,* we think it must have had an effect on all who participated. And this was by design. It's no accident the entire assembly was there. Both those who chose and those who were chosen were now assembled in front of the holy apostles. Why? Because God put them there. Their heavenly Father arranged for all of them to be there to witness what was about to happen. But for what purpose? To indelibly etch these things into their minds, these are things they cannot forget. But why? While we don't pretend to comprehend the whole matter, we suggest it was at least in part to *enhance their perception* of the *work* of the new office and of the men chosen to serve in the new office.

---

125 Robert H. Mounce, *Word Biblical Commentary* (Nashville: Thomas Nelson, Inc., 2000), Pastoral Epistles: 263.

An enhanced perception of the work

Following a series of Spirit-orchestrated steps, steps that ensured both member participation and candidate qualification, the church stood before the apostles with the chosen seven. Before their watching eyes and listening ears, the apostles laid hands on the seven. As the assembly of disciples stood silently, the apostles prayed fervently for the men and the success of the work they were chosen to accomplish. We can only imagine the impact this solemn service had on the church. Can there be any doubt that the events that culminated in the installation of the new deacons *enhanced their perception* of the work these seven men were chosen to do on their behalf?

An enhanced credibility of the men

Not only would the installation service affect their perception of the work, but it must have enhanced the *credibility of the men* as well. Yes, the multitude chose the seven, but the apostles approved of their selections and then solemnly installed, or set in place, just those seven men. No more, no less, and the seven were now standing before the apostles.

How could this not have changed their *perception* of these men? How could they not have thought more *highly* of them after the ceremony than before? How could they not know the full approval and authority of the apostles rested upon these wise and Spirit-filled men? What an impact the ceremony must have had on the *credibility of the chosen men*.

To summarize everything in Step 3, *installing the qualified*, we shifted our focus from the two responsibilities of the church to the first of two responsibilities of the spiritual leaders: the responsibility to *install qualified candidates*. We infer from the text of Acts 6 that spiritual leaders of the church must ensure the installation service is public, corporate, and solemn. We also considered the impact this has on the church, specifically the enhanced perception of both the office and the men who serve in the office. If we follow the pattern established by the apostles, the needy will be better served, pastors will be less distracted, deacons will be highly esteemed, and God will be glorified in the *installation* of *qualified candidates*.

And now the final step -

Step 4—Directing qualified candidates.

Step 3—Installing the qualified.

Step 2—Electing qualified candidates.

Step 1—Finding qualified candidates.

2 Then the twelve called the multitude of the disciples unto them, and said, It is not reason that we should leave the word of God, and serve tables. 3 Wherefore, brethren, look ye out among you seven men of honest report, full of the Holy Ghost and wisdom, whom we may appoint over this business. (Acts 6:2-3).

Whom they set before the apostles: and when they had prayed, they laid their hands on them. (Acts 6:6).

Once candidates have been selected by congregational vote and installed into office, whose responsibility are they? Who gives *direction* to their work? Or are they an autonomous body without direction or oversight, a kind of rogue band of untrained do-gooders, like Robin Hood, taking from the rich and giving to the poor?

And here's another thing. On "Installation Sunday," as the last prayer ends the service, are they supposed to know exactly what to do? Naturally, if you have a band of faithful and trained deacons already in place, the introduction into service can go very smoothly. But still, does the church pat the newly installed deacon on the back and say, "Oh, don't worry brother. You'll figure it out!"?

While there is no verse that explicitly states who's responsible for the deacons, thankfully, God did not leave us without direction. According to His Word, there are only two legitimate offices in the church, and there is only one office that is described as the "ruling" or "overseeing" office. That is the office of pastor/elder or, as we have been referring to them throughout this book, the "spiritual leaders." Peter writes, "The elders which are among you I exhort . . . Feed the flock of God which is among you. Taking the oversight thereof" (1 Pet. 5:1-2). Paul wrote, "If anyone aspires to the office of overseer . . ." (1 Tim. 3:1, ESV). And the book of Hebrews directs the church, "Obey them that have the rule over you, and submit yourselves: for they watch for your souls, as they that must give account" (Heb. 13:17).

These passages require the spiritual leaders to exercise some level of direction over every aspect of the church. The office of deacon, on the other hand, is never described as an office of oversight. We know that there is some degree of oversight exercised by deacons as they manage their work. But their ministry is to serve the physical/material needs of the body, not govern the body. The only officer of the church that "oversees" or watches over the entire church is the office of the pastor/elder. Because of this, all members of the church, including deacons, seek the support of and direction from the elders.

As it relates to the oversight of diaconal ministry, Johann Bengel stated, "It was the *primary duty* of the apostles, evangelists, and bishops to preach God's word; it was their *subordinate duty* to exercise a kind of fatherly care over the maintenance of the poor in particular, of strangers, of widows, and others"[126] (italics added). One very important aspect of the church, over which elders exercise "a kind of fatherly care," is the ministry of the deacons.

---

126 Johann Bengel, *The Critical English Testament.* Third edition (London, 1876), Book of Acts: 49.

Please do not misunderstand the point here. We are not diminishing the value, necessity, or nobility of the office. Deacons do exercise real oversight. Their job is to "watch over" the needy and other areas of practical ministry. Their general oversight of the work is implied when the apostles stated, "[W]hom we may appoint over this business." In order for deacons to carry out their responsibilities, there must be some measure of self-direction. If they are indeed Spirit-filled and wise leaders, they ought to be listened to and allowed some degree of freedom. They should not be afraid to take the initiative to solve problems as they arise. In fact, no member of the church should feel constrained when it comes to lovingly meeting each other's needs and know that the designated resources of the church are at their disposal. However, everyone should know that these things are under the general oversight of the elders of the church.

When Pharaoh appointed Joseph over his affairs, he said to him, "I have set thee over all the land of Egypt" (Gen. 41:41). He then gave him his ring, fine garments, put a gold chain around his neck, had him ride in the chariot right behind his own, and then "made him ruler over all the land of Egypt" (vv. 42-44). The word *set* in verse 41 means "to administrate." As the administrator of Pharaoh's affairs, clearly Joseph exercised authority, yet is there any doubt as to who was in charge? Joseph carried out his duties under the authority of Pharaoh.

In the same way, when the apostles said of the chosen servants "whom we may appoint over this business," they indicated that they still clearly functioned under the oversight of the apostles. So it has been with deacons throughout church history: they function under the authority of the "overseers" of the church. Why? Because the primary responsibility of the spiritual leaders is to devote themselves to Word and prayer, not "serving tables" or, more broadly, serving the needy. Deacons should not consider themselves an autonomous governing body. They are not self-directed to the exclusion of the overseers. They receive their directions from the spiritual overseers as they exercise a watchful, "fatherly care" over every aspect of the church, both spiritual and physical.

How this balance is maintained is tricky at times. There is a real temptation on the part of the spiritual leaders to either micro-manage the deacons or let them function as spiritual overseers. We think both of these are a mistake and out of sync with the directives given by the apostles. It is up to each church to work out these things in a way that is faithful to the Word and glorifying to God.

Beyond the Scriptures discussed above, we find further support for our understanding of the relationship between spiritual and servant leaders by *observing* some of the details recorded in Acts 6.

First observation

The chosen servants were brought to the apostles, not the other way around. The apostles did not bring the candidates to the assembly and say, "Appoint them." It was understood by everyone the apostles were the God-ordained leaders and teachers of the body of Christ. The church devoted themselves to the apostles' teaching (Acts 2:43). The apostles were the shepherds, and new believers were their sheep (John 21:15-18, Acts 20:28). There is no hint that the members of the newly planted and growing church were taking matters into their own hands. When it came time to set the chosen into office, the entire scene flowed toward the apostles to work out these things.

Second observation

Not only did the assembly bring the qualified candidates to the apostles for approval and appointment, but it was the apostles who chose the entire course of action for the assembly, even the selection process. It wasn't those who were serving the needs of the Hebrew widows, or a "social-justice" committee, or the disenfranchised who felt they were underserved who came up with the solution. It was the apostles. They determined who the church could and could not put forward for consideration by "posting" the requirements. They gave all the directions and told the assembly to come back after choosing *seven* men, a number, by the way, determined by the apostles. The entire process, from finding to installing, was directed by the twelve spiritual leaders of the church.

The point is the apostles directed the entire process. This establishes the biblical precedent that servant leaders are under the direction of the spiritual leaders of the church. Today, whether we refer to them as elders, overseers, pastors, or any other title, they are the "spiritual leaders" of the congregation who are entrusted with the oversight of the church, which includes the deacons or "servant leaders."

Third observation

When it comes to the *details* of diaconal ministry, the Scripture is mostly silent. Acts 6, while helpful, doesn't give us any specifics. This silence, however, should not be interpreted to mean that attention to detail is unwarranted. In order to be both effective and efficient, there must be structure, planning, and careful preparation if the ministry is to serve as God intends.

Among the most important contributions that spiritual leaders can make is ensuring that every deacon is adequately equipped to carry out his God-given responsibilities. Deacons come into the office with varying levels of prior preparation. Some have innate skills that have been developed over the years. But this isn't true for every deacon. Nor are these skills among the biblical requirements. A particular deacon might lack leadership and administrative skills but excel above others in compassion and the ability to see a need when no one else does. What is a strength in one deacon, might be a weakness for another. This is why a plurality of deacons is so important.

The question we're asking now is, "Who is responsible to make sure that every deacon is adequately prepared to carry out their appointed ministry?" This is a detail that falls on the shoulders of the spiritual leaders. They alone have the responsibility to both prepare, and *direct* the chosen servants.

We're not going to get into the "nuts and bolts" of diaconal training under the direction of the elders of the church. The nuts and bolts of training are out there. Not only do we have resources on our own shelves, but additional resources on the office and work of a deacon can be found very quickly on the Internet, everything from books to training videos. Areas to target for training would include things like these:

- Budgets
- Leadership
- Communication skills
- Conflict resolution
- Biblical counseling
- Community resource awareness

Keep in mind that the training process can, and perhaps should, begin long before the deacon is chosen to serve in the office. Since every Christian is called to serve others, every member of the church is either a deacon or a deacon in training. The entire church can benefit from the same training programs that deacons go through. Let every willing member of the church enjoy the benefits of developing skills that make for good servants.

To summarize Step 4, *directing qualified candidates*, we have simply highlighted the fact that diaconal ministry, and deacons in particular, are under the direction of the only authorized overseers of the church: the spiritual leaders. As such, spiritual leaders are responsible to give direction to their work and to make sure they are both qualified and fully equipped to succeed in their appointed sphere of ministry.

CHAPTER SUMMARY

We trust that our study of Acts 6 has been helpful as we seek to serve the needy around us or, as we put it earlier, to move from needing deacons to having deacons. The passage reveals the following *four-step process*:

Step 1—*Finding* qualified candidates.

Step 2—*Electing* qualified candidates.

Step 3—*Installing* qualified candidates.

Step 4—*Directing* qualified candidates.

The first two steps, *finding* and *electing*, are congregational responsibilities. The last two, *installing* and *directing*, are spiritual leadership responsibilities.

The fact that we have drawn our lessons from a biblical-historical narrative should not discourage us from seeing these events as God's plan for the church today. As David Wells put it, "The importance of the story form in the Bible does not lie in the story form itself. Its importance lies in the fact that as a narrative of God's acts in the external world, it has yielded truth that is as objective as the events to which it is wedded." Remember it is God's story, not ours. The record of the early days of the church, in many instances, is our guide to do likewise. We do not think it is simply coincidental that, within a few years of the events of Acts 6, we find both a reference to the office and the qualifications for the office (Phil. 1:1; 1 Tim. 3; Titus 1). Acts 6 is more than a description of what happened. It represents a model of what will become a full-blown diaconal ministry. It is a model given to us by God and a model we would be wise to follow today. *Find, elect, install,* and *direct* only *qualified candidates*.

CHAPTER 5

GETTING ORGANIZED

As the "Installation Service" draws to a close, Peter says the last "Amen." Immediately, some of the assembled multitude begin to press forward, crowding around the seven. Some are wishing them well. Some embrace. But some immediately begin demanding help for either their loved ones or themselves. A few in the crowd are shouting out needs, names, addresses, each hoping to be first on the list. It's loud, it's joyous, it's serious, and it's intimidating all at the same time. Peter, always the man of action, grabs Nicholas by the arm and shouts to the others, "Come with me!"

Along with James and John, Peter leads them to a secluded spot, away from the crowd. "Brothers, I sensed you needed a little breathing room to gather your thoughts. We have no doubt you are up to the task, but time is of the essence. You must act quickly. We are here to assist you in any way we can. We will meet with you tonight to go over some details. But for now, we will leave you alone. We are all counting on you to fulfill your calling and resolve the reported issue." He and James quickly hurry away. John, however, takes time to embrace each man, giving an encouraging smile and a squeeze on the shoulder before heading off. Stephen, Philip, Prochorus, Nicanor, Timon, Parmenas, and Nicolas are left standing in a quiet side street of Jerusalem. Now what? What will these respected men, men full of the Holy Ghost and wisdom, do now?

For a moment there's an awkward silence, but it doesn't last long. Nicholas speaks up: "We can meet at my house; we'll have some privacy there. We need to discuss how we're going to help the Grecians, and we need to spend time in prayer. Sarah will prepare a meal. Let's meet there in one hour."

Over the course of the afternoon, they spend their time *getting orga-nized.* Nicholas sketches out a map of the city and marks where most of the Grecians are known to live according to the list of names given to them by the apostles. He then puts an "X" where each of the seven live. Noting a correlation, Timon suggests dividing the work geographically, with each man serving an area closest to his home. Since Nicholas lives outside the city walls to the south, he will cover that area as far as Bethany. The city and other outlying areas are then divided accordingly.

At a side table, Prochorus and Nicanor begin making a list of needed supplies. They are aware of some supplies that are in storage. They also con-sider supplies that will be culturally and practically appropriate for Grecian widows. They soon realize more exact information is needed: names, addresses, number of children living in the home, ages, known relatives, etc. They will also need to know the exact nature of each need. Stephen wisely suggests that he and Philip go meet with the family members who first murmured against the Hebrews. Not only can they fill them in on the exact nature of the neglect, but it will be important for the murmurers to spread the news that the appointed men are taking care of the situation.

Philip, meanwhile, is concerned about unbelieving family members. He offers to speak to each one about believing in Christ. He asks that names and addresses of unbelieving families and known friends be collected and sent on to him.

For several hours, they collaborate on the work that has been assigned to them. Each of the seven men contribute to the discussion and planning. They have different skills and abilities, but each one demonstrates the spiritual wisdom for which they are known. After prayer, they unanimously agree the next thing they must do is meet with both the apostles and the leaders of the Hebrew benevolence fund. They are certain that much wisdom and information will come out of those meetings. Before leaving, Nicholas cries out to the compassionate and merciful God, asking for grace and strength to carry out this critical task. With that done, they slip out into the city to find the apostles. There's no time to waste.

Now, do we know for sure that any of this actually happened? Not exactly, but something happened at the end of the Installation Service. And whatever happened, it worked. Verse 7 tells us, "And the word of God continued to increase, and the number of the disciples multiplied greatly in Jerusalem, and a great many of the priests became obedient to the faith." The need was met, and the church once again began to prosper.

So, what *did* they do? Here's what we think happened first: somehow, someway, they *got organized*. That's what the above scenario is all about. With the goal of caring for the neglected widows clearly in mind, they met together, came up with a plan, put the plan into action, and followed up. These are the things that spiritual and wise men would do. That's just reasonable to assume.

The goal of this chapter is to encourage deacons to enjoy the benefits of *getting organized* and to offer some help in getting there. Since *getting organized* is the goal, we should start with a definition. What is organization? *Webster's Dictionary* defines *organized* as "having a formal organization to coordinate and carry out activities." In simplified contemporary terms, to "get organized" means taking something with a lot of parts and arranging them in a way that makes everything work together in a more effective and efficient way. To state it another way, organization means having a goal, planning to reach the goal, and managing all the necessary details of the event or action. That's what it means to "get organized."

Whether the details are few or complex, there are obvious benefits to *getting and staying* organized. A few benefits are listed below, and we will pick up on some of them in this chapter. We encourage you to take time to discuss the full list and add to the list other benefits of organization that come to mind.

Benefits of Organization

- Keeps the goal in mind
- Leads to planning necessary action steps
- Speeds up decision making
- Enhances time and resource management
- Improves focus
- Increases productivity
- Reduces stress
- Frees up time for other activities (family, church, hobbies)
- Provides a framework for follow-up

A critical aspect of getting organized is the planning process. Simply put, *you cannot get organized without a plan.* While a myriad of planning protocols is available, if you need a starting point, the following will at least point you in the right direction.

The Planning Process

1. Clarify the goal.

2. Establish steps to reach the goal.

3. Identify and secure the necessary resources.

4. Execute the steps.

Once the plan has been executed or put into action, three more steps must be taken:

5. Verify that the steps have been taken.

6. Correct any missteps.

7. Confirm that the goal has been met.

These are the basics of organizational planning, and its importance cannot be overstated. Without an organized planning process, diaconal work will suffer from a lack of direction and run the risk of failing to meet the goals of caring for the needy, protecting the spiritual leaders, and serving the more general, practical needs of the church. We cannot let our lack of organization keep us from reaching these goals. If every aspect of servant ministry is arranged in a manner that makes the whole ministry function in the most effective and efficient way, the needy will be served, the church will be blessed, and God will be glorified.

Yes, God will be glorified. Organization brings order, and God is a God of order. In 1 Corinthians 14:40, Paul exhorts, "Let all things be done decently and in order." We must see that behind this exhortation lies the nature of God: "For God is not the author of confusion, but of peace" (v. 33). Everything about God, from His nature to His acts, is nothing if not orderly. From creation, to redemption, to the final consummation of all things—everything points to the orderliness of God. Chaos and disorganization are contrary to His nature, whereas the result of order is peace. God could rightly be called "the God of organization" (arranging all the parts in a way that makes everything work together for good, Romans 8:28). Therefore, if diaconal work is to reflect the nature of God and honor His name, it must be a well-organized ministry. The principle of "decently and in order" demands it.

We realize that many churches are organized far beyond what we discuss here. However, from our experience, we know there are many who could profit from some practical assistance in *getting and staying organized.* Even if you are privileged to serve in an organized and structured ministry setting, if you keep reading, you might enjoy thinking about the first deacons and how they might have organized the early church's effort to care for the Grecian widows, an effort that grew in complexity as the church grew.

Before getting into some of the "nuts and bolts" of getting organized, let's take some time to go back to Acts 6 and the first deacons again. We want to think about the details of their organization and planning process. We would like to do that, but we can't. As any discerning reader of Acts 6 knows, there are no details. We don't know how they organized the work. We don't know their plan. We don't know what specific steps they took to reach the goal of caring for the Grecian widows. It's just not there.

That's interesting. The appointment of the seven is the starting point for diaconal ministry for the next two thousand years and counting. Given the significance of their appointment and the implications for the future, we might expect some details concerning their work. Specifically, how did they get organized, and what steps did they take to resolve the issue? These are the kinds of details that might be helpful as we evaluate our own care for the needy and other diaconal responsibilities.

But no, the details are missing. Think about it for a minute. Luke, recognized by both church and secular scholars as a reliable historian, who goes into great detail concerning other matters, says nothing about the actions of the seven. But Luke is not the only one whose lips are sealed. What about Paul? He wrote three "Pastoral Epistles," numerous general letters, refers to the office in Philippians 1:1, expands the list of qualifications in 1 Timothy 3, but says nothing about the actual work of the deacon. Both Paul and Peter write concerning the work of the overseer, as does the writer of Hebrews. But no one describes the work of the deacon.

You might be thinking, "These men wrote under the inspiration of the Spirit." Thank you for bringing that up! Why didn't the Holy Spirit communicate these details or at least something concerning the organization and planning process of the chosen seven? We're not second-guessing God. We're just wondering why He chose to leave us in the dark. We know the *nature* of the office, the *value* of the office, and we know the *requirements* for the office, but we don't know how they actually carried out the *specific responsibilities* of the office.

Okay, we don't know *how*, so let's go down another path. Can we say with any certainty *why* the details are missing? Again, the answer is no. However, let's think about this too for a minute. The question is, "Why are the details missing?" There might be many reasons, but we will suggest just two.

First, the servant ministry of the seven was *a work in progress*. The transition recorded in Acts, from the Old Covenant to the New, from Judaism to Christianity, is changing everything, and that includes the churches' response to the poor and needy brethren. Regarding the poor and needy believers, what do we find the church doing in Acts 2:4 and 5? Selling houses, lands, and possessions and bringing the proceeds to the feet of the apostles. Talk about a change! They didn't teach that in the synagogue. Everything in the early church, which is the church we find in the New Testament, is a *work in progress*. At this early stage of the church, the seven did not have a detailed plan ready to be put on display for the ages to come. It shouldn't surprise us then that the details concerning their organizational planning are missing.

The second reason why the details might be missing is that there is a *cultural divide* between the early church and nearly every church that followed. Every church exists in its own *time* and *place*. Exactly where we find ourselves on God's green earth and the specific time that He has ordained for us to be here change things. What was appropriate for Grecian widows in the first century is not the same for Haitian widows in the 21st century, or anyplace else for that matter. Diaconal responses in Queens, New York, will be different from diaconal responses in a little village in Zambia. It's doubtful that what worked in Jerusalem two thousand years ago would work in every age and in every place. The point is, we need appropriate cultural sensitivity when serving the needy.

Therefore, whether it is the fact that everything was a *work in progress* or the *cultural divide* between them and us, we question how useful the specific organizational details of their ministry would be to diaconal ministries today. These may be among the reasons why the Holy Spirit left out the details. And given our proclivity to make rules where no rules are intended, perhaps we should be glad the details are missing, regardless of the reason.

Briefly, we bring up one more question. How did the seven know *what* to do? Did they run around willy-nilly looking for a widow to help? And if they found one, then what? Suppose she needs a meal for herself and her children? Did he go home and tell his wife, "Hi, honey, guess who's coming to dinner?" Willy-nilly is not a strategy. So how did they know what to do or how to even start?

In answering the question of how, there are two groups to keep in mind: the *Hebrews* and the *apostles*. The whole business of caring for the needy was not new to the *Hebrews*. The Law of God contained very specific directives concerning Israel's responsibility to care for the needy among them. They had fifteen hundred years of practice by this time. These seven men, though having Grecian names, no doubt knew all about scriptural charity. Their Hebrew background would inform them of the mechanics of both collection and distribution of supplies for the needy.

But even so, dramatic shifts have already taken place: the shift from the synagogue to the church and the shift from the rabbis to the *apostles*. We find the church bringing their charitable contributions to the apostles' feet, not to the rabbis. The apostles are now responsible for the collection and distribution of supplies. As Jews themselves, they have a pretty good idea of how this is done. As apostles, they now have firsthand experience to draw on. We think this experience would prove to be invaluable to the seven. Remember, in our fictional portrayal at the opening of this chapter, after meeting together for planning and prayer, they head out to find the apostles. Being both *Hebrews* and *apostles*, with loads of knowledge and experience, that seems like the most likely place to start.

Let's get back to the main issue: organizational planning to reach the desired goal. That's the missing information we wish we knew. But just because the details are missing, it doesn't mean they weren't organized. Common sense tells us they had to have a plan; we're just not told what it was.

Although we do not have the details, we think there is a window of information embedded in the text that verifies our hunch that the seven chosen servants understood the need for getting organized. In Acts 6:3, we have the phrase, "over this business." This is their commission, their appointed assignment. This is what they must do to carry out the purpose for which they were chosen.

The Greek word for "over" is *epi*, which in context means "to superintend"[127] and suggests they must be over or carry out the given assignment. They are now personally responsible to manage, supervise, give direction, to be "in charge of " (NASB), and see to it that this duty is carried out.

---

127 James Strong, *Strong's Exhaustive Concordance of the English Bible* (Grand Rapids, MI: Zondervan Publishing, 2001), under "over," no. 1909.

The apostles are saying, we "turn this responsibility over to them."[128] In a word, they are now "over" the work entrusted to them. We think "over" implies organization and planning. How can they manage, supervise, or be in charge of the whole business without organizing or planning the work?

And what were they over? The phrase tells us they were "over this business." The Greek word for "business" suggests employment or necessary business.[129] The idea is that they were appointed over a work that was necessary. It was now their duty, their "business," to make sure the needy have the things that are necessary.

Making it *their* "business," *their* responsibility to carry out this necessary ministry, implies the authority to be "over," superintend, carry out the work they were chosen to do. We deal with this implied authority in another place, but we thought we should at least point this implication out while we're here. When the apostles turned this whole business of caring for the neglected widows *over* to the chosen seven, everyone understood they were also granting them the authority to make it happen.

Back to the text. The words *over this business* tell us they were over a specific kind of necessary work, a certain realm of responsibility. The word *this* suggests "this and not that." It separates the work of the apostles as spiritual leaders from the work they were assigning to the seven servant leaders. They were essentially saying, "This is your business now. We are assigning it to you. Manage all the details, and see that it gets done." And what business was that? Caring for the needy in the church. Our point is this: the phrase "over this business" not only implies but would seem to require organization, planning, communication, and good management of the entrusted responsibility.

---

128 Barrett, C.K. *A Critical and Exegetical Commentary on the Acts of the Apostles, ICC, Vol. 1* (Edinburgh: Clark, 1994), p133.

129 Strong, *Strong's Exhaustive Concordance of the English Bible*, under "business," no. 5532.

As we have shown, the window of information called verse 3 sheds light on their assignment. Knowing the goal, they must put together a plan, and in order for them to plan a course of action, what must they do? Meet and talk, of course. While it seems obvious, they must meet to *get* organized, and they must meet regularly to *keep* organized, but have you ever thought about it? Have you thought about those men meeting to discuss the work they were to oversee? The point we're stressing is this: just because the details are missing, it doesn't mean they are not there. We're just not told exactly what they are. But we can be fairly confident they did not carry out the work without first meeting to plan it all out.

As we consider the language of the commission and what the seven must do to fulfill it, we think the following three steps might summarize their initial response and serve as a pattern for our own diaconal ministries:

1) *Meet regularly* to get and stay organized.

- Organization doesn't manage itself; it takes human effort.

2) *Constantly review* the needs and available resources to stay current.

- God alone can create order out of chaos with a simple word; we must constantly communicate and manage information if we are to do our best work.

3) *Record everything* from decisions, to actions, needs, contact information, resources, etc.

- Few in this world possess the mental capacity to retain the various and sundry details of business meetings and planned actions. But most cannot.

Up to this point we've been laying the groundwork, or making the case, that organization is essential for an effective diaconal ministry. From Acts 6, we've drawn out implications that led to the three steps mentioned above:

meet, *review*, and *record*. We think of the steps as being inseparable. It is in your *meetings* that you *review* and *record* your diaconal work.

In the remainder of this chapter, we will give our attention to each of the three steps. This is mostly in the form of practical advice. As we said earlier, you may already be highly organized and running an effective and efficient servant ministry. Praise God if that is the case. For everyone else, we offer the following suggestions on getting and staying organized.

Getting Organized

Let's take a brief look at each of these three steps: meet, review, record.

STEP 1: THE MEETING

Both personal experience and feedback from others tell us meetings are often less fruitful than they ought to be. A valuable exercise for any organization trying to improve its current effectiveness is an overall self-evaluation. This should include an evaluation of the organization's meetings. The reason is simple. Planning, which is necessary if we are to reach our goals, usually takes place in a meeting. The meeting, then, must help us, not hinder us, from reaching our stated goals. Generally speaking, an organized meeting is more effective and helpful than an unorganized meeting. We recognize that impromptu meetings are often necessary and can actually be quite effective. However, they should be the exception, not the norm. In the context of diaconal ministry, meetings ought to help you care for the people and practical ministries entrusted to your watch-care. If they don't, then you have a problem.

Since ministry meetings often fail to accomplish their intended purposes, maybe a little self-evaluation will help. Here are five questions to ask concerning your meetings. We add a few comments to each question.

First Self-evaluation Question:
Are your meetings organized?

Organization is a tool to help deacons achieve their reason for existing, which is to serve. If any aspect of the organizational process hinders the pursuit and accomplishment of that purpose, then it must be corrected. A critical aspect of *getting organized* is the wise management of time, specifically the time when we meet together.

Time is a gift from God and cannot be taken for granted or wasted. The Bible is very clear about our responsibility to be wise stewards of all that God has given us, and that includes our use of time. In this regard, organization saves what belongs to God: *time*. To waste time simply because we are not organized is to waste the gift of time and reflects poorly on us as stewards. Deacons are to be men who distinguish themselves for their wisdom. Wasting time is not consistent with the characteristics of wisdom.

We feel the need to temper what we're saying by adding that deacons can enjoy some fun and relaxation when they get together for those purposes. Whether it's socializing around the coffee pot, on the golf course, or going on a camping and fishing retreat together, these moments can be a very profitable use of time. Relationships are strengthened not only by working together on a common project, they can also be reinforced through social activities. In fact, enjoying these other activities can draw us closer together as Christian brothers, strengthen our unity, and make us more effective as we serve in the office together. However, a deacons' meeting should be structured to maximize the time set apart for ministry purposes.

We realize this is sometimes hard to achieve. We know that from personal experience, and it's not always the other guy who's guilty of wastefully killing time. But as hard as it might be, we have to remember why we're there and strive to not waste the precious gift of time. Men are taking time away from families, recreation, hobbies, and even other spiritual pursuits. You know the frustration of arriving at a meeting on time only to spend a portion of it on something other than the stated purpose.

With that in mind, everyone must come to the meeting ready to get down to business. It might mean someone speaking up and respectfully suggesting, or even insisting, that the meeting get started. That might be one of the spiritual leaders, the chairman, or any deacon for that matter. And if you find yourself being encouraged to set other interests aside so that the meeting can get started, receive the nudge with a gracious and thankful spirit, demonstrating the fruit of the Holy Spirit with your response.

Second Self-evaluation Question: Do you have an agenda?

An agenda is an excellent way to keep the meeting moving in the right direction and making the most of the time you have. Not every meeting of every diaconal team will require an agenda. Most of the time, however, it's wise to prepare an agenda for the meeting. If your team is so effective that you have nothing to talk about, it may be time to look for opportunities to advance diaconal ministries in your church and community.

What the agenda looks like might vary from meeting to meeting but not necessarily so. If you find a list of agenda questions, for example, that work well for your ministry team, it's okay to use it from meeting to meeting. Also, the agenda will vary from church to church. The main thing is having an agenda that helps you reach your intended purpose: meeting the needs of those you serve.

Agenda items can be either statements or questions. As a sample only, here are some questions that could be rewritten to be used as an agenda, or use them as they are as another way of evaluating your current ministry. If used as an evaluation tool, then the results might indicate good agenda items for future meetings.

- How effectively are we handling the present needs within our church?

- Are there new needs that require our attention?

- Do we have reports on other ministries that are under our supervision? Are they effective? What can we do to improve them? What is their present funding status?

- Are there budget issues that we are responsible to manage?

- Are there any concerns regarding property maintenance, improvements, or expansion (assuming you are responsible for the management of property)?

- Are there needs outside the church family or in the community that we need to consider?

If there are many items for discussion, it would be helpful to give the agenda out before the meeting. This gives everyone time to think about and pray over the coming discussions. It goes without saying that printed agendas need to be guarded. Some of the topics for discussion may involve sensitive information that needs to be kept private.

Remember that agendas are not divinely inspired, but simply a guide for your meetings. Sometimes an issue comes up that isn't on the distributed agenda but needs your attention. It is also important to recognize when a topic under discussion deserves more time than was originally planned. While they are helpful in managing our time, they should not be allowed to control our time. Agendas are tools, not rules.

Third Self-evaluation Question: Do you have a moderator?

Your response to this question will depend on the structure of the office in your church. The chairman of the deacons may automatically serve as the moderator, or you may rotate this responsibility. Some churches have one of the pastors moderate all business meetings. Regardless, meetings need a moderator.

A moderator by definition is responsible for managing every aspect of the meeting, and usually that includes discussion time. Rather than a written summary of the moderator's responsibilities, here is a simple list of suggestions for moderating a meeting:

- Keep the goal in mind, and redirect the conversation when it veers off course.

- Encourage participation from everyone; discourage domination by anyone.

- Welcome comments; discourage judgmental or critical responses.

- Calm heated emotions, especially your own.

- Paraphrase difficult ideas to ensure understanding.

- Take everyone seriously; belittle no one.

- Look for common ground among the various opinions.

- Listen for useful action steps.

- Remember you are a moderator, not a ruler; be open to helpful suggestions.

- Be open to exploring unexpected, fresh ideas and solutions.

- Bring the discussion to a beneficial conclusion.

- Display the fruit of the Spirit toward all.

While we have focused on the moderator, it is extremely important for everyone in the meeting to respect and yield to the leadership of the moderator. When it's your turn to lead the meeting, you will appreciate this advice. As officers of the church, it is imperative that love for one another rules over every meeting. A good verse to remember, and perhaps quote before discussion begins, is 1 John 4:7-8, which states, "Beloved, let us love one another. For love is of God, and everyone who loveth is born of God, and knoweth God. He that loveth not, knoweth not God, for God is love."

Fourth Self-evaluation Question: How is the workload divided?

The final two questions aren't exactly about making your meetings more effective but making your diaconal ministry more effective. Yet, since they are both related to your meetings, they are good evaluation questions.

As for this fourth question, assuming you have more than one deacon, eventually someone will ask, "Who's going to deal with it?" It's a question concerning the division of work among the deacons. How much "serving" is required of each servant depends on a number of things: the number of requests for care, the availability of resources, and other practical needs that require a deacon's attention. Generally, this will be determined by the size of the church, as well as the creativity and extent of your church's diaconal outreach.

How much each one has to do is one matter, but how effective they are is another. Division of labor studies have indicated that effectiveness is related to how the work is divided. Similarly, it seems reasonable to assume the effectiveness of a church's servant ministry will be influenced by the way the work is divided among its deacons. The same studies show that it is not just a matter of sharing the load, but dividing the work so that each person's skills are maximized by matching individual skill sets with corresponding needs. The matching of skills isn't always practical in ministry, yet these are the kinds of issues that need to be ironed out ahead of time. Otherwise, you might end up having to deal with hard feelings, exhausted deacons, or even ineffective servant ministries later on. The time and place to "iron out" sticky issues like this are beforehand, in your regularly scheduled meetings. While it is important for deacons to discuss these things among themselves, it's wise to seek input from the spiritual leaders of the church, especially when it comes to individual giftedness and the important topic of having a servant's heart.

When we think about the workload facing the seven appointed servants of Acts 6, it's only reasonable to assume they had some mechanism for dividing the work. It's hard to envision all seven men hooking up one oxcart and going from member to member gathering money, food and clothing for the needy. It's equally hard to imagine that all seven men then took that one oxcart of supplies and went from house to house distributing to those who had needs. While this might work on a small scale, it's hard to conceive of a group of deacons doing this in a church of thousands or in a large city like Jerusalem. Nor is it likely that the majority of work was put upon just one or two of the men. While the text does not say that the workload was divided, common sense tells us it was.

Our "oxcart" illustration is just that, an illustration. In actuality, the text seems to indicate that property and possessions were sold and the proceeds, or money, was laid at the apostle's feet. This is more practical than collecting tangible items that require storage in a pantry or shed until they are needed. Paul collected financial contributions from church to church that could then be carried to the church in Jerusalem. However the contribution is made, whether financial or physical, it still needs to be distributed, and that distribution requires effort, and that effort should be carefully divided among the deacons.

It's only a guess, but we imagine in their first meeting they spent time discussing how to collect and distribute either funds or supplies to the neglected widows. Remember, Jerusalem was a very large city, and its population swelled during the annual feasts with hundreds of thousands inside its walls and many more thousands encamped outside the walls. Acts 6 occurs in the context of Passover and Pentecost, and afterward the many new believers who decided to stay close to Jerusalem.

For a moment, imagine you're the chairman of the deacons of "The First Christian Church of Jerusalem," and the other six are looking to you for suggestions. Faced with such a daunting task, how would you divide the work? Would you divide the city and its surrounding area into sections and ask each man to oversee one of those areas? Maybe you would divide the work according to the neighborhood where each man lived. That way, he could use his home as a base of operation in his own community, keep a close eye on those with ongoing needs, and have funds or supplies ready at hand. Maybe you would choose to divide the work according to each man's special gifts, abilities, and experiences. Some are better with the elderly, or with children, or home repairs, or cooking meals, or evangelism. Or maybe your division of labor is going to be based on the number of volunteers you can sign up in each section of town. You have to decide; the needy are waiting. How will you divide the work?

And here's another thing. What if one deacon is tired of always being the one who goes out at night or to the rough side of town or asked to handle the difficult situations and the habitual complainers? The point is, wouldn't it be wise to decide these things ahead of time so that there are no delays, no quarrels, and no resentment among the servants? Isn't this what you would expect from wise and spiritual men?

Another important factor when considering who does what are the deacons' wives. They are a God-given asset to their husbands when dealing with sensitive issues that are awkward or inappropriate for a man. On some occasions, the deacon's wife may be the one handling the entire situation. They should be remembered when the labor is being divided. Their age, spiritual maturity, special giftedness, life experiences, and more are important factors to keep in mind. For instance, an elderly deacon whose wife isn't able to do much physically may be more of a prayer warrior or counselor to younger women. A younger woman might be more of an organizer, or late-night companion, or scrubber of floors than an elderly deaconess. Among the other wives, one might be a gifted cook, another might have the gift of comforting the needy, while another loves to teach women to sew, cook, and clean, or grow vegetables. These are the kinds of things that can be taken into account when dividing the labor among deacons.

As far as we know, there is no "best way" to divide the labor. Deacons are servants first. Serving is the nature and function of the office. So, no matter how the work is doled out, biblical deacons are willing to serve. Nevertheless, dividing the work is an important issue, and each group needs to pray for wisdom when dividing the workload. Even if this was the only issue on the agenda, this in itself would be a good reason to meet regularly: to decide who's going to do what.

There is one more thing to consider. With the approval of your spiritual leaders, you might even ask for help from a sister church. Deacons serving in another ministry might have more experience and a measure of expertise in areas that you are still trying to figure out. This would especially be true for a new or growing church, one that is facing certain kinds of ministry issues for the first time, including the question of dividing the work. This is an important issue and must be decided as early as possible. As always, deacons should be willing to first seek counsel from their own spiritual leaders.

Fifth Self-evaluation Question:
Are you personally ready for a meeting?

Up to this point, we've been focusing on the meeting. This question focuses the spotlight on you, the deacon, and your personal spiritual preparation before the meeting ever begins. Deacons are to be known as men who are full of the Holy Spirit, meaning that every part of your life shows evidence of being under the influence of the Spirit, not perfectly but you are being led by and yielding to the Spirit in every area of your life. In other words, there are no gaping holes. But here's the thing: being in a spiritual frame of mind and soul is not something you suddenly get into by simply walking into the meeting room. There isn't a switch on the wall marked "spiritual."

Being a spiritually minded person is something you constantly work at. It's who you are as a Christian leader. You bring it with you as you come.

The difficulty lies in the fact that we carry with us this body of sin, and we live in a sinners' world. We live with, work with, talk with sinners every day, yet every time we meet, the church is counting on us to be "full of the Holy Spirit and wisdom." This is work that concerns the body of Christ. It is imperative that you walk into that meeting with a mind and heart that has been prepared before you ever get there. Anything less and you are not prepared to do the work you were called to do.

It's not like we're saying anything new here. You not only know this is right, you also know what to do about it. If you didn't, you probably would not have been elected to the office. We also know that you have spiritual leaders in your church who are equipped to help you with spiritual matters. If you find yourself regularly showing up for meetings in a state of spiritual weakness, humble yourself and ask the Lord and a stronger brother for help.

If we would offer any help toward being spiritually ready for your deacons' meetings, we might just suggest that you ask yourself the following questions.

- Have I fellowshipped with God this week in Word and prayer?
- Have I cried out to God for help as I seek to serve others?
- Have I asked Him for wisdom to fulfill my responsibility?
- Have I turned to the Word for answers to difficult questions?
- Have I prayed for those I serve?
- Have I submitted myself to the leading of the Spirit?
- Have I been a spiritual leader at home?

Your answers to these questions will let you know if you are spiritually ready for the next deacons' meeting. We know we are pressing a high standard here. But in reality, these questions are applicable to every believer, not just deacons. But you are a deacon, and you are indeed held to a higher standard. In fact, that's why you were chosen to serve in the church, because you distinguish yourself as being "of good report, full of the Holy Ghost and wisdom." Spirit and wisdom—that's what you need to be ready for every meeting. Otherwise, you run the risk of meeting in the flesh.

The previous five self-evaluation questions were all about "Step 1: The Meeting." We covered a lot of information in Step 1, but don't worry; we will quickly cover the next two steps with just a few comments on each.

STEP 2: REVIEWING

Reviewing is a simple way to stay on top of everything. As a team, you need to watch over every detail. Constantly ask questions: are needs being met, are resources keeping up with disbursements, are previous decisions being carried out, are volunteers working out, etc. How frequently you review each detail is up to you, but every aspect of your ministry must get reviewed with some regularity. Otherwise, you will lose control of both effectiveness and efficiency, and both are necessary for a well-ordered ministry.

STEP 3: RECORDING

In order to *review everything*, something else has to exist: a *record of everything*. Your board of deacons probably has a secretary. If not, appoint one—soon. Someone needs to keep a record of both discussions and decisions. Even if your church has just one pastor and one deacon, one of you needs to take notes.

These "notes" are usually referred to as the "minutes" of the meeting. Discussion notes can be general, but decisions should be spelled out in detail to avoid any misunderstandings or confusion in the future. Notes should be taken of the entire meeting. Typically, following prayer, the meeting will start with a reading of the "minutes" of the last meeting, and notes will be kept until the closing "amen." Because the notes include both past and present discussions and decisions, they add up. Therefore, they need to be recorded.

Not only will they add up, they must also be kept or stored someplace. Over time, they become a history of your work. Keeping a copy in a lockable filing cabinet in a church office is a good idea. The problem with that, however, is two-fold. First, keeping all the "minutes" under lock and key in one location means they are not readily available to every deacon. They often need certain details of their meetings at a moment's notice. Second, it can be laborious poring over handwritten notes kept in the typical ledger.

Therefore, in order to manage this historical record and other important information relating to your diaconal ministry, and to do so in a way that is both effective and efficient, we recommend a *deacons' operations manual*, or DOM. The DOM is a handy reference manual for past, present, and future work. Each Deacon is given a DOM and is responsible to keep the information both up to date and secure. One of our churches has been using the DOM for a while now, and the deacons have found it very beneficial!

The primary benefits of the DOM are as follows:

- a recorded history of past diaconal work

- a handy reference for current work

- a more effective and efficient ministry tomorrow

- improved accountability for all responsible parties

You might consider having two manuals for each deacon: one kept at the church for safekeeping and one kept at home for quick reference when a need comes up. That's just a thought.

We know that two questions will quickly come to mind. First, what kind of information should you keep in your DOM, and perhaps more importantly, how will the information be organized? Drawing from our own experiences and discussions with deacons and spiritual leaders in other ministries, we recommend at least nine sections in your manual. We will briefly comment on each of the nine recommended sections. Even though most of what follows is common sense, sometimes a fresh perspective or a simple reminder is all we need to nudge us in the right direction.

Here is a list of the nine recommended sections in your DOM:

- Section 1: Needs
- Section 2: Resources
- Section 3: Volunteers
- Section 4: Follow Up
- Section 5: Problems
- Section 6: Church Property
- Section 7: Budget
- Section 8: Future Plans
- Section 9: Written Policies

SECTION 1: NEEDS

It's hard to imagine, with the many thousands who were being added to the church, that the newly appointed servants memorized all the names, addresses, and lists of needs. If they had phones back then, they would have been blowing up! It seems to make perfect sense to think that these men would compile a list of names, where they lived, and what they needed.

The word *need* raises an interesting question. Maybe you've asked, "What constitutes a need?" Webster defines a need as "those things that are essential for living; that helps to minimize suffering in a person's life."[130] Helpful as this definition is, it requires some discussion. What constitutes as "essential"? And there are many things that "minimize suffering." What about preventing suffering? Would that be essential?

So, what does a need look like? If we don't agree on this, it can lead to both confusion and division. We all know from experience that this is a subjective thing, as it seems everyone has their own opinion on what constitutes a "need." However, there are some things that are obvious. Having enough food to feed yourself and your family is essential. Sufficient clothing and adequate shelter are essential. But what about medical care or a functioning vehicle so the primary breadwinner can get to work to provide for the family? Then there is the matter of education, both for school-age children and parents who lack job skills. Does the need for job training qualify for assistance? We know of churches that provide the cost of job training under certain circumstances as a means of helping others reach self-sufficiency.

The issue is complicated by the fact that there are too many who are happy to let others take care of them. This is a complicated issue that only the Gospel of grace can address. But even among some believers, it is difficult to change generational, ingrained patterns of thinking and behaving that the welfare system, or a soft-hearted church, helped create. Having a welfare system supported by taxation is not in and of itself evil. The nation of Israel was a theocracy under the rule of God, yet the people were taxed, and part of the collected taxes went to care for the poor and needy.

---

130 2 Webster, *American Dictionary of the English Language* (1828 ed.), under "need."

We are not living under a theocracy. Instead of a tithe to support the government and the poor, we pay taxes. When Jesus was asked if it was right to pay taxes, he summoned a coin. After drawing attention to whose likeness was on the coin, he said, "Therefore, render unto Caesar the things that are Caesar's, and unto the God the things that are God's" (Matt. 22:17-21). Today, we are still under God, we are required to pay taxes, and part of that money goes to the poor. To say that we don't have to pay our taxes to help others is wrong. It's complicated, but it's wrong.

Public taxation to assist the poor is one thing. Caring for poor and needy church members and helping unbelievers around us, as we are able, is another thing. The Bible is very clear about this. John writes, "Whoever has this world's goods and sees his brother in need, yet closes his heart against him, how does God's love abide in him? Little children, let us not love in word or talk but in deed and in truth" (1 John 3:17-18, ESV). Helping the needy is clearly required.

What's missing is a careful explanation of what constitutes a need. Furthermore, there's no list of acceptable and unacceptable circumstances. In the parable of the Good Samaritan, Jesus teaches us that the injured person in our path is our neighbor and therefore ought to be helped. How? Medical care, food, housing, and anything else it takes to bring him back to good health. On the other hand, Paul urges us to not help the person who won't work (2 Thess. 3:6). This is an entirely different situation and calls for a different response. In other words, there is no comprehensive one-size-fits-all definition of a need. Nor is there a nice and neat list of circumstances to tell us when, or when not, to get involved. No, each situation needs to be evaluated on its own merits.

Let's get back to Section 1 in the DOM: Needs. From certain New Testament passages, it appears the early church maintained a "needs list." One such passage is Acts 6:1. Here, we may have a reference that points to the existence of a list of qualified widows. The phrase "the daily ministration" is interesting. The Greek word for "daily" refers to time.[131] It speaks of a "quotidian" or daily quota. It's something that occurs daily. In the passage, there is a group that is not receiving the "daily distribution" of food. The Hebrew widows, however, were receiving their daily quota. Combining the idea of a daily quota and what we know about Hebrew benevolence practices, it seems likely that the Hebrews were working off of a list. Being a daily need, it must have been both proportional and perpetual. A certain amount, every day, for certain widows—sounds like a list.

Another passage that informs our thinking about a list is 1 Tim. 5:9. We wish we could spend more time on this, but we will let a few words suffice. It reads, "Let not a widow be taken into the number under threescore years old, having been the wife of one man." The word translated as "number" is *katalego*. Literally, it means "to lay down." Here, it is used figuratively, meaning "to write down or enroll." Accordingly, the ESV reads, "Let a widow be enrolled . . ." The qualifying widows in the church at Ephesus were added to an existing list of those who needed regular assistance.

Returning to Acts 6:1, this may be the origin of the "needs list" as it existed in the early Christian church. The "enrollment" in 1 Timothy may be rooted in the neglect of certain widows in Acts 6, which itself is rooted in Judaism. Maybe that is how they were neglected in the first place; because they were Grecians, they were never put on the Hebrew's list of widows to care for to begin with.

Luke does not tell us what criteria, if any, were used to determine how a Grecian widow got her name on the list. Any qualifying criteria for being on the list may have come later. What we do know is that a culturally different group is not receiving their daily quota of supplies. The fact that there was a daily quota suggests it must have been written down. We might wish there was more concrete information to go on, the kind of information that would spell out who, when, and how much we should help. But

---

131 Strong, *Strong's Exhaustive Concordance of the English Bible*, under "daily," no. 2522.

that information is not given. Even the Greek word translated as "daily," while helpful, still requires discussion and judgment.

Here are some suggestions for when you find yourself forced to make these kinds of subjective decisions about a "need."

First, gather sufficient information:

- Who needs help?

- Why do they need help? (Is there an underlying cause?)

- What kind of help do they need?

- When do they need this help?

- What specifically can we do to help?

- How often will they need our help?

- What is the solution (both short and long term)?

There's nothing special about our list of questions. They might just serve as a starting point for your discussions. The point being made here is to collect adequate information before making a decision.

Second, do the following once you have the necessary information:

- Discuss the need with your fellow deacons, and pastors when necessary.

- Carefully weigh the relevant Scriptures.

- Prayer for wisdom.

Third, make a decision. If you decide to move forward and help, make sure you spell everything out: how much, when, how often, and any conditions you might place on being helped. This will become invaluable information not only for the current situation, but as a record for future situations.

If you decide not to help, make sure you can clearly explain your reason for turning down the request for assistance. This too should be recorded in your DOM.

Beyond the obvious physical need, every situation is an opportunity to minister to people on a spiritual level as well. If, for instance, the person or family is a member of your church, are they embarrassed, defensive, angry at God, or resentful of others who have more? Is there a discernible underlying root cause that needs to be addressed? If the answer to any of these questions is yes, then you have both an opportunity and a responsibility to help your brother or sister on a spiritual level. Lifting up a brother out of a ditch is one thing; edifying his soul is another thing. Look for these opportunities to minister to the whole man.

If the needy individual is an unbeliever, this presents a unique opportunity to point the person to Christ. Wisdom and discretion are needed in this situation. Often probing questions are required, and if we're not careful, we can go off in the wrong direction. We don't want to come across as setting up a "trap" to catch a needy soul. Each situation is unique, and if there is any question, then seek help from the spiritual leaders of the church. They can help guide you through these difficult opportunities. But again, whenever you are called on for help, see it as an opportunity to serve the whole individual, body and soul.

Coming back to the needs list, your working list of current needs will undoubtedly be mostly material things such as food, clothing, utilities, health care. But you will also list whatever resources you might take along to meet spiritual needs: Bibles, tracts, books, etc. These kinds of needs will be addressed in the following sections, but they are needs, and as such they need to be recorded for future reference. Another need along this line might be individuals you can call on to assist you. They will be found in another section, but you can make a note here to remind you that they will be needed to help resolve a particular spiritual problem. If someone needs light bulbs replaced, you need light bulbs and someone to put them in. So it is with spiritual things. If, for example only, a woman is needed to help another woman deal with sensitive spiritual issues, whom do you need to contact, and do they require printed resources? You need a place to record all these various and sundry needs.

For the reasons given above, we recommend your DOM has a section to keep a record of the existing needs in your church. It's hard to imagine being organized without it.

SECTION 2: RESOURCES

Once you determine who has a need, you must then determine if you have the resources to meet the need.[132] The seven in Jerusalem undoubtedly took into consideration what supplies were currently available or perhaps needed to be either donated or purchased. The seven men didn't personally assume responsibility to supply the goods for the widows. Not that they didn't help. All we have to do is look at Acts 2-5. They were, after all, members of the church who were selling houses, lands, and possessions so that no one among them went without. And that brings up an interesting possibility. They were among those who were bringing their gifts to the apostles' feet for distribution. Although it's just a guess, perhaps this had something to do with their selection. They had wisdom, the Holy Spirit, and a good reputation. Maybe a part of that "good reputation" had to do with being known for their generous contributions for the needy. As the narrative indicates, these were public actions. They weren't done in a closet. Is it possible that, as the church looked for qualified men, they chose men whose reputations for generous giving and thoughtful actions preceded them?

As the early church was made aware of particular needs, we assume they either had the supplies on hand or had the financial resources to

---

132 There is some evidence that the apostles collected only money; money from savings or from the sale of goods or land, which was then distributed directly to the needy. We are assuming they collected both money and goods, as might be suggested in the following passages: 1 John 3:17-18; Ja.2:15-16; Matt.25:35-46.

purchase them. Those resources, both monetary and physical, had to be kept somewhere. Someone had to know both what and where they were. Someone had to keep track of them all. Which likely means someone managed a list of resources. And if they were getting low on, or ran out of either cash or an item in high demand, someone had to go get some more. Did they pick it up at a storage location or go buy it? Did they keep reserves at home? We don't really know, but they must have dealt with these kinds of issues, the kind of issues that soup kitchens and church pantries deal with all the time. And wouldn't you expect men who are full of the Holy Spirit and wisdom and men who are placed "over this business" to know how to manage the resources at their disposal?

That's what this section in your DOM is all about—keeping track of resources, both needed and on hand. Most churches are able to keep a few pantry supplies on hand, but even so, not all needs can be met with a pantry. An elderly widow has different needs than a young single mom. And what if the need is a new light switch or dead-bolt door lock? Sometimes it's better to purchase the resources as they're needed or go shopping with the individual to make sure they get what they need.

Beyond the obvious, there might be creative options for managing resources. One church had several members who volunteered to be ready to give to the needy at a moment's notice whatever they might need. Another church had a signup sheet for members to list things they were ready to donate to the needy. The items were kept by the family making the donation. This let the deacons know these resources were already designated and available. These are just a couple of creative options that can be replicated by any church. If you have creative ideas along these lines, don't be afraid to share them with other churches. And those churches might have creative suggestions for you. You might even consider interchurch sharing of resources. It might be a blessing to you both. All of this resource information can be recorded in your manual, along with detailed contact information.

Concerning these nontraditional ways of managing resources, before implementing them, you will want to clear them with the spiritual leaders first. It's not a matter of micro-managing the deacons. Pastors sometimes have private information concerning people that might directly bear on the collection or distribution of resources, either through or to these individuals. Deacons are encouraged to be creative and resourceful with their servant ministry, but if they go outside the established norms of their particular church, they should seek the approval of the spiritual leaders before moving forward.

The main point here is the value of having a place to record what resources are either on hand or readily available and where the resource is located. And not just physical supplies, this would be the place to keep an updated total of money available in your deacons' fund. Keeping that figure current is essential if recording it as a resource is to mean anything. There are also human resources to record, like deacons or church members who are qualified to offer spiritual guidance, child care, cooked meals, and so forth. Having all of this information in one place will speed up your response time.

Concerning available resources, we add a couple of thoughts. *First,* it may be appropriate to involve immediate and/or extended family members of those who are in need. Some of them may not be members of your church, but it seems appropriate to ask family, and perhaps even friends, to assist their own loved ones. Paul instructs his young protégé, Timothy, "But if any widow have children or nephews, let them learn first to shew piety at home, and to requite their parents: for that is good and acceptable before God" (1 Tim. 5:4). As far as God is concerned, it's good for the family to take care of the family, especially when they are all believers. But even if they are unbelievers, it's still a good idea to ask children, grandchildren, and other family members to help if they are in a position to do so. This is especially important when a long-term need exists or if it will require more resources than the church has available. If they refuse, or are not able to help, then the needy are considered desolate and in need of the church's assistance.

Obviously, much wisdom needs to be exercised in these situations. This kind of plea can easily backfire, and good intentions can be misread. However, it can also become a way to minister not only to the person in need, but to many others through their need. Your leadership and example in helping a family member can be a powerful witness. The added benefit to you as a deacon may simply be that, from your contacts with the family, you were able to gain valuable insight concerning the situation. As you seek to serve the whole person, body and soul, you may be able to address things like discipline, work ethic, finances, and time management, things you may not have known if not for speaking to family members and close friends.

The *second* observation concerning available resources for the needy is this: while Rome gave nothing back to the poor under its rule, we are privileged to live in a country that provides assistance for those who qualify. Every American citizen contributes, either willingly or unwillingly, to these programs and agencies through tax dollars. In a sense, we are investors into the system, and if necessary, we have the right to get back some of the dollars that we put in.

The well-deserved criticism is that the system is often abused. True enough, but we don't think the abuses prevent believers from accessing the available funds when absolutely necessary. It's also true that the church has the responsibility to care for its own. But what if the church has no resources or if the problem is chronic and the resources have been strained? These are difficult questions to answer. All things considered, it is our cautious recommendation that these programs and agencies be used without abuse or neglecting our own responsibilities. Because this suggestion is controversial, it requires input from the spiritual leaders of the church.

This section in your notebook, Available Resources, provides the kind of information deacons need to enable a quick response to calls for help. Response time is always critical, and the more organized you are, the quicker you will be able to respond. This would also be the place to keep contact information for your local agencies, like the Salvation Army, Goodwill, homeless shelters, women's shelters, county health department, and so forth.

SECTION 3: VOLUNTEERS

Numerous biblical studies on the office have rightly concluded that deacons represent the entire church body in the work of serving others. But the representative does not entirely take the place of those who are represented. They are not a branch of service unto themselves. They not only serve on behalf of the body, they also seek ways to engage the whole body in serving others. Remember, serving is a universal call. It is not a diaconal call only. As those who serve as role models of service to the church, they are always looking for ways to bring others into compassionate obedience to the command to serve.

The words in Acts 6:3, *over this business*, suggest the responsibility to superintend, manage, and direct any and all necessary actions. This would naturally include the oversight of the servant volunteers within the church. One of the exciting opportunities laid upon the diaconate is to organize and direct volunteers from the congregation.

Volunteers are an indispensable resource for diaconal ministry. It's hard to imagine the first deacons attempting to meet all the needs of the rapidly growing church in Jerusalem by themselves. In fact, it sounds downright impossible. They had to have help. But don't think that yours has to be a rapidly growing church like the one in Jerusalem in order to find and direct volunteers. Even a diaconate of one can lovingly enlist the help of others. In doing so, he is lovingly bringing others into obedience to the universal call to serve and experiencing the joy that serving others brings.

Let's look at the challenge of recruiting volunteers under the following five headings:

1. Getting volunteers

2. Evaluating volunteers

3. Training volunteers

4. Organizing volunteers

5. Contacting volunteers

1. Getting volunteers

A typical method for soliciting help is to announce an immediate need for volunteers. Sometimes this is all it takes, but not always. Sometimes we get qualified volunteers; sometimes we don't. Some people don't like to be put on the spot; they need a little time to prepare. Others might be concerned about their ability to help. They need more information, or encouragement, or training, before they raise a hand to help. On occasion, the needy individual is sitting there in the room or auditorium and feeling quite awkward, even if they aren't mentioned by name. At such times, you cannot go into further details without embarrassing the brother or sister.[133]

Instead of making a general announcement seeking volunteers when they are needed, we think there is a better way to recruit. Simply put, do it beforehand.

What if you had a list of volunteers who are already trained and "on call" at a moment's notice, a team of "first responders," like FEMA, or the Red Cross?

What if this list of volunteers included specialists, like a team of "special ops" in the church, individuals who have specific gifts in certain fields—plumbers, electricians, carpenters, nurses, biblical counselors—or a woman who has demonstrated wisdom and skill as a biblical wife and

---

133 This brings up questions concerning things like pride versus the blessings of openness, but we will let you wrestle with these things on your own.

mother; or a business owner, or computer tech, or any number of church members with special skills who have been recruited ahead of time to be available to serve in their field of giftedness? Note: Remember to update this information from time to time.

What if your list of volunteers included people who are great organizers or natural leaders, people who could step in and spearhead a project on a moment's notice?

What if this recruiting of volunteers started in your New Members Class so that every person coming into the church starts out with an opportunity to get connected to an area of service?

Wouldn't this army of volunteers at the disposal of the deacons be a powerful resource and a blessing to the church, the community, and perhaps beyond?

As an example of diaconal work going beyond the local church and community, at the time of this writing, one of our churches has a deacon serving in Haiti as a diesel mechanic on a large mission compound (he does much more than keeping the engines running so that the electricity stays on, but we won't go into all that he does). As a deacon sent from the church, he not only ministers to the needy, he serves as the eyes and ears of the church back home, keeping them informed of the evangelism, church planting, and relief efforts going on in that country. The point being, they have a deacon serving the needy in *another country* on their behalf. He's not a missionary. He's not a church planter. He's a deacon. He and his wife are exciting examples of utilizing the special skills of church members who are ready to serve the needy wherever God calls.[134]

When we think of gifted and willing volunteers rising up within the church, can we do anything but give all the glory to God? Think about

---

134 Update: He now senses God's call into full time ministry and has returned to the states to be trained under the leadership of his Pastors. God willing, they will soon return to Haiti where he will focus on church planting and the training of Haitian pastors.

this for a moment. The church is His church. We are the body of Christ. This amazing story of the church is then entrusted to humans. God calls men and appoints them to lead His people spiritually as under-shepherds of the Great Shepherd. God also gave His church a second office that is responsible to watch over the practical and material needs of the flock. The church is no ordinary organization—it is God's. And from this group of humans come pastors and deacons, all put into place, in His church, for His own glory.

But there's more to the story of His church. He also provides a variety of servants with various gifts who can help in the work of the ministry and edify the body of Christ (Eph. 4:11-12; 1 Cor. 12), not only pastors and deacons, but a church full of gifted men and women who should always be ready to volunteer to serve in the place of Christ. This is the "pool" from which deacons find help. Remember, serving is a universal call and the Holy Spirit has gifted every member for the "common good" (1 Cor. 12:7, ESV).

This is the amazing body from which volunteers come. At this point, the obvious question is, "How do we get this well-trained and organized army of volunteers?" Ah, good question! We will try to answer that question with a few thoughts.

First, it is primarily up to the spiritual leaders and teachers to create an atmosphere in the church where members are ready and willing to serve. This is, after all, a concern of the benevolent God. He cares for the poor and needy and has done everything to see that they are served. And one thing God has already provided is under-shepherds to watch over them. Pastor/shepherds can cry out to the church on behalf of the Great Shepherd, to feed, clothe, and shelter the needy brethren—not only cry out but instruct. A public appeal for help may get some volunteers, yet public instruction from the Scriptures on serving will inspire many more. This kind of public teaching may drive some away, but true servants will step forward. This is so because the Spirit of truth uses the Word of God to work on human hearts as truth is taught. This is God's way! The entire process of getting, inspiring, and keeping volunteers is first and foremost the result of the Holy Spirit working through the ordinary means of the teaching of the Word of God on this subject. When you see volunteers lining up and signing up, something has inspired them: the Spirit and the Word! Therefore, the responsibility to rally volunteers from the membership lies primarily with the spiritual leaders/teachers of the church. However, "primarily" does not mean exclusively, which leads us to the next observation.

A *second* avenue for inspiring others and building a culture of volunteerism are the deacons who are presently serving. This is so simple that it can be overlooked. Deacons who are called to serve and are demonstrating their love for the work and the joy in serving the needy will inspire others to follow them in the work. Their love and zeal will naturally be on display to those they serve and those they represent. But when they are given opportunities to share their stories, and when they are publicly recognized for their work, as Paul recognized Stephanas (1 Cor. 16:15-16), along with the biblical teaching on serving, deacons will become more noticed and the nobility of serving will become more prominent in the church. So, by their own example and enthusiasm, along with the proper recognition for faithful service, others will be inspired to follow their lead and respond to their calls for volunteers.

This transitions us into a *third* suggestion for getting volunteers: the public testimonies of those who have been blessed by serving, as well as those who have been served. To let insecurity or the fear of public speaking keep us silent on what God is doing in and through the church is to rob God of the glory due His magnificent name. While a testimony of praise does not always need to be made publicly, there are times that it should be public. God is exalted when His children display His compassionate mercy to the broken and needy. The Triune God is glorified and the church is blessed to hear stories of how our Father is using others to serve in the name of Christ and in the power of the Holy Spirit.

Frankly, it's not easy to get either humble servants or needy brethren to speak up: we all get it. But they both need to be encouraged to do so, which means they need a venue for speaking up. There might be a place in your worship service for giving praise, or after a communion service, or during a fellowship meal. The point is, find a time for deeds of mercy to be made known to the whole church. We can tell you from experience the rich blessing it is to God's people to hear these testimonies and the praise that goes up to our glorious God (2 Cor. 9:12-15; 10:17).

Our *fourth* suggestion was mentioned earlier, but it is more effective after these other things have been done first: public appeals for volunteers. While it doesn't always produce the kind of response we're hoping for, when preceded by public teaching, the example of the deacons, and public testimonies, a general appeal may be the very thing that nudges a member into volunteering for service. To be clear, by "volunteering for service," we mean volunteering to assist the deacons in serving the needy. This whole section has to do with diaconal assistants in the church.

We find it necessary to specify "in the church" because decades of ministry experience have taught us that some who have an interest in serving others, or perhaps have special abilities that facilitate helping others, end up using their gifts outside the local church. They often volunteer to use their gifts in community-based outreach programs like food pantries, homeless shelters, or other not-for-profit organizations, or perhaps even other church-based programs. This is not necessarily a bad thing. In fact, it can be a good thing. They can become a beacon of mercy in this dark world and bear witness to Christ through showing mercy to those in need. However, sometimes it's because they are not first being utilized in, or through, their church. We have seen situations where church leaders failed to understand and appreciate the gifts and talents of people and squandered the opportunity to involve them in diaconal ministry in their own church.

The point we're making here is this: find ways to encourage a spirit of volunteerism among the members of the church to ensure they are available to serve those in their own church family when a need arises. If your church is small, there may not be a lot of opportunities to minister to the needy, in which case, they may indeed be encouraged to serve first in the community. In doing so, you are stirring up their spirit of volunteerism and heightening their sense of the necessity of serving others. And if the Lord adds new members to the church or opens up new opportunities for service, the deacons will have plenty of experienced volunteers who are available for diaconal ministry.

2. Evaluating volunteers

Now that you have a list of volunteers, what comes next? You have to evaluate your army of ready servants. You quickly learn that every volunteer is unique. Many will possess similar gifts and abilities, yet, because of gender, age, experience, and spiritual maturity, they will also be very different from each other. This is a good thing; it is a God thing!

God adds to the church and gives gifts for building up the body. As leaders in the church, it is our responsibility to recognize each person's giftedness, be attuned to the various needs in the body, and then bring the two into alignment. That being said, it doesn't always need to be orchestrated. Sometimes these things happen organically as believers make themselves available and are sensitive to both the leading of the Spirit and the needs of those around them.

But it doesn't always happen like that, does it? As leaders in the church, both spiritual and practical leaders, we often have to bring the two together. In doing so, we try to match the right volunteer to the right need. That means that, on some level, *every volunteer must be evaluated*. We are mindful of obvious things like gender, age, and abilities, but we are also evaluating things like experience and spiritual maturity. We also need to know the basic personality traits of every volunteer. Some will be willing to explore new and challenging opportunities for service. Others will not. Some will be outgoing and willing to serve in unfamiliar situations. Others will not. Some, who are more reserved and quiet by nature, might be more suited for certain situations than the gregarious and outgoing person. The only way to know these things is by knowing your volunteers.

Evaluation is also important because it helps the deacons as they look ahead and consider future ministries. It seems to be presumptuous for a church to start a new ministry or outreach, and then hope to get the necessary volunteers. Usually, God provides workers who already have the desire to serve in a certain way before a new ministry gets started. That would be like starting an ethnicity-based outreach ministry when no one in the church speaks that group's language. We know that there are always exceptions to the norm, but it is wise to know beforehand if you have the right people in place. A prior evaluation will tell you if you do.

Another advantage of evaluating and knowing your volunteers is that it allows you to match untrained volunteers with experienced servants. This one-on-one training can be invaluable in bringing volunteers along in their personal and spiritual development. And the benefit flows both ways. It can be a means of challenging growth in your mentors as well. An additional benefit of a mentorship program is that you are training future deacons. Tomorrow's deacons will usually be found among today's volunteers.

Quickly, one more advantage of knowing your volunteers well is diminishing the possibility of putting the individual in a situation that might discourage them from volunteering in the future. Carelessly sending out a volunteer with another novice to handle a situation that calls for experienced and spiritually mature leadership is a sure-fire way to discourage the spirit of volunteerism in the church. This kind of information gets around! Although the circumstances were a little different, I (Mark) remember as a young man getting a late-night call from the senior pastor to see if I wanted to go on a "ride along" to deal with a domestic situation. I'm glad he had me stay in the car to make sure it was okay for me to come in. I'm not sure how I would have reacted when the handgun came out! I think I avoided late-night calls from him for a long time. These kinds of things can't always be avoided, but we need to exercise wisdom when putting our volunteers into action. We not only want to avoid putting them in harm's way, we do not want to do anything to discourage them from serving in the future.

The evaluation process that we have in mind is more informal than formal. We're not suggesting an exam or an intense interview of your volunteers. It is simply knowing and taking note of strengths and weaknesses, level of spiritual maturity, knowledge of the Scriptures, particular areas of giftedness and interest, personality traits, and so forth. What this means, of course, is that you must study and know your church. From your knowledge of every member, you can develop a profile of congregational skills, talents, and areas of interest. As mentioned earlier, some of this knowledge can be gathered during your church membership classes. As you informally gather this information, you will need a place to write it all down. This is another benefit of having a DOM.

The obvious information to have on your volunteers is their name, address, phone number, and hours they are available. You'll make a few notations about what they have volunteered for, along with a general description of their personality, spiritual maturity, known giftedness, and so forth. Perhaps someone will want to make a spreadsheet to organize this kind of information. You will also keep notes on any past occasions they were called to help out, how the service went for both the volunteer and the one being served. We're sure you can find a way to structure this aspect of diaconal ministry in a way that works for your church. This will be invaluable information for yourselves, the church, and future ministry opportunities.

3. Training volunteers

Volunteers can be both intimidated and discouraged by the thought of volunteering for service. The uncertainty of what will be expected of them, the fear of failure, doubts about their ability, or past bad experiences will keep some from making themselves available to the deacons for service. Most volunteers are not interested in leading an effort, at least not at first. They simply want to offer their help to the servant leaders of the church. Some may become deacons in the future, but others, for various reasons, will continue as reliable volunteer servants. But getting them to volunteer in the first place is the first challenge.

If the members see a well-organized and user-friendly ministry, they are more likely to join the ranks of the army of volunteers who are ready to go into service. There are things the leaders of the church can do to encourage a spirit of volunteerism, such as offering a "ride along" program, producing a well-written informative pamphlet, developing a fun and engaging training course and the aforementioned testimonies of ongoing servant ministries in the church. These are the kinds of things that will encourage members to step forward when volunteer team members are needed. Whatever the reason, deacons must be prepared to overcome the hesitancy that many people have about volunteering for servant ministry.

Keep in mind deacons are the face of diaconal ministry in the church. As such, beyond their own sacrificial service, they will either encourage or discourage members to pitch in when more servants are needed. Exactly how they do this will be worked out in each ministry. However, what we're talking about is the opportunity to mentor a new crop of servant leaders.

In the secular world, just the mention of mentoring a trainee is met with a sigh, a groan, or a rolling of the eyes. But in the church, it ought to be received differently. Don't think of mentoring others as a burden, but as a blessing. It's a blessing to train others to serve the needy in and through the church. To go back to a previous chapter, it is a calling that is universal, necessary, and noble. As a deacon, you have the opportunity—yea the blessing—of enlisting and mentoring others in noble work, to give on-the-job training to new workers, and to leave your fingerprints on the servant ministry in your church. Volunteers often need the benefit of experienced and patient mentors. Deacon, if not you, then who will be their mentor?

Examples of mentoring are found over and over again in the Bible. We know about Old Testament examples like Moses and Joshua, and Elijah and Elisha. This was also the pattern of the apostles who were constantly taking others under their wings to help prepare future servants in the church, men like Timothy, Titus, Epaphras, John-Mark, and others. Jesus Himself trained twelve to continue the work He started, who then entrusted the work to other qualified and faithful men. Likewise, pastors and deacons must be committed to training and developing (mentoring) servant volunteers in the church.

It takes much wisdom to do diaconal work in the church. If you have any doubt about that, see the list of requirements for the office. It also takes wisdom to train others. Some things are fairly simple and straightforward. There are practical things like caring for church property or helping an elderly widow with tasks around the house. Other things are more complicated, like helping a woman who lacks certain domestic skills or helping a man overcome a natural laziness or a lack of home-repair skills with no money to hire someone. Many people who struggle need basic financial counseling. It takes both skill and wisdom to help people. This is why it is so important for deacons, and even their wives, to be committed to training others for diaconal work.

While we're thinking about mentoring others, always keep watch over your attitude. The attitude with which something is done is just as important as the action itself. Any on-the-job training ought to reflect well on the organization. But when the organization is the church of Christ, the trainer ought to reflect the fruit of the Spirit as he serves. The whole point of mentoring is to train others to serve as you serve. But if the training leads to a bad, negative, critical attitude toward the needy and vulnerable members of the church or the community, mere outward action alone will never rise to the level of being pleasing to God. Volunteers must be trained to serve in a spiritually edifying atmosphere, an atmosphere of "unfeigned love of the brethren" (1 Pe.1:22).

The entire training process must be a blessing to everyone concerned: the deacon, the volunteer, the one being served, and the entire church family. And above all else, it must glorify God. We say these things as an encouragement to make sure that you are not only mentoring others, but that you do so in a way that is spiritually profitable.

Here are a few more practical thoughts on training volunteers:

- Always connect a seasoned servant with a volunteer.

- Be careful about sending an untrained and unprepared volunteer out to serve without a training partner.

- Some situations may allow you to use an entire family to serve another family in need. This can be a huge blessing to both.

- Look for opportunities to involve your teens, like yard work, painting, help with shopping, or other age-appropriate jobs.

- Find things for senior volunteers to do, such as visit the sick and shut-ins, send out birthday cards, and be ministry "prayer warriors". Don't overlook the fact that many seniors are great at using social media and can be instrumental in sharing information concerning the church.

- Develop specialized teams: cleaning team, transportation team, home repair team, and so on. This gives volunteers an opportunity to do the kind of service they are most comfortable with and puts them "in the field" more quickly. Some volunteers are willing to do just about anything, while others prefer to "stay in their own lane." Keep those things in mind when calling on available helpers.

- If, for whatever reason, you, as a deacon, are unsure or uncomfortable with using a certain volunteer, get counsel from your spiritual leaders before giving out an assignment.

These are just a few things concerning the training of volunteers, and this information can be kept in your DOM.

4. Organizing volunteers

Most people are drawn to order and away from chaos. That's why most people recognize a poor plan when they see it. They also recognize a plan that has been well thought out ahead of time. If you want to discourage volunteers and keep them from enlisting in the future, give them an unorganized assignment. They will feel their time is wasted and that you don't know what you're doing. On the other hand, if you want to encourage volunteers and give them the sense that you value them and their time, and that you care about the people they are serving, you should give them an organized, structured assignment. You must have a plan, give easy-to-follow steps to execute the plan, and follow up on the plan after the assignment is completed. This kind of organization results in the best use of time, resources, and energy. In other words, it results in an efficient and effective ministry. So, before you even sign up, let alone send out your volunteers, make sure that you have carefully thought through all the details. Volunteers will love you for it!

Most of the time, the planning phase will be worked out and come together in your regular deacons' meetings. Therefore, you will have the opportunity to record all the details of the planned outreach, including the minutes of the discussions, in your DOM. This will ensure you are presenting a carefully planned activity to everyone involved.

5. Contacting volunteers

As stated above, you will need to keep volunteer *contact information* handy. The last thing you want is out-of-date information when you need to get in contact with someone. At the risk of stating the obvious, make it your practice to constantly update this information. Not only do people occasionally change their numbers and/or social media accounts, but your list of available volunteers will change from time to time as well. Volunteers go through seasons of life like everyone else—physically, spiritually, mentally, emotionally—and this might change their ability or willingness to be called on for assistance. It can be both embarrassing and discouraging to call on people who have requested to be removed from the volunteer list or, in the other direction, to never call on a willing servant because someone forgot to put their name on the list. We also need to be sensitive to what people are going through in their own lives before picking up the phone. Think carefully about the individual you are about to call. Have they been missing church? Have they gone through a devastating loss? Has their health been poor? Has their financial situation changed owing to a loss of income? These are the kinds of things we have to think of when we look through the volunteer list. It would be helpful if the deacons kept each other abreast of these kinds of situations that occasionally befall us all, not only for the sake of keeping the information up to date, but for the sake of the brother or sister as well. These won't all be diaconal situations; some will be pastoral in nature. But the deacons have to think about these things as they seek to serve the needy in the church body. Yes, this takes time, but in the end, it will serve you well.

Volunteers are an important asset to the church. Thinking back on the seven men in Acts 6, they must have had help. And if so, where did the help come from? Surely, some of them volunteered. And two thousand years later, deacons still need volunteer help.

In this section, we addressed *getting, evaluating, training, organizing,* and *contacting* volunteers. It is the deacon's unique privilege and responsibility to recruit, assess, prepare, and send out into service those who volunteer to serve the needy.

SECTION 4: FOLLOW UP

This section in your DOM is for evaluating your diaconal ministry and should be updated on a regular basis. We all need "feedback" to make sure we are on point with our efforts. Without following up on our work, how will we know for sure if the need has truly been met? Not just our opinion, but the opinion of those we are serving. We don't want to be the proverbial "ivory palace" kind of leaders: grand plans in the office but no idea of what's actually going on in the rest of the church. We're not saying this is always, or even often, the case. It's not. But let's be honest; it can happen. We need to stay on top of every situation and the effectiveness of our ministries by hearing back from everyone involved: the needy, the deacons, and volunteers if there were any.

Asking for feedback can be scary for the one receiving it and intimidating for the one giving it. But it needn't be. It all depends on how it is managed. If we're defensive, argumentative, or in any way upset when people are honest with us, then they will stop being honest. However, if we lovingly and humbly receive both praise and criticism and use it to make us more Christ-like, then we authenticate the confidence that was placed in us in the first place.

How you actually do the follow-up is up to you. Basically, the deacons and volunteers who were directly involved should follow up with the one who was served, and deacons should follow up with the volunteer. If it was handed off to an experienced volunteer, then the deacon will want direct feedback from the volunteer and the individual served. Feedback can be gained verbally by asking questions and taking notes, or through a written evaluation sheet. In either case, the feedback needs to be kept in your DOM.

It may not be necessary to follow up on every diaconal action. But it is a good idea to regularly follow up as a way of evaluating the effectiveness of your ministry. Self-evaluation is a good thing, but it is just as important, if not more important, to get input from those who are on the receiving end of your servant ministry.

SECTION 5: PROBLEMS

A "problem" is any harmful or unwanted situation or matter that needs to be addressed yet remains unsettled. The seven in Acts were appointed because of a problem or a harmful situation that needed to be addressed: the neglected Grecian widows. What were they commissioned to do? Address and settle the problem and, if possible, prevent its recurrence.

While that was the starting point, no one really thinks it ended there. Not every problem was resolved by simply putting food on the table. Most problems have underlying causes that are not always evident at first, like the issue of not serving the Grecians. Why were they neglected? Racial bias? Resentment? Arrogance? Selfishness? Or perhaps all the above?

Whether they discovered an underlying cause or not, they no doubt had other issues to deal with. The people they were serving were real people with real problems. As they solved one problem, they had to solve other problems as well. That's what happens to problem solvers. They're asked to solve more problems. The same thing happens to servants—they serve. From one issue to the next, they serve others by solving problems.

Although this detail is missing, it's reasonable to think this is how the office developed. From one problem to the next, they became known as the problem solvers. Often, they dealt with just material problems and sometimes the underlying spiritual causes.

Solving problems takes both practical and spiritual wisdom, hence the requirement to be "full of the Holy Ghost and wisdom." Some problems are resolved immediately; others require long-term solutions. Some are caused by the needy themselves; others involve family and friends. Some are simple matters; others are complex. And what about those who ask for material help, but refuse spiritual help?

Then there are the servant leaders themselves. Too often they are dealing with their own problems. They have to solve their own "harmful or unwanted" situations and, at the same time, find solutions for other people's problems. It can be taxing physically, emotionally, and spiritually. Being a problem-solving servant of others can be difficult work. A universal, necessary, and noble work, but difficult nonetheless.

The Scripture tells us, "Without counsel purposes are disappointed: but in the multitude of counselors they are established," and, "in the multitude of counselors there is safety" (Prov. 15:22; 11:14). Being spiritual and wise individually is a gift of grace, but the collective wisdom and spirituality of a team of servants is God's plan for the church. This is true of both offices of the church. God led the apostles to put into motion His solution to the problem of neglect, not just one, but seven problem solvers. Together, as a team, they attacked the problem, and not just that one problem, but many more problems that would arise. Furthermore, as they served the Grecians and met the immediate need, and then more needs as they came up, they gained collective wisdom that comes from experience. The same is true for deacons today. As you pool your collective wisdom and spiritual insights, insights that become sharper through experience, you will become more effective as problem-solving servants of the needy.

The wisdom, the leading of the Spirit, the lessons learned are all shared in your meetings and recorded in your DOM. All of this can be preserved in the Problems section of the manual. This is the place to record everything related to the problem itself. By recording everything, you will preserve your discussions, biblical references and insights, proposed solutions, recommendations, necessary steps, and so forth. The outcomes will be recorded in the Follow Up section. As you deal with current problems and refer back to your notes on past problems, you will become more skilled at untangling and solving the problem in front of you. That is the value of the Problems section of your DOM.

Before moving on, we should point out that problems should not always be viewed negatively. *First*, a problem can be the doorway that leads to dealing with an underlying cause. If it weren't for the presenting problem, we might not have gotten to the root cause. We should be thankful when a problem leads to real, lasting solutions. *Second*, a problem dealt with biblically often leads to spiritual growth. For one thing, when sin is involved and it is acknowledged and repented of, and forgiveness and cleansing follow, grace and growth are sure to follow. Also, when God graciously supplies the needs of His people, they instinctively give thanks and praise His name. These are good outcomes that began with a problem. We should look for and celebrate the positives that come when a problem is solved.

SECTION 6: CHURCH PROPERTY

While nothing is said in our narrative, or anywhere in the Scripture for that matter, about church property, it is reasonable to assume this practical ministry would fall under the oversight of the deacons. It's important to remember that the primary concern of the apostles was not that they didn't like caring for the needy. No, that was the occasion. Their chief concern was protecting their own time. Acts 6:2b-4 reads, "It is not reason that we should *leave the word of God*, and serve tables. Wherefore, brethren, look ye out among you seven men, full of the Holy Ghost and wisdom, whom we may appoint over this business. *But we will give ourselves continually to prayer, and the ministry of the word*" (italics added). In essence, they were turning over to the seven the administration of everything that interfered with their first priorities of prayer and Word. We think it's possible that the apostles had a broader range of service in mind than just "serving tables." Knowing, as we do, that the real issue was being freed from distractions, wouldn't both groups, the Hebrews and the Grecians, draw the conclusion that they should do everything possible to protect the apostles' time? Keep in mind, the "whole multitude" was in attendance that day, not just the Grecians, and the whole multitude heard them say it's not right that they should be distracted by this because they have more important things to do. And isn't it possible, even likely, that the church understood there was more to this than just feeding widows? Perhaps this explains the expanded list of qualifications in 1 Timothy 3, some of which come with explanation. Surely, more than just feeding widows is envisioned, as important as that responsibility is to the church.

Here's the point we are getting at, and we doubt there will be much objection. We should be open minded to broadening their sphere of ministry (as demonstrated by both Stephen and Philip). As we have been saying all along, this does not mean that deacons must do all the work, not at all. Rather, they are generally responsible, as good administrators, to make sure that everything in their care gets done. In the end, not only do they serve the needy, they also absorb other distractions. One of those distractions is caring for church property. This keeps pastors from having to worry about and overseeing this important aspect of body life.

In some cases, deacons are handy and enjoy taking care of the building and property and have the time to do so. But that's not always the case, nor is it biblically required. Some deacons shouldn't be allowed around power tools and paint rollers. That's okay. But they can oversee a building maintenance committee of men and women who know how to take care of the property. Maybe a deacon is better at organizing a work day and making sure lunch is provided. He makes it his business to make sure, in every way possible, that the pastors aren't pulled away from ministering in prayer and the Word. Of course, some spiritual leaders enjoy rolling up their sleeves and getting sawdust in their hair. They might even need to be nudged back into the study if need be. That too can be a way of protecting the pastor from distractions.

This section in your DOM should be organized to call attention to various aspects of property management, things like Immediate Attention, Future Projects, and Scheduled Maintenance. This would be the place to keep names and other emergency contact information of contractors and church members who can be called when a property emergency comes up. As a preventative measure, deacons should also schedule a periodic walk-through or visual inspection of the property. If an issue is spotted, it can be noted in your manual, prioritized, and the necessary steps to deal with it identified.

Again, the important thing here is to shield the spiritual leaders from unnecessary distractions. That is why deacons typically oversee church properties.

SECTION 7: BUDGETS

This chapter is about *getting organized*. The best way to organize the collection and distribution of benevolent giving is with a budget. When asked, "What is the purpose of a budget?" a retired Air Force master sergeant, now working as a civilian on a military base, immediately answered, "Accountability." His point can be boiled down to this: those who spend the funds must answer to those who give the funds. Concerning diaconal work, deacons are accountable first to God, then the church, and finally the needy.

In order to be faithful stewards who confidently give an account to all concerned, deacons must budget and wisely manage the money and resources entrusted to their care. Beyond accountability, a few additional benefits of budgeting are as follows:

- Planning for future needs

- Tracking past expenditures

- Prioritizing limited resources

- Revealing problem areas

- Visualizing available funds

- Protecting everyone with access to the funds

Since the benefits of budgeting are obvious and have been valued by civilizations in one form or another for thousands of years, we wonder if the seven were given a budget by either the apostles or the church. No one knows. However, it would make sense. We know they collected money that was allocated for the poor and needy and then distributed those contributions as necessary. Did they ever look at what was available, compare that to what was needed, and plan accordingly? As wise and spiritual men, they surely wouldn't spend or commit more than they had available or what they expected to collect in the future. What's that called? Budgeting.

Think about the apostles. One of them was a tax collector, some were commercial fishermen, and one, Judas, kept track of benevolent giving. He even had a purse to keep it in. Wouldn't Matthew, the tax collector, or Peter, the fisherman, know the value of a budget? But those were apostles; what does this have to do with the seven?

From the narrative, it seems they all came through Chapters 2 through 5 together. They witnessed the sacrificial and joyful giving that was laid at the apostles' feet. The monetary value of their collective gifts must have been enormous. Surely, someone kept a record of these things. Someone had to know what was actually on hand, what was needed, and where it all went. In other words, this is what came in, this is what went out, and this is what is needed, so let's control the flow. That's a budget. Surely, the apostles, the church, and the seven men of good report knew that a budget of some kind was necessary to be good stewards of the given resources. Remember they had to be men of good reputation, and maybe one of the reasons the seven were chosen was their reputation for sound financial management of their own money. According to Paul, this is a qualification for office (1 Tim. 3:8,12).

Whether or not the deacons of the early church worked from a budget, it is important for today's deacons to follow a budget. While a budget is not an iron-fisted tyrant never allowing any deviation, it is a valuable tool for all the stated reasons and should be followed.

This is the section in your DOM where you will record your expense with a watchful eye on your available balance. Think of this section in your manual as a checkbook ledger: money in, money out, and a running balance. When a need comes up, every deacon can know if the resources are available. In order for this to work, this information needs to be shared and updated at least monthly and perhaps every time the deacon board meets. It might be tedious at times, keeping track of receipts and making sure the balance in the DOM is updated. But it will be a blessing if you keep it up.

Always keep in mind that your first priority is the church family. Remembering that will come in handy when you are forced to make difficult choices over who gets what and how much. If at all possible, keep a reserve on hand for "the household of faith" (Gal. 6:10). A budget will help you do that.

SECTION 8: FUTURE PLANS

As deacons meet together, pray together, and serve together, they inevitably dream together. They share visions, possibilities, personal passions, fields of interest, and so on. Some refer to this process as "vision casting."

Sometimes these visions for the future come from deep within, but sometimes they are planted by others and take root in the mind and heart of a sensitive and forward-thinking deacon. New ministry opportunities can come from discussions among deacons, suggestions from church members, the example of another church, and immediate needs in the community. Concerning church members, deacons should be listening to everyone, but especially to those who volunteer to assist in the work.

When planning future ministries, keep this in mind: some people by nature dream big. We need big dreamers in the church to stir us up to attempt big things for God. Others, by nature, are cautious and perhaps even fearful of wasting resources on the ambitious dreams of others. We need cautious people as well. They make sure we are counting the cost and investing God's resources wisely. Big dreamers left unbridled can get us into undesirable situations. The overly cautious would rather maintain the status quo. The church needs both. Diaconal ministries need both. They balance each other. And when they both are full of wisdom and the Holy Spirit, they allow themselves to be open to the wise contributions of the other.

Giftedness is another factor. God gives gifts to the church for the common good (1 Cor. 12:7; 13:12). While there are many potential pitfalls to avoid down the path of "giftedness," we must be careful to not dismiss the interests and passions of others simply because we do not share them. A dismissive attitude might be a covering for either arrogance or ignorance, arrogance in thinking our interests are the only ones that matter and ignorance in not knowing that God gives us a variety of gifts for the good of the entire church (1 Cor. 12-14; Eph. 4:11). Giftedness creates interest, and interest often turns into fulfilling ministry opportunities. This is true even among deacons. Why wouldn't it be? Unless they are promoting unbiblical or unrealistic avenues of ministry, let them enjoy a servant ministry that is both interesting and fulfilling.

As you discuss future possibilities, this section in your notebook is the place to record those discussions. Each deacon can record his own thoughts/visions for the future in his own manual and bring them up at the appropriate time. It might even be wise for the moderator to make this a regular agenda item, not that you will always have something to discuss or that every idea needs to be brought up again at every meeting. Some ideas will never be acted on and will eventually be dropped as potential areas of service. Others, when returned to, will gather interest and eventually lead to a new way to serve the needy.

The point here is that you need a way to record all suggestions for future ministry opportunities. How often has a good idea been forgotten because no one bothered to write it down? With a section in your DOM earmarked for these suggestions and with discussions balanced by the natures and giftedness of each other, deacons will have a journal of future ministry opportunities.

SECTION 9: POLICIES

Without getting technical, policies are the written set of guidelines that manage the behaviors of a group of people. Although some churches function without written policies, this seems unwise. A short list of some of the benefits of written policies points this out:

- Clarify member expectations.
- Improve individual accountability.
- Prevent impulsive actions.
- Speed decision making.
- Protect against bias.
- Focus on core objectives.

We will resist the temptation to comment on each of the above benefits of written policies. We do suggest that you discuss the benefits and compare them to either your practices or policies. If you do not have written policies to manage your servant ministry, begin by asking your spiritual leaders if they think it would help your ministry. Suffice it to say, we think written policies that relate specifically to diaconal ministry are beneficial.

Your policies will be kept in this section of your DOM for quick reference when making decisions.

We realize in a small church, deacons may not be dealing with multiple issues at the same time, as is often the case in larger churches. However, getting organized is always a good thing, and forgetting important details is always a bad thing, even if the details are few.

We think diaconal ministry is important enough to justify the effort it takes to put together a DOM and manage the nine sections. Perhaps you already have a DOM, or something similar; if so, great. If not, we hope you find these suggestions helpful.

CHAPTER SUMMARY

This chapter has focused on the value of *getting organized*, which by definition means taking something with a lot of parts and arranging them in a way that makes everything work together in a more effective and efficient way—like God does. God is a God of order. Organization leads to orderliness, and orderliness reflects the nature of God.

Using the historical data we have in Acts 6, we speculated that following the Installation of the Seven, they got organized. We think that's what "men of honest report, full of the Holy Ghost and wisdom" would do: get organized. *Getting organized* doesn't just happen. It starts with a plan. Therefore, we included some thoughts about the planning process and stated, "*Without this organized planning process, diaconal work will suffer from a lack of direction and runs the risk of failing to meet the goal of caring for the needy.*"

Although the details of their organizational planning are missing, we suggested that today's deacons must *meet* together, constantly *review*, and *record* everything. This led us into the DOM and the recommended *nine sections* for your manual. Obviously, we are not suggesting the Seven in Acts 6 had their own DOM. We are, however, suggesting that the magnitude of the work assigned to them must have required meetings, catching up, and record keeping. That's the value of the DOM: keeping the work organized as you *meet*, *review*, and *record* everything.

As deacons, your time is valuable. You have many legitimate matters clamoring for your time, especially those individuals you have been chosen to serve. Organization saves time, and time belongs to God. We dare not waste the gift of time for want of *getting organized*.

CHAPTER 6

THE NEGLECTED

I n the early days of the New Testament church, most believers were of Jewish descent. Hearing the Gospel message, they believed in Jesus Christ, the Messiah, the Christ of God. The Great Warrior and Deliverer defeated Satan, the one who reigned over the human race through the power of sin and death. As the Spirit went out breathing life into dead souls, God was forming a new congregation of believers called the church.

As the church was being formed, the Jewish converts demonstrated a genuine readiness to share all things with their Jewish brethren who lacked the basic necessities of life. Whether families, widows, or orphans, they were ready to help. As the story of the church unfolds in the early pages of Acts, their care for one another gives off the sweet fragrance of genuine love. Peter was front and center during these days and later referred to this kind of love as "unfeigned love of the brethren" (1 Pet. 1:22). An unfeigned love is a sincere love, a love without hypocrisy. As we read Acts 2 through 5, it's their sincere and sacrificial love that gets our attention and draws us into the narrative. Let's look at two of those remarkable scenes.

The first is found in Acts 2:42-47.

> 42 And they continued steadfastly in the apostles' doctrine and fellowship, and in breaking bread, and in prayers. 43 And fear came upon every soul: and many wonders and signs were done by the apostles. 44 And all that believed were together, and had all things common; 45 And sold their possessions and goods, and parted them to all men as every man had need. 46 And they, continuing daily with one accord in the temple, and breaking bread from house to house, did eat their meat with gladness and singleness of heart, 47 Praising God, and having favour with all the people. And the Lord added to the church daily such as should be saved.

We're almost stunned as we discover the total sharing of earthly goods among the first believers. Verse 44 tells us, they "had all things common," meaning whatever they personally owned was now common property. Nothing was untouchable or hoarded as private property. The only thing that mattered was that no one went without the basic needs. Whether they secured a storage facility or distributed the goods immediately and directly to the needy is uncertain. What is certain, however, is that, out of great love for their brethren, not one of them was allowed to go unsheltered, unfed, or unclothed. It's hard to imagine such a community, such love. Truly, the remarkable beginning of the early church was producing a remarkable and "unfeigned love" for one another.

The second scene is found in Acts 4:32-37.

> 32 And the multitude of them that believed were of one heart and of one soul: neither said any of them that ought of the

things which he possessed was his own; but they had all things common. 33 And with great power gave the apostles witness of the resurrection of the Lord Jesus: and great grace was upon them all. 34 Neither was there any among them that lacked: for as many as were possessors of lands or houses sold them, and brought the prices of the things that were sold. 35 And laid them down at the apostles' feet: and distribution was made unto every man according as he had need. 36 And Joses, who by the apostles was surnamed Barnabas, (which is, being interpreted, 'The son of consolation,) a Levite, and of the country of Cyprus, 37 Having land, sold it, and brought the money, and laid it at the apostles' feet.

Here we find the church continuing in the same spirit and practice of genuine love. Again, we are told "they had all things common" (v32), which, in practical terms, is to say that no one "lacked" (v34) any basic need—amazing. Under the supervision of the apostles, every material need was being met. No doubt the selfless actions of Barnabas brought glory to God, but also recognition to himself for his unusual gift of loving and encouraging others (vs. 36-37). Who cannot but stand in awe of genuine Spirit-led love in action?

Just as Peter called for unfeigned or sincere love, so do others who were eyewitnesses of the events recorded in Acts 2 through 5. Take John, for example. Who can think of biblical love without remembering his first Epistle? Clearly, John sees an inseparable link between God's love for us and our love for one another. Of the many passages that could be referenced, we draw your attention to just two. 1 John 3:16-18 reads

> 16 Hereby perceive we the love of God, because he laid down his life for us: and we ought to lay down our lives for the brethren. 17 But whoso hath this world's good, and seeth his brother have need, and shutteth up his bowels of compassion

from him, how dwelleth the love of God in him? 18 My little children, let us not love in word, neither in tongue; but in deed and in truth.

God demonstrated His love by laying down His life for us, and John sees this as a pattern to be followed by every believer, a pattern that was on display in the early church. And in chapter 4, verses 7 and 8, John writes, "Beloved, let us love one another: for love is of God; and every one that loveth is born of God, and knoweth God. He that loveth not knoweth not God; for God is love' (1 John. 4:7-8).

John learned from both the life and the death of Jesus that genuine love is sacrificial. Another disciple of Jesus was his half brother, James, the writer of the Epistle that bears his name. Following the resurrection, James quickly emerged as a leader in the church in Jerusalem. Witnessing genuine love years earlier helped him discern when love was merely feigned. You can hear the frustration in his complaint with church members who pretend to love one another but give no real evidence to support their boast (see 2:1-17). James remembers the contrast between the love that was inspired by the Holy Spirit and the kind that was lying to the Holy Spirit. Peter asked, "Ananias, why hath Satan filled thine heart to lie to the Holy Ghost?" (Acts 5). James seems to be filled with righteous anger when he queries, "If a brother or sister be naked, and destitute of daily food, And one of you say unto them, Depart in peace, be ye warmed and filled; notwithstanding ye give them not those things which are needful to the body; what doth it profit?"

Neglecting the needs of the brethren is never an option. Love always acts. When the love of God is effectually working in us, it will lead us to help our brothers and sisters who have needs, all of them. This is a Holy Spirit-led response.

This brings us to the focus of this chapter: "The Neglected" in Acts 6:1. The words *but in those days* signals a contrast is coming. Broadly, the contrast is between the days when love was on display and the Lord was adding great numbers to the church and the day it all came to a halt because the Grecians were being neglected. This issue sparks an outcry on behalf of the neglected and requires a swift response from the apostles.

Did you notice that the problem occurred when "they had everything in common" (4:32) and "more than ever believers were added to the church" (5:14)? This is a harsh reminder of how flawed we are even when we are busy doing good things. Obviously, the Hebrews had not fully welcomed all believers into the church as equal family members. The Grecians were allowed to be among them but were not given the same privileges as the Jews. Apparently, the unfeigned love the Jews were expressing had cultural, ethnic limitations. These barriers would not be easily overcome. Eventually the church must open wide its doors for all nations, tribes, and tongues. Besides the Grecians, many Gentiles will soon be brought into the church through the Gospel. They were included in Christ's finished work. The Holy Spirit was already living in those who were once called by the Jew "the unclean." But full acceptance, if it ever does come, will take time, more teaching, and a whole lot of love.

As already pointed out, the fact that there are neglected Grecian widows is a significant contrast to what's reported in the previous chapters when "they had all things common." In Chapter 6, "there arose a murmuring." But that was the early church. What about the church today? Unfortunately, the problem of neglecting certain groups is still a challenge. The church will always find it difficult to love all the brethren with sincere love because of indwelling sin. And the office that will be challenged the most to ensure that the love of Christ is shown equally to all is the office of the deacon. For this reason, we think it is important to spend some time on this crucial issue, the problem of neglect. We've broken the remainder of this chapter into the following four divisions.

First—Words that need to be defined and explained

Second—Possible causes for neglect

Third—Inherent dangers of neglect

Fourth—Preventing neglect

FIRST—WORDS THAT NEED TO BE DEFINED AND EXPLAINED

"Neglected"

The Greek word for "neglected" in Acts 6:1 is *paratheoreo*[135]. The Greek prefix *para* means "beside," "alongside," or "next to." Together with the root word, it conveys the idea of choices or options being placed side by side for the purpose of selecting one over the other. The process of choosing requires due diligence, but eventually a conclusion is reached and a choice is made. In his *Word Pictures in the New Testament*, Archibald Thomas Robertson had this to say about the Greek word translated as "neglected" in Acts 6:1: "*Were neglected (paratheoreounto). Imperfect passive of para-theoreo*, old verb, to examine things placed beside (*para*) each other, to look beyond (*para also*), *to overlook, to neglect*."[136] We're not suggesting that the Hebrews making the choice had a full understanding of all their options, or of their own ulterior motives, or even a mature set of values from which to make a godly decision. We will look at some of those things in the following sections. For now, we're pointing out that they had some information, they interpreted that information, they looked at their options, and they made a choice. That's what the word *neglected* tells us. They deliberately

---

135 Strongs, 3865

136 Robertson, A.T., Word Pictures in the New Testament, (Nashville, Broadman,1930) 1: under neglected.

chose one group over another. In choosing one group, they neglected the other group.

"Priority"

Even though this word, like the words that follow, is not found in our text, its connection to neglect is obvious. *Webster's Dictionary* defines priority as "[t]he state of being antecedent in time, or of preceding something else" and "[p]recedence in place or rank."[137] We should always consider our priorities when making a decision to do one thing and not another thing. Vain and selfish desires can influence and even dictate our choices. That's the nature of our carnal flesh. Therefore, we always need to evaluate the decisions placed before us and determine, to the best of our ability, which is most important. Jesus speaks of choosing the best thing over other things in Matthew 6:33: "But seek ye first the kingdom of God, and his righteousness, and all these things shall be added unto you." We can't help but wonder if *"The Hebrew Benevolence Committee"* made the decision to care for their widows and not the Grecian widows because they believed their widows were their priority. Or did they make their choice on the basis of a more unholy reason? While we don't know for sure what motivated the Jews to neglect the Grecian widows, we do know from the word *neglected* that something influenced their choice. They placed both groups side by side and concluded that the Hebrew widows took "precedence over" the other group.

"Symptom"

The word *symptom* is used primarily as a medical term but not always. A symptom is a sign or an indication that a particular condition or underlying problem exists. The condition itself may not be visible, but the symptom tells us that a problem is real and needs attention. In our text, the symptom

---

137 Webster's Dictionary, 1828, under "priority."

is "murmuring" (vs. 1). Murmuring is not the problem, but it indicates that there is a problem. When symptoms are ignored, problems generally get worse, even in church life. Discerning between symptoms and root causes is not always easy.

"Problem"

Webster defines a problem as "a matter or situation regarded as harmful and needing to be overcome."[138] It's obvious that the decision to give priority to one group of widows over another group of widows caused a problem: a harmful situation needing a solution. The murmuring against the Hebrews proves the point.

Stepping away from Acts 6 and that particular problem for a moment, there is an important point to be made for those who serve as deacons: problems can arise even when you make the right decision with the purest of motives. A situation can be "regarded as harmful and needing to be overcome," which is not harmful or needing to be overcome at all. Sometimes, doing the right thing will upset those who wanted another outcome or expected a different course of action. At that point, the original problem has been dealt with, but a new problem has surfaced: the sinful response that some have chosen. Responding to unwarranted criticism takes wisdom and may require help from the spiritual leaders of the church, at least in the beginning. Hopefully, as men who are full of wisdom and the Holy Spirit, your response will be God honoring.

"Solution"

A solution refers to "the means used to solve a problem."[139] As far as God was concerned, the only solution to solve the problem of neglect as reported in Acts 6 was appointing an adequate number of men to deal with

---

138 138 Webster's 1828, under "problem."
139 139 Webster's, under "solution."

the situation or, as we believe, the establishment of the office of the deacon. Going forward, the deacon and his work are the appointed means to solve the problem of neglect, and, at the same time, eliminate the cause of the complaining spirit before it ever begins.

These five words—*neglected, priority, symptom, problem,* and *solution*—are important to our understanding of what happened in Acts 6 and are helpful as we seek to avoid a similar situation in our own churches.

SECOND—POSSIBLE CAUSES OF NEGLECT

In this section, we want to take a little time to talk about some of the things that might have caused, or at least contributed to, the problem of neglect recorded in Acts 6. We've already hinted at a few possible causes, but we hope this closer examination proves to be helpful as we strive to avoid the problem of neglect in our churches today.

Is it possible to know why the early church neglected the Grecian widows? Not exactly. In fact, the text focuses on solving the problem, not what caused it to begin with. But we know this situation did not develop in a vacuum. Something caused it. Once again, we are dealing with missing details. Yet, even though these details are missing, we believe it is worth considering some potential causes of neglect. These causes pose a danger to all of our churches, and it is especially important for those who serve as officers in the church to be constantly on the lookout for these troublemakers. Sometimes, finding the cause of a problem is essential to finding the solution.

FIRST POTENTIAL CAUSE FOR NEGLECT: HUMAN LIMITATIONS

No doubt the apostles recognized their own limitations at this point in the narrative. This was not a new experience for them. Their experiences, as the disciples of Christ, as told in the Gospels, had revealed their limitations many times. With the addition of Matthias, the same men were now the twelve spiritual leaders of the early church. They must have felt an enormous responsibility for the expanding church. Christ made it very clear he was passing on to them the work that he began. They were now responsible for the oversight and continued development of the assembly of believers, both spiritually and physically. Can you imagine the multitude of tremendously important decisions they must have faced every day? This is where we find them in Acts 6. We find the apostles comparing responsibilities, looking at them side by side, and choosing one set of responsibilities over the other, these duties over those duties.

In Chapters 2 through 5, we find them overseeing the collection and distribution of goods. The problem, however, was that those activities, as important as they were, were distracting them from their God-given priorities. They make it very clear, in verses 2 and 4, that they were concerned about the danger of neglecting the more important things like "prayer and the ministry of the word." Whatever other responsibilities they shouldered, these two must stay at the top of the daily to-do list.

But it was a struggle. As the church grew, or rather exploded, the apostles faced new demands on their time, energy, and resources. Day by day, they were faced with important decisions. Decisions lead to actions. They must have asked themselves many times over, "What decisions do we need to make today?" There were so many challenges, so many issues. How many times did they ask, "Can that wait until tomorrow?"

In the narrative leading up to Acts 6, we learned that the Hebrews were doing a good job of taking care of their widows, but others were lacking the necessities of life. The "fly in the ointment" of their brotherly love was that the Grecian widows were not receiving help. Their neglect had caused a problem, and the apostles must address it immediately. This cannot be put off!

We can't imagine that the twelve apostles made a conscious choice to allow the Grecian widows to be neglected. Yet, it happened. The Hebrews knew very well the Old Testament commands of God concerning widows, and the apostles were doing everything they could to see that no one went without. It would only be speculation to try to figure if and when the apostles were aware of the neglect. We are inclined to believe—and this is only a guess on our part—that the apostles were aware of the situation before the murmuring began. They were personally overseeing the funds, they certainly knew there were Grecians in the growing church, and they were Hebrews, so they are members of the group that the Grecians have a complaint against. Peterson writes, "Since the apostles appear to have administered the community resources at this stage (cf. 4:34-37; 5:2), complaints about the *daily distribution of food* were thus also a challenge to their leadership"[140] (italics original). And, as we observed before, the fact that they immediately went into action when the murmuring began might suggest prior knowledge, discussion, and the necessary remedy.

Supposing for the moment that they knew about the situation, then what went wrong? Although they may have been aware of the problem, there is only so much a person, or even a group of people, can do. We only have so much time, so much energy, so much gas in the tank. Even though these men were filled with the Spirit of God, they were still men with limitations. Even Christ, in His humanity, had limitations. So yes, the simple fact that every human has limitations could have contributed to the problem of neglect in the early church. In fact, the passage suggests as much. The twelve apostles had come to the realization they could not deal

---

140 Peterson, *The Acts of the Apostles*, (Grand Rapids, MI, Erdmans, 2009), 232.

with this problem and still devote themselves to their God-given priorities of Word and prayer. Something had to give. Humanly speaking, they came face to face with their own limitations. The problem of neglect forced the apostles to find a solution outside of themselves. As it turned out, it was a solution for the ages. Behold the wisdom and kindness of God in establishing an office to accommodate the limitations of the other officers of the church. This would be true regardless of when the office officially began.

It might be instructive for our own ministries to think about some apostolic activities that stretched their limitations to the max. Remember, even though they are apostles empowered with great gifts, they were still fallen humans and, as such, experienced human limitations even as God was using them as foundational stones in the church. Every day they were forced to prioritize their calling, their lives, their responsibilities, and every decision, all to the glory of God and the good of the church. As we think through the brief list of competing priorities below, it may explain how a group of widows in the church were neglected.

Competing priority no. 1: Proclaiming the Gospel

The commission to proclaim the Gospel (Matt. 28:18-20) was not optional for the twelve; it was their duty. This commission had been stamped upon their consciences by the life and words of Jesus Christ, and they were compelled to fulfill every command. As soon as we open and begin to read the pages of Acts, we are confronted with the importance of proclaiming the Gospel. All of them were commissioned to preach, beginning in Jerusalem and then to all the world. This is evident by what takes place in the opening chapters of Acts. In Acts 2, Peter preaches on the day of Pentecost. In Chapter 3, he preaches in Solomon's Portico. In Chapter 4, Peter and John are arrested for proclaiming the resurrection in Jesus' name. In Chapter 5, the apostles are thrown into a common prison, beaten, and then charged to cease speaking of Christ. Yet, "they did not cease teaching and preaching that the Christ is Jesus" (Acts 5:42 ESV). So, when the twelve got out their "to-do" lists every morning, proclaiming the Gospel was right at the top of the list. It was t a priority. Neglect this? Never!

Competing priority no. 2: Discipling new converts

Initially it was the apostles who shouldered the responsibility to reach people with the Gospel, baptize them, and then see to it that they were thoroughly taught or indoctrinated in their new faith (Matt. 28:18-20). The mandate was clear! Go, make disciples, baptize them, then teach them. Teach what? All that Jesus commanded them. It was their responsibility to make sure this mandate, in its entirety, was accomplished. They could not neglect the new believers. When we think of the demands on their time and energy, we begin to realize how organized they must have been. There were thousands of people who put their faith in Jesus as the Christ of God and Redeemer of mankind. Each one was baptized and began to learn about the "all things" that Christ commanded them to do. Not all of the new converts had been educated in the Old Testament Scriptures. Grecians and even gentiles were responding to the Gospel. To one degree or another, all of them needed to be discipled. Can you imagine the Bible studies going on in Jerusalem? Exactly how they organized and accomplished this task we don't know. The details are missing. But one thing is certain: the new converts must be discipled, and it was their job to see that they were! Neglect this? Never!

Competing priority no. 3:
Counseling those who had special needs

Everyone has baggage! By "baggage," we mean the problems that new converts bring with them into the church. And all new disciples are entitled to the comfort and care of shepherds, problems and all. It doesn't seem to matter where, or when, or how a person comes to faith in Christ; they all come with some measure of problems needing pastoral care. Life can be very harsh on people and deeply scar the mind and emotions. We know that many of these problems, if not most, are corrected over time as the believer submits to the ministry of the Word and Spirit. They will also benefit from the normal process of "Formative Discipline" that comes from being in a spiritually healthy church.

However, in the first few days and weeks of the church, how equipped were most of them to give spiritual, Scriptural help? Even if they knew the Old Testament Scriptures, would they know how to apply them to the lives of new believers? The point is, there were problems that the multitude of new believers weren't equipped to handle—the same kind of problems we face today, things like marriage problems, child-rearing concerns, work-related issues, cultural tensions, sexual temptations, drunkenness, etc. New believers came seeking biblical solutions to these and many other life-related problems. Initially this house-to-house counseling ministry fell on the shoulders of the apostles. If you were converted under the preaching ministry of one of the apostles and you had a problem, who do you think you would turn to for help? And remember how many were being saved under the preaching of the apostles: thousands, tens of thousands! Neglect them? Again, never!

It's not difficult to see how a specific group within the church could be neglected. The leaders were men with limitations. No matter how dedicated a servant is, when the workload is overwhelming, they cannot do everything that needs to be done. As the events in Acts 6 indicate, because of their limitations, they were forced to prioritize and come up with a plan to utilize the giftedness of other leaders in the church.

Competing priority no. 4: Dealing with social issues

The apostles labored in a society that was greatly affected by such things as poverty, slavery, and ignorance. *Poverty* was, and still is, a fact of life. *Slavery* was the backbone of that first-century economy. As for overcoming *ignorance*, Imperial Rome had no interest in providing either formal education or vocational training for the impoverished or slaves. These, and other social ills, impacted the work of the apostles.

Take education, for example. It is possible, according to many studies, that illiteracy in the Roman Empire was as high as 90 percent. This might explain why Paul insisted that his letters and other Scriptures be read in public. Why? Most of them couldn't read. We can't help but wonder if the apostles and other church leaders encouraged education and literacy for the masses. Over the centuries, missionaries have understood the value and benefit of educating the people they are called to disciple. Believing the preached message of salvation in Christ is one thing, but reading and studying it on your own, "that ye may grow thereby" (1 Pet. 2:2), is another thing. The ability to read the pages of the Scripture for one's self must not be undervalued. The apostles too must reach them through the Gospel and then "teach them to observe all things whatsoever I have command you" (Matt. 28:20). Limited education would only complicate their mission. Many of the new converts would come to be taught the Scriptures in a gathered assembly. But discipling them would require a lot of time and patience because of the impact of the various social problems of the day.

Once again, as we think about the cultural/social context of the early church, we understand how stretched the apostles were for more time and energy, stretched to the point of possibly neglecting their own God-given priorities of Word and prayer. Even godly men have limitations.

Competing priority no. 5: Home and family life

Have you ever wondered how many apostles were married? We know that some were. Other apostles were not. Did they have children? We can only speculate, but let's assume that at least some of them had children. Yet, somehow, in the midst of all their many nonnegotiable duties, they must find time for the family. Did they own their own home? Were they renting? Were they living with other family members or church families? Somehow, in the midst of all their other duties, they must find time to keep up their home, take care of maintenance and repair issues, manage their finances, keep everyone safe, and a host of other home and family responsibilities that require constant oversight. We know these things didn't take care of themselves, nor could they push these responsibilities off onto someone else. As husbands, they were the head of their homes, loved their wives, and brought up their children in the "nurture and admonition of the Lord." As apostles, they no doubt felt the pressure of being role models for family life in the church. Being called by Christ to a foundational role in the church was not a free pass to neglect home and family. This is just another example of the fact that the apostles, like the rest of us, must have felt the pressure of limited time, energy, and resources to get everything done. Neglect home and family? Never!

As leaders in the church, we've all experienced the challenges of juggling priorities. Sometimes we are even forced to make a choice between competing responsibilities. That's never easy. These are real-life experiences that even the apostles had to work through. It's only speculation, but did they ever confide in one another and discuss the difficulty of juggling ministry and family? Perhaps. Maybe they faced these issues early on as they left everything to follow Jesus, and then there was the ever-growing realization of their own impending suffering and death for His sake. These things have to weigh on a man, even an apostle. Conflicting priorities indeed.

Competing priority no. 6: Prayer and Word

The apostles state, in no uncertain terms, what their priorities must always be: the ministry of prayer and Word. Yet, at the same time, they would never minimize the problem of the neglected Grecian widows. They too must receive attention. From a human standpoint, it was time for them to recognize their limitations and enlist the help of others.

Think about it for a moment. When did they find time to pore over the pages of the sacred Scripture to prepare their lessons and sermons? Remember, the church was meeting daily and "continued steadfastly in the apostles' doctrine" (Acts 2:42). The New Testament era came with its unique Christological lens for interpreting the Old Testament and would require serious study. Paul himself instructed Timothy to "bring the books," a possible reference to the Old Testament Scripture (2 Tim. 4:13). Jesus taught them many things, and the Holy Spirit confirmed these things to them, but they still needed time in the Word and, later, to give proper attention to the new writings of the apostles and others. And when did they carve out the time for prolonged and emotionally draining prayer for Christ's rapidly growing church, the kind of agonizing prayer demonstrated by Jesus when he was with them? These things were not only important; they were their primary duties. The narrative suggests that these were two things that would suffer if the apostles did not take steps to protect their time. It was because of their human limitations that they appointed the seven men in the first place. Simply put, they couldn't keep up with the ministry of the *Word* and *prayer* plus "waiting on tables." They must choose one over the other, and they did.

All six priorities listed above were important to the apostles. Every day they must decide which one comes first today, then second, and third, and so on. Their call to preach the Gospel everywhere and still "feed the flock" of God (Matt. 28:19-20; Acts 20:28) could not be accomplished unless they devote themselves to constant prayer and digging into the Word.

It seems reasonable to believe, and is suggested by the text, that human limitations were a factor that contributed to the problem of the neglected widows in Acts 6. We often think of the apostles as superhuman. Yes, they were special men indeed, in the sense that Jesus Christ chose them to be His special disciples. He would eventually send them as apostles to carry on the work He began. The redemptive work was his alone to complete, but the proclamation of that work, which was the Gospel, they must take to the world. The apostles were told to spread that message not only throughout Jerusalem, but then to all the nations. In this sense, the apostles were indeed special men. They were trained by Jesus Christ himself and then filled with the Holy Spirit in order to do the work that had been entrusted to them. Along with their commission to preach the Gospel, He gave them a special grace and power to do the work. But even with all of these advantages, we must not forget they were still just men who had human limitations. At some point, these twelve men would be maxed out. They could not do everything! The work of the Lord had exceeded their available time, resources, and energy. Why? Because they were human, and every human has limitations.

LESSONS FOR TODAY

Acknowledging we have limitations is a good thing, not a bad thing. But we must also remember that just acknowledging limitations does not solve any problem. Feeling overwhelmed is understandable, but neglecting the needs of our brethren is not an option where "unfeigned love" is practiced. When the murmuring arose, the apostles first acknowledged the reality of the neglect and then took action to resolve it. That's what wise and spiritual leaders do. This should be what wise and spiritual deacons do, as well. See a need, and meet it.

In the process of owning and overcoming human limitations, we discover that knowing our limitations can actually be good for us. Here are a few benefits of knowing our limitations.

First Benefit—Knowing our limitations tends to cultivate a deeper dependency on God.

Speaking from experience, Paul wrote, "[A]nd he said unto me, my grace is sufficient for thee: for my strength is made perfect in weakness. Most gladly therefore will I rather glory in my infirmities, that the power of Christ may rest upon me. Therefore I take pleasure in infirmities..." (2 Cor. 12:9-10; see Phil. 4:13; Eph. 6:10).

Paul acknowledged his weaknesses, found strength in Christ, and in the end, Christ was magnified. Discovering and owning our limitations is a good thing. It is truly, according to Paul, a thing to "glory in."

Second Benefit—Knowing our limitations forces us to "prioritize our priorities."

Above, we mentioned six activities that were on an apostles' priority list. Every day they had to evaluate and prioritize their various duties. Like the apostles, every believer should strive to make God, Word, and prayer a priority. On top of their devotional relationship to God, what if the deacon is married, a father (or mother in the case of deaconesses), an employee, a church member, or active in the community as salt and light? How does a deacon *prioritize* these various God-given responsibilities? Is it even possible? Absolutely! Is it easy? Absolutely not! The answer lies in prioritizing our priorities.

Practically speaking, many people find it helpful make a list of the various priorities and then rank them in their order of importance. This is "prioritizing your priorities." Remember, there are many things competing for your attention. Some are important, some will even be urgent, but they are not all necessary. Every day, and sometimes several times a day, we can check our actions against the priorities we have determined to live by. And we must always tenaciously guard our priorities from being hijacked by important but lesser things.

This is what happened in Acts 6. The apostles clearly understood what their priorities were and caring for the widows could no longer be on their list. That decision did not demean the widows; if anything, it honored them by saying they cannot be neglected. How would they resolve the conflict of these very important, God-given responsibilities? Their solution was to create an entirely new office, which we know as the office of the deacon. As a result of this wise transfer of oversight, the widows were now at the top of the deacon's list. An old proverb says, "Necessity is the mother of invention." It may not be a biblical proverb, but on a practical level, it describes the actions of the twelve.

Deacons need to frequently ask themselves, "Does my list of priorities (which will be revealed in the way I live my life) reflect God's intention or design for the office?" If not, among the possible reasons as to why, might be the restraint of several human limitations. While we never want this to become a well-used door for making excuses, sometimes we have to admit our limitations for the glory of God and the good of those we serve.

To illustrate the point, let's look into the life of an imaginary deacon. We'll call him Joe. He was recently appointed to be a deacon in his church. He is quickly becoming aware of all the duties and responsibilities placed upon the deacons. He's a little surprised at how many things fall under the care of the deacons. Every month the chairman gives Joe a list of jobs that he will be responsible to either do or make sure gets done. He is free to do the work himself or organize a team of volunteers to help. As he looks over the items on the list, he tries to calculate the amount of time required to complete all the jobs. Like most deacons, Joe works fulltime in order to fulfill his God-given mandate to provide for the needs of his family. His work is generally limited to forty hours per week, but occasionally he has to put in some overtime. Joe is married to a wonderful Christian woman, Margaret, who is very supportive of his appointment to the office of a deacon. They have a strong marriage and are very committed to spending time together. Joe also has three children, and they are involved in different activities that he and Margaret feel are valuable for their development. They have been members of their church for a long time and are faithful to the services and occasional activities. Even before Joe was appointed a deacon in the church, the entire family was involved in joyfully serving others who have needs. They were somewhat unique in that regard, always looking for someone to serve.

All of these things are important to Joe. They are on his unwritten list of priorities, and he works hard to live accordingly. Owing to the demands on his time and attention, and feeling pulled in different directions, he strays off the list from time to time, but because of their mutual love for the Lord, each other, the children and the church, Joe and Margaret confess their failures and encourage one another to live according to their priorities. Even so, he occasionally feels overwhelmed and stressed as he struggles to keep his life in balance.

Most deacons relate to the stress Joe feels as he compares his God given responsibilities to the very real limitations of time, energy, and resources. As we've stated, owning your limitations is a good thing and can force you to prioritize your priorities. Then, with the strength that Christ supplies, do the next important thing.

Third benefit—Knowing our limitations propels us to consider the value and giftedness of others.

It's not unusual to discover that an item on our to-do list would be better on someone else's list. This is not necessarily a sign of weakness or failure. In fact, giving up a task to someone else who is better suited to handle it can be an expression of humility and wisdom. This is exactly what the apostles did when faced with their own limitations. They took steps to identify qualified, gifted individuals who could relieve them of a particular responsibility.

It is true that sometimes our limitations are designed by God to stretch our faith and teach us to live more dependent on His grace. However, the unwillingness to give up a task that we may not have the time or necessary skills to perform may reveal a prideful spirit. While our intentions may begin honorable enough, pride can prevent us from acknowledging our limitations. This self-protective attitude can reveal itself in our marriages, employment, relationships, and our diaconal work.

This is one reason why a team spirit is so vital among deacons. Sometimes it's just a matter of recognizing our weaknesses and handing off a project, or need, to someone more qualified. This requires that each deacon not only knows his own strengths and weaknesses, but those of the other deacons as well. This would make a great group exercise: list the strengths of every other deacon and discuss them among the group. With caution, you might have each deacon acknowledge one or two of his own weaknesses that might hinder the effectiveness of his service. This could be useful information if you find it necessary to ask another deacon for help.

Something more difficult, yet vitally needed, is for deacons to have the love and courage to speak up when they see a fellow servant hindering the work of the office owing to pride, the kind of pride that refuses to hand responsibilities off to more qualified or perhaps more available deacons. This reminds us of the prayer of David when he writes, "Let the righteous strike me; it shall be a kindness. And let him rebuked me; it should be an excellent oil; let my head not refuse it" (Ps. 141:5). This incredibly humble prayer flows out of a heart well acquainted with its own weaknesses (v. 4). The apostle Paul says a similar thing in Romans 12:3, "For I say, through the grace given unto me, to every man that is among you, not to think of himself more highly than he ought to think; but to think soberly, according as God hath dealt to every man the measure of faith." May all servants of the church have the same self-awareness and willingness to be reminded of their limitations and be reproved when they go astray. This disposition is the fruit of the Spirit and is seen in wise and humble servants of the church.

Every church is made up of members who are gifted to serve the local body of Christ. Furthermore, all of these gifted members have been placed in the body by God to serve one another. There is a God-initiated orderliness to all of this. To the church at Ephesus Paul writes this:

> 11 And he gave some, apostles; and some, prophets; and some, evangelists; and some, pastors and teachers; 12 For the perfecting of the saints, for the work of the ministry, for the edifying of the body of Christ: 13 Till we all come in the unity

of the faith, and of the knowledge of the Son of God, unto a perfect man, unto the measure of the stature of the fulness of Christ:14 That we henceforth be no more children, tossed to and fro, and carried about with every wind of doctrine, by the sleight of men, and cunning craftiness, whereby they lie in wait to deceive;15 But speaking the truth in love, may grow up into him in all things, which is the head, even Christ: 16 From whom the whole body fitly joined together and compacted by that which every joint supplieth, according to the effectual working in the measure of every part, maketh increase of the body unto the edifying of itself in love. (Ephesians 4:11-16).

Everything pertaining to the church is initiated by God for His glory and the good of the church, and this includes all the members serving one another. On an applications level, this only happens when everyone under-stands this responsibility, knows their own gifts and limitations, and sees and values the giftedness and service of others. Bring this thought down to the office of the deacon. The office will only function as God intends when every deacon knows his gifts and limitations and sees and values the gift-edness of his fellow deacons.

Fourth benefit—Knowing our limitations will encourage us to develop and train others.

This benefit flows out of the previous thought. When we, as leaders, are open and receptive to the value and giftedness of others in the church, then we are ready to either develop and train them for further service, or imme-diately use them as the gifts of God that they are to the church. As more are ready and available for service, more workload is shared. We are looking beyond those who are currently serving as deacons. Our sights are set on finding and mentoring both future deacons and the army of volunteers that sits in every church.

Moses was directed by God to take a young man named Joshua under his wing to prepare him to eventually take over the leadership of Israel. Elijah was strengthened in his service when God led him to mentor a young Elijah who would not only assist him, but eventually take up the mantle of a prophet of God. The apostles either directly or indirectly mentored the new core of elders and servant leaders in the early church. Paul and Barnabas, for instance, mentored young men for ministry. Thus, future leaders were raised up who, in turn, invested themselves in the lives of others who were equipped to take their place. Christ Himself set the example for all of us as He spent a large portion of his ministry developing and training men to be co-laborers in order to take up the work when He departed.

Mentoring is a biblical model and necessary for preparing the next generation of servant leaders of the church. Owing to our human limitations, the only way to multiply the work is to multiply the workers. Therefore, developing and training new leaders should be the norm in the life of a church, not the exception. This is not a sign of weakness but of faith. It says that the leaders of the church have a vision for greater opportunities to serve the assembly, the community, and the world as God allows, and demonstrates that we believe God sovereignly places individuals in the church, and that each member is gifted by God to serve in that assembly.

APPLICATION FOR DEACONS

It has always been a challenge to keep up with every God-given priority. Occasionally they collide and we are tempted to neglect a responsibility that deserves our attention. Often the cause is owing to our *human limitations*. Our limitations, however, when squarely faced, bring opportunities for growth and spiritual enrichment for those who serve the church.

- They cultivate a deeper dependency on God.
- They force us to prioritize priorities.

- They propel us to value the giftedness of others.

- They encourage us to develop and train others to do the work of serving.

SECOND POTENTIAL CAUSE FOR NEGLECT: IGNORANCE

Ignorance is not the same as limited mental capacity. The deficiency is in knowledge, information, raw data. That's what ignorance is, a lack of information or knowledge.

While we don't know how much knowledge the apostles had about the neglect of the Grecian widows, the events that unfolded are still instructive as we think about the problem of ignorance as a *potential cause* for neglect. Yes, the Grecians murmured. The Scripture is clear in condemning a complaining spirit. Yet, as far as the apostles were concerned, there was no justification for ignoring them, or denying their right for assistance. We think this is worth noting. While our response may vary depending on the depth of our knowledge of the situation and any extenuating circumstances, our first instinct should always be to relieve the suffering. Afterward we can deal with related sinful issues. While the hurt feelings of the neglected might need to be addressed, if our lack of attentiveness is due to a lack of interest or effort on our part, that is our sin and also needs to be addressed.

Because ignorance (lack of knowledge) is so germane to the office and work of the deacon, here are a few practical thoughts on overcoming it. We're thinking specifically of ignorance that leads to the neglect of the needy in the church. While being a bit simplistic, we think it basically comes down to this; a breakdown in communication.

The actions of the apostles and the mission of the seven sent a clear *message* to the church: God just opened a channel for having your needs both known and met. No more neglect, no more murmuring, no more excuses—these men and the army of volunteers behind them are here to serve your needs. The needy can now *communicate* their need, and the servants will take action. Our churches should know the same thing. If there is a need, make it know to those who have the responsibility to help: the deacons. Of course, an atmosphere of genuine love and concern must be nourished and carefully guarded by the leadership of the church. The needy must constantly be reminded that the deacons, and the entire church family, stand ready to help. This is the message sent to the church in Acts 6. The entire episode communicates this message.

Occasionally, those with needs have to be reminded that communication is a two-way street. We can only respond to what we know. This is a problem that takes patience, gentleness, and teaching to overcome. That being said, when the entire assembly understands and values the work of those who serve as deacons, and consistently practices biblical Christ-like love for others, those with needs will be encouraged to speak up.

Remember, the only way to overcome ignorance is with knowledge. Knowledge is the light that casts out ignorance, and knowledge springs up through information. We have to work at being both informed and current concerning the needs of those around us. The open communication of *readiness* by the servant leaders, and the open communication of *needs* by the needy, is a giant step toward overcoming the ignorance that can cause neglect.

Another simple observation from the passage is that some people knew about the neglect. The text doesn't say the neglected were complaining, although they may have. It says, "[T]here arose a murmuring of the Grecians against the Hebrews, because their widows were neglected" (Ac. 6:1). This seems to suggest that others, probably family members, took offense on their behalf and complained about it. Isn't this often the case? Someone knows of the situation but instead of telling the only people who can do something about it, they immediately resort to complaining.

Because of the way the apostles wisely handled the situation, the entire assembly of believers now had someone—seven someones to be exact—to go to when they became aware of a need. Instead of frustration, or fear of getting involved, or any number of sinful and unhelpful responses, the members were now given a clear course of action. Given the involvement of the entire church in the process of selecting servant leaders as recorded in Acts 6, could there be any excuse for anyone going neglected?

So today. The church knows who the deacons are, don't they? And they know what deacons do, don't they? And deacons know why they exist, don't they? And every member understands their responsibility to serve others, don't they? The answer to these rhetorical questions requires open communication between the needy and those who's task it is to meet their needs. It is this pipeline of information that can assist the deacons in overcoming the potential problem of ignorance that can easily lead to neglect and murmuring. The lines of communication need to be flowing freely through the entire church. Both spiritual leaders and deacons can be unaware (ignorant) that a problem even exists, or if they have limited knowledge, they may not know the severity of the situation. In either case, because of the potential damage that ignorance can cause, it should never be taken lightly. We should never shrug it off with a "Hey, I didn't know." Whether it's fair or not, they expect us to know. As we have suggested all along, they have a right to expect help from their church family. The old adage "ignorance is bliss" has no place in the family of God.

This open interaction between members and deacons comes with some cautions.

Two brief cautions for deacons

1. Never forget that you were elected by the members of your congregation to be their representatives in this ministry of mercy, and you are ultimately accountable to them as their servant leaders. Always be gracious and appreciative of the information

they share with you. If it mattered enough for them to share this information, make sure that it matters enough to you to follow up on it. Also, be discreet with the information. Never allow it to become an opportunity for gossip, judgmentalism, criticism, or other such sins.

2. Be watchful for the sin of pride. We can be so sure that we have a handle on everything that we may resent the hint that we might not know that a fellow member has an unmet need. Don't take it personally. Humbly accept any information that helps you accomplish your primary task of serving the needy.

Four brief cautions for members

1. Always be discreet with the information that you share, and keep it as brief as possible. This prevents gossip from putting on "airs of concern" for the needy. Deacons need to search out the matter for themselves and take the appropriate action. If they need more information, they will ask.

2. Once you briefly share your concern for a needy brother or sister, guard yourself against imposing your own expectations of how the need should be met. The relationship between officers and the assembly is built on trust. You choose your deacons on the basis of the fact that you believe them to be "full of the Spirit and wisdom." Trust them to do the right thing even if it's not what you expected. Deacons have to guard against pride, but so do members.

3. Remember that serving is a universal call. If you know of a need and you are able to meet it, do so. This is especially true for small financial or material needs. The benevolence fund (assuming your church has one) should be a fund of last resort in most situations. Serving the needs of our brothers and sisters is everyone's duty as God supplies the means. If you can't meet the need, then by all means inform

one of the appointed servant leaders in your church. Even if you take care of a need on your own, it is often wise to let a deacon know about it. Along with what you tell them, they may have additional information that needs to be considered in the future.

4. If you personally meet a need, but the problem persists and you suspect there are contributing factors that need to be addressed, proceed with caution. Scripturally, you are bound to go to a struggling brother or sister you suspect has been overtaken in a fault (Gal. 6:1). At the same time, be ready to bring others into the situation for help. In situations concerning material needs, a deacon would be an excellent first choice. If the problem is severe, however, it would be wise to inform the spiritual leaders of the church.

APPLICATION FOR DEACONS

If there's a good thing about ignorance, it's this; it can be overcome. It is overcome by knowledge. But it often involves a lot of work, asking a lot of questions, digging for answers, and keeping the ears and eyes open for clues. All of the necessary information is achieved by maintaining open lines of communication throughout the church. As deacons, you must make the effort to communicate with those you serve and do everything you can to encourage those you serve to communicate the material needs of the body back to you. Often, those who need your help are reluctant to let you know they are struggling. It is your job, as servants, to know who needs help and to welcome those who provide helpful information so that you can accomplish your God-given task.

THIRD POTENTIAL CAUSE FOR NEGLECT: WRONG ASSUMPTIONS

An assumption is taking something for granted without sufficient evidence or proof. This definition does not say that all assumptions are evil and always wrong. There are, in fact, times when we must make assumptions on the basis of limited information and they can turn out to be spot on. Seasoned spiritual leaders and experienced servant leaders are generally able to spot a phony almost as soon as they walk through the church doors.

On the other hand, there are times when we draw perfectly rational assumptions that nevertheless turn out to be mistaken. Even the apostles could be guilty of making ill-informed assumptions. A good example of this happened to Paul. He made an assumption regarding a certain young man whom he wanted to accompany him on one of his missionary journeys. Paul assumed that the young man's interest in doing God's work, along with supportive seasoned leaders around him, would be sufficient to get him through the hardships of church planting in hostile territories. Paul's assumptions proved to be mistaken. Young Mark eventually abandoned the work and returned home. Anyone can make what appears to be a good decision on the basis of the available information and yet be wrong. Then, following Paul's split with Barnabas, some, perhaps even Paul, might have assumed that Mark could never be counted on again. That assumption would have been a mistake, as Mark goes on to prove to be a faithful and useful ministry partner to both Paul and Peter (2 Timothy 4:11; 1 Pet. 5:13).

So, what does the danger of making assumptions have to do with the problem of neglect in Acts 6? It's possible the twelve apostles made assumptions concerning the situation facing the widows. Knowing that the Hebrews, along with the entire church, were already assisting their needy fellow Hebrews, including widows, it's possible they simply assumed the Grecians would be taken care of as well. Or, maybe they assumed the

Grecians would step up and take care of their own without assistance from the Hebrews. Although both groups were now Jewish Christians, they worshipped in different synagogues, spoke different languages, and moved in different cultural settings. Without being in constant contact, maybe it was a case of out of sight - out of mind, assuming they would take care of themselves.

There are many possible scenarios that might have led to false assumptions concerning the Grecian widows. Regardless of what assumptions were made, once the problem bubbled up to the surface, the apostles knew they must find a solution and find it now. No more assuming, just solve the problem, which is exactly what they did.

APPLICATION FOR DEACONS

If apostles can be guilty of mistaken assumptions that can hinder the work (like Paul regarding Mark), then surely it can happen to deacons. When it comes to caring for the broken and needy saints among us, deacons must never assume anything! Granted, it seems reasonable to assume that those who know of a need or are the closest to the situation will see to it that the need is taken care of. But there is a big difference between what people should do and what they actually do. Even among those who have been taught that serving is a "universal call," deacons must take nothing for granted. It might seem obvious to you that family members would be eager to take care of Grandma, but that just isn't always the case. That's why Paul deals with that exact problem in his letter to Timothy (1 Tim. 5:4). The truth is, both deacons and spiritual leaders sometimes find themselves going to family members, both believers and unbelievers alike, to remind them of their obligation to care for their own. You can't just assume that because they share blood, they're willing to share their goods.

When it becomes apparent that your assumptions have been wrong and someone has been neglected, what should you do? You have a choice to make. You can either focus on the failures of those who should have responded, or you can immediately focus on the neglected. Regardless of whether the apostles were guilty of mistaken assumptions or not, when the murmuring started, they immediately focused on the neglected, not the murmuring. Solving the problem, took care of the murmuring.

As deacons, you must guard yourselves against the impulse to make quick assumptions. Whether it's assuming someone else will do it, assuming the need is not that great, or any of a myriad of other excuses, it is never a wise thing to do. Assume nothing! The needs of your brothers and sisters depend on your wise watchcare.

FOURTH POTENTIAL CAUSE FOR NEGLECT: PREJUDICE

Our comments here are meant to be a simple examination of the *potential* for prejudice in the office and work of a deacon and how it can lead to the problem of neglect. We trust you will tackle the deeper issues of unjust prejudice in society and the church as you serve the needy in your particular context. This is simply a starting point for further thought and discussion.

Prejudice, by definition[141], can be good or bad, right or wrong, of little or great consequences, and generally influences our actions. Obviously, as we think about it as a potential influence on the Hebrews in Acts 6, we're looking on the negative side of the definition as an opinion or frame of mind that leads to the dislike and mistreatment of a person or group of people formed without a full and due consideration of the facts. Restated, the Hebrews, without gathering the necessary facts, which could have been learned from the Scriptures or the apostles, let their long standing negative opinion of the Grecians influence their decision to neglect their widows.

---

141 141 Webster's 1828, under "prejudice."

Truthfully, we are all predisposed, biased, or "prejudiced" concerning some things. However, our ignorant prejudice against people whose only offense is being different than us is of great moral consequence and ought to be guarded against at all times. Some of us grew up thinking our school, neighborhood, or church was the absolute best. And we sometimes held harsh opinions of those outside our own group. On closer examination, there was no basis in fact for our opinions. We were just ignorant enough to think our little corner of the world was better than any other corner of the world. That's the way prejudice is: it thrives on ignorance and leads to hurtful attitudes and actions. Our sinful hearts are naturally filled with pride and prejudice against others. Jane Austin, seeing this inclination in the human heart, wrote the beloved novel *Pride and Prejudice*. The two seem to go hand in hand. Sadly, human history is filled with both. There is a sinful tendency to treat people badly on the basis of things like skin color, nationality, education, economic standing, culture, and so forth.

Coming back to the situation in Acts 6, the fact that the Hebrews took care of their own is both commendable and enlightening. It shows they understood the duty to show charity to the less fortunate. That's good. On the other hand, they only took care of their own. We have to believe the Hebrews were aware of the fact that the Grecians were being overlooked in the daily distribution of food, yet, for whatever reason, chose not to serve them. That's bad. But why did they neglect them? They were, after all, Hebrews just the same! Was it a case of *human limitations* preventing them from serving the Grecians? Was it due to *ignorance*? Maybe they didn't know. What about forming wrong *assumptions*? Did they assume the Grecians would take care of their widows? Or, is it possible they passed over the Grecian widows simply because they were Grecian?

Clearly, there were long-standing problems between Palestinian Hebrews and Grecian Hebrews. Their prejudice against them was deeply rooted and no doubt learned from early childhood. As far as most of the Palestinian Jews were concerned, absolute loyalty to their multifaceted heritage was the same as loyalty to God—a loyalty not shared by the Grecians. Based on their shared history of bitterness toward each other and the wording of the text, we think that pride and prejudice was indeed the *actual* cause for the neglect.

Again, it is interesting to note that the assembly chose seven men with Greek names. Their choice of these seven suggests several things. First, it suggests that the seven Grecian servants would look over the needs of only the Grecian widows. We think this can be inferred from the text. Second, the Hebrews would continue to take care of their families, as they had been doing all along. And finally, it suggests that the apostles were not going to force one cultural group to take care of another cultural group, even though they were one family in Christ. The twelve will force this issue in time as they teach the inclusive nature of God's family, and the gospel itself will begin to break down the walls that divide as God calls His sheep, by name, from every tongue, tribe, and nation. There simply is no reason for any form of prejudice in God's kingdom. But for now, the apostles solve the problem by appointing seven men to serve the needs of a different cultural group: the Grecians widows. Not only does it solve the problem, it also models the principle of inclusion which is so necessary for the advancement of the gospel until Christ returns for his Bride.

APPLICATION FOR DEACONS

Deacons are well aware of the fact that many Christians are guilty of prejudice in one form or another. But this should never be true of a deacon. You have been called to serve without distinction and you must examine your own thoughts, feelings, and behavior toward all people. Anyone who has a sinful prejudice against others is sinning against God, the church, and the individual. As deacons, you must not only guard your own heart against prejudice, but you may have to help others overcome it as well. This is not easy. It takes gentleness, humility, knowledge of the relevant scriptures, and prayer. But it must be confronted like any other sin. If you have dealt with it in your own heart, you may be able to share your testimony of victory with those who struggle in this area. You may have to enlist the help of the spiritual leaders in your church. But one way or another, it needs to be removed from the body of Christ. The Gospel demands it.

The best place to begin a battle against prejudice is God's Word. Wrong thinking leads to wrong feelings, which lead to wrong actions. Paul writes, in Romans 12:2, "[B]e ye transformed by the renewing of your mind." The Greek word for "renewing" is used only two times in the New Testament, here in Romans 12 and in Titus 3:5, "and renewing of the Holy Ghost." Putting these two passages together, the Holy Spirit changes us by changing the way we think, which we are responsible to be changing as a matter of gratitude for the mercies of God. We know that the Spirit of God uses the Word of God to accomplish this work of renewal. All sinful thinking must be confronted with God's Word in order to bring about the "renewing of the mind."

Here is a partial list of biblical passages that will help us fight against and overcome sinful prejudice if we submit ourselves to Christ and His Word. Rom. 12:9-10; 1 Cor. 1:26-31; 1 Cor. 12:18-27; Gal. 3:26-29; Eph. 2:11-22; James 2:1-9; 1 John 3:14-24; 1 John 4:7-21.

FIFTH POTENTIAL CAUSE FOR NEGLECT: LAZINESS

While laziness does not seem to have been a problem for the apostles, it certainly could have been a problem for the Hebrews and Grecians. The church rapidly expanded in the first days and weeks to include a wide variety of people groups: Jews, Grecians, and Gentiles. Thousands of people were added to the church in a very short period of time. If the burden of work fell on the newly converted Christian Hebrews alone, they may have very quickly reached a breaking point. Serve a few—no problem.

Serve thousands—no way! And what about the Grecian family members? Perhaps they were just too lazy to deal with it, too lazy to get involved and do the hard work of caring for the needy all around them. We don't know if this contributed to their neglect, but it is one possible explanation. It wouldn't have been the first time, nor the last, that laziness led to the neglect of the needy, even among families.

The Bible has much to say about this sinful tendency. God's Word needs to be heeded if you hope to keep this sin from hindering your ministry. Here are a few references that may be helpful in the evaluation and correction of this tendency: Prov. 15:15-19; Prov. 20:4; Prov. 21:25; 1 Thess. 3:10; 2 Thess. 3:6-12.

APPLICATION TO DEACONS

The office of the deacon is no place for a lazy person. For clarification, there are people who are lazy by nature, yet, because of the grace of God working in their lives you wouldn't know it. Through the enabling work of the Holy Spirit they have mortified, or are in the process of mortifying, that particular inclination of the flesh. But the lazy person who finds it too much trouble to serve the needy has no business in the office. How many needy people will go neglected because of this sin in your ministry? Hopefully none!

This has been a long section, so in review, these are the five *potential causes for neglect.*

1. Human limitations

2. Ignorance

3. Wrong assumptions

4. Prejudice

5. Laziness

There are more causes for neglect than just these five, but these represent the primary underlying causes that deacons of every age have faced. It would be helpful to discuss these five issues among yourselves. You might also see if you can come up with other contributing factors not mentioned here.

THIRD—THE INHERENT DANGER OF NEGLECT

The murmuring recorded in verse 1 is like a dorsal fin of a shark sticking up out of the water: a sign of imminent danger. Instead of a loud airhorn piercing through the air to warn all swimmers, murmuring itself is an alarm that immediately sends the apostles into action to protect the church from an imminent danger of another kind, a danger that threatens to tear the fabric of the expanding church into pieces—*the danger of division.* One large group, the more powerful group, decided to ignore a smaller, more vulnerable group. When that happened, the seeds of division were planted. The murmuring of the Grecians against the Hebrews reverberates back to the apostles. If the apostles do not act immediately, what likely comes next? Stronger accusations? Hard feelings? Slander? Bitterness? Hatred? And ultimately where does this lead? A divided church; perhaps even the walking away of a hurt and disillusioned group of members.

For a brief moment, Satan laughed with evil delight. He saw an opportunity to divide the church, and the outcome was exactly what he wanted: an ineffective church. How so? Let's play this out just a little longer. If this infection of division was allowed to fester, what immediate effect would it have on the church? Actually, we don't have to guess because the passage tells us. We looked at this in a previous chapter, but notice again how the whole scene is bracketed. Verse 1 tells us, "And in those days, when the number of the disciples was multiplied," and verse 7 tells us the same thing, "And the word of God increased; and the number of the disciples multiplied." Something happened in between these verses to bring church growth to a screeching halt! What was it? "There arose a murmuring of the Grecians against the Hebrews." But when the situation was resolved, all speed ahead once again. On the one hand, Satan danced. On the other hand, God immediately withdrew His blessings from the church until it was resolved. Of the renewed increase and growth of the church in verse 7, Joseph Alexander wrote, "It seems implied, though not explicitly affirmed, that this effect was promoted by the measure just before described, the ordination of the seven almoners or deacons."[142] He goes on to suggest that the action of the apostles and the church reinvigorated their Gospel outreach "by allaying the incipient divisions in the church itself, and thus removing one chief obstacle to its advancement."

To say that much was at stake is an understatement. The future of the church, the foundational ministry of the apostles, a great harvest of souls from all nations, and so much more was in the balance. The fact that God had a plan for the ages that could not be thwarted by man should not keep us from seeing the obvious implications. God hates division in the church, and division affects our impact on the world. Perhaps the most divided church spoken of in the New Testament was the church in Corinth and how quickly its candlestick was removed. But before the Gospel was ever preached in Acaia, the church in Jerusalem was being tested as to the genuineness of its faith and love. Would they embrace the entire body of Christ, or be divided over the neglect of some of its most vulnerable members? Would the Gospel continue to triumph over the forces of evil, or would the schism in the church grow and deny the power of the Gospel to overcome evil? The solution was the deacon, and the result was, "And the word of God increased; and the number of the disciples multiplied." Division in the church is ugly—sharks in the water ugly! But unity in the

---

142 J.A. Alexander, Commentary on The Acts of the Apostles, (Klock & Klock, Minneapolis, MN, 1980), p247-248

church, manifested by loving care for every member, is a beautiful thing, a God-glorifying thing.

The *inherent danger* of neglect, a danger that is the outcome of neglecting the needs of some, is the danger of tearing to pieces the delicate fabric of unity in the body of Christ. It is up to the leaders of the church, both spiritual and servant leaders, to guard the church against this incipient danger.

FOURTH—PREVENTING NEGLECT

Over the years, both of us have been bi-vocational pastors. When we were younger we both worked for a large residential and commercial cleaning service. We spent countless hours watching videos, taking quizzes, and sitting through live demonstrations, all to make sure we learned to clean the "Service Master" way. Without knowing it at the time, we learned something that goes beyond fabric and hard-surface care, something that applies to pastoral care over the church: the difference between prevention, correction, and restoration. We can hear Ron, the owner, saying something like, "If the carpets are new or newer, a good *preventative* maintenance program will keep them looking good for a long time. If they are moderately soiled or older and in of need immediate attention, a *corrective* program is called for. If, however, they are heavily soiled and damaged due to neglect, the only thing left is the full *restorative* program. In this case, an aggressive and deep cleaning is necessary. However, make it clear to the customer that the damage is permanent and may require complete replacement. As the old saying goes, 'an ounce of prevention is worth a pound of cure.'" Thanks, Ron, those were good lessons!

As pastors, we are responsible for something more valuable than carpet. We "shepherd the church of God" (Acts 20:28) "as those who will give an account" for their souls (Heb. 13:17). If we neglect their spiritual condition and progress, there is the danger of their relationship with God and the church falling into a state of spiritual decline. As deacons, you are responsible for watching over the material needs of men, but the same principles apply. If you neglect their physical needs, there are the ever-looming dangers mentioned in the previous section, and it is always better (and easier) to prevent a problem than correct a problem due to neglect. And remember, if the situation is not corrected, you run the risk of division, and restoration is always much more difficult.

So, the pressing question is, how do we prevent neglect from happening in the first place? It would be nice if there was just one answer to this question, like a magic key that unlocks every lock. However, instead of a single key that prevents neglect from occurring, it takes a keyring. In other words, there are several important (key) steps that church leaders, both spiritual and servant leaders, can take to prevent us from neglecting our needy brothers and sisters.

Here is a short list of practical, interrelated, and codependent "keys" for preventing neglect.

KEY #1: APPOINT DEACONS.

Go back to Acts 6 and see what the apostles and the early church did to both overcome and prevent the problem of neglect. What did they do? It's obvious, isn't it? *They appointed deacons*, servant leaders who not only solved the immediate problem, but served to prevent the problem from reoccurring. It is so important for the church to appoint deacons full of wisdom and the Holy Spirit to serve as the eyes and ears of the church, ever looking, ever listening, for a needy member. And this applies to both inside and outside the church. This is the first key, and you most likely have taken this step. But if you haven't, do what the apostles did: appoint deacons.

KEY #2: ACT IMMEDIATELY.

We don't know for sure how much time elapsed after the murmuring started before the apostles acted, but the text seems to indicate that as soon as the apostles heard of the situation, *they acted*. The word *against* indicates a wedge was being driven between the two groups. With this word, we have the beginning of division in the church: this group against that group. As soon as the complaint "against" the Hebrews arose, time was of the essence. The clock was ticking. Would the situation be resolved? How long would it take? This is a very important lesson for deacons in every age, in every church. *Act immediately*. Do not give Satan an opportunity to drive a wedge of division in the church between the neglected and those who have the primary responsibility to care for them, the deacons.

KEY #3: SHOW GENUINE LOVE.

This brings us full circle - back to where this chapter began: the need for genuine love. Deacons, above all others, must labor to create an atmosphere of *genuine love* for the brethren. When we respond in unfeigned love toward those with material needs, we demonstrate our love for God. Pointing out the inseparable relationship between loving God and helping the needy, John wrote this:

> In this the children of God are manifest, and the children of the devil: whosoever doeth not righteousness is not of God, neither he that loveth not his brother. (1 John 3:10).

> We know that we have passed from death unto life, because we love the brethren. He that loveth not his brother abideth in death. (3:14).

> But whoso hath this world's good, and seeth his brother have need, and shutteth up his bowels of compassion from him, how dwelleth the love of God in him? (3:17).

Beloved, let us love one another: for love is of God; and every one that loveth is born of God, and knoweth God. He that loveth not knoweth not God; for God is love. (4:7-8).

Herein is love, not that we loved God, but that he loved us, and sent his Son to be the propitiation for our sins. Beloved, if God so loved us, we ought also to love one another. (4:10-11).

In a similar fashion, James wrote the following:

What doth it profit, my brethren, though a man say he hath faith, and have not works? can faith save him? If a brother or sister be naked, and destitute of daily food, And one of you say unto them, Depart in peace, be ye warmed and filled; notwithstanding ye give them not those things which are needful to the body; what doth it profit? (James 2:14-16).

And Peter wrote:

Seeing ye have purified your souls in obeying the truth through the Spirit unto unfeigned love of the brethren, see that ye love one another with a pure heart fervently. (1 Peter 1:22).

Can there be any doubt that there is an inseparable relationship between loving God and helping our needy brothers and sisters. Isn't it also true that our love for God is manifested by our love for the brethren? The exhortations in these verses do not exist because we find these things easy, but rather, they exist because we find these things hard, very hard. However, the more we teach, urge, and model biblical love for God and one another, the more likely it is that we will see the fruit of genuine love in our churches. This responsibility falls primarily on the spiritual leaders of the church. However, deacons are the hands and feet of Christ to the needy, and as they demonstrate the love of Christ for our brothers and sisters in need, they encourage everyone around them to follow suit and demonstrate their own love for God by showing love for the needy. As this happens, the entire church begins to breathe in the atmosphere of love, an atmosphere that is the fruit of the Spirit in the life of every yielded heart. If ever there was a single key to preventing neglect in the church, perhaps *love* is that key.

KEY #4: KNOW GOD'S WORD.

Know, and submit to, the mind of God on the subject of caring for the poor as it is revealed in *His Word*. This may be the most important thing deacons can do to stay focused on their calling and avoid the problem of neglect. The truth of *God's Word* serves as a watchman over our hearts and minds. Truth cries out and warns us that we are violating the will of our Father in heaven. Truth shapes and reshapes our thinking, which, in turn, directs our actions to be more conformed to God's mind for the church. Deacons fit into God's plan for the church as special emissaries on assignment from Jesus Christ. Therefore, it is essential for deacons to know the will of God regarding the poor and needy around us, and His will is revealed in His Word. God's will concerning the needy matters to the needy, it matters to the church, and it matters to God.

Here are a few references from both Testaments that deacons, whose job it is to prevent neglect, would do well to know:

Ex. 23:11; Lev. 19:10-15; 23:22; Duet. 15:7,11; Prov. 14:31; 21:13; Isa. 58:7; Lk. 3:10-11; 6:38; Ro. 12:13; Eph. 4:27-28; 1 Tim. 6:17-18; Heb. 13:16; Ja. 2:1-20; 1 John 3-4

CHAPTER SUMMARY

This chapter began with an examination of the first few chapters of Acts to remind us of the amazing generosity of the first believers toward their needy brothers and sisters in Christ. We then examined a few important words: neglect, priority, symptom, problem, and solution. We thought about these words in relation to the situation that occurred in the church, the problem of neglect. The church went from generously sharing with everyone to neglecting some.

We then examined some possible causes of neglect. While we don't know exactly what caused the Hebrews to neglect the Grecian widows, we looked at five potential causes: human limitations, ignorance, wrong assumptions, prejudice, and laziness.

From there we considered some of the inherent dangers of neglect, using the metaphor of shark-infested waters to hit home how dangerous neglect can be to the church.

And finally, we looked at some keys to preventing neglect: appoint deacons, act immediately, show genuine love, and know God's Word. Drawing from our "tent-making" experience, we learned the value of preventing damage before it occurs, thus allowing us to avoid correction and restoration.

We hope this practical chapter on the problem of neglect proves to be helpful as you determine to serve the entire body of Christ—neglecting no one.

CHAPTER 7

A DIALOGUE ON TEAMWORK, PART 1

INTRODUCTION

Sadly, one of the most difficult aspects of ministry is the problem of maintaining Christ-honoring relationships among church leaders. This strain is often felt between the spiritual leaders of the church and the servant leaders of the church, between pastors and deacons. Not only is this sad, but it is all too common.

Our original intention was to write a practical chapter on the subject of teamwork with the goal of helping deacons navigate the difficult terrain of dealing with the friction that sometimes exists not only among themselves, but also between the two offices. That was our intention. Somewhere along the way we asked ourselves: what if we put it in story form, a kind of parable? Voila! Chapters 7 and 8 were born. We're going to tell you about a deacon named Joe, his wife Margarette, and their pastor Gary.

As you will discover, Joe has not been a deacon very long, yet his soul is vexed by the lack of teamwork, and ultimately by the ineffectiveness of the deacons in his church. He often confides in his godly helpmeet, Margarette, who lovingly and patiently listens, encourages, and prays with Joe. They love their church, and they want to see things get better, but they're not sure what to do. Finally, Joe arranges a meeting with Pastor Gary. One meeting turns into several. Their pastor-led conversations in these meetings get to the heart of our original intention of offering guidance to deacons on the subject of teamwork.

The story begins with a PROLOGUE to introduce the characters and the situation. Here, we eavesdrop on a particular Sunday in the life of Joe. The story progresses to the DIALOGUE scenes that focus on Pastor Gary and Joe. Gary fleshes out the biblical teaching on teamwork, yet in the course of their discussions, Joe discovers much more than teamwork. The story then concludes in a brief EPILOGUE. In a little twist on the PROLOGUE, we find out if Joe's concerns have been resolved.

PROLOGUE

As Joe collects his children from their various Sunday school rooms to gather for worship in the auditorium, he notices a spirit of joy and excitement in his own soul. It's been a good morning. The drive to church was uplifting as Margarette led the family in the singing of choruses. Joe likes the idea of the family SUV being a Spiritual Utility Vehicle unto the Lord. There was a noticeably good spirit in the adult Sunday School this morning. Joe was especially grateful for that. As his family slips into the pew, his eyes are once again drawn to the stained-glass cross behind the pulpit. As preparation for worship, Joe often looks on the cross as a reminder of

Christ and the privilege of coming to the Father through His Son. A good morning indeed!

In a matter of seconds, his spirit of worship is shattered. In the time that it takes for his eyes to move from the cross to the worship bulletin, his heart sinks into his stomach and his stomach rises up into his throat. There it is in black and white, and there is nothing he can do about it. It reads, "DEACONS' MEETING, Thursday night, 6 p.m." He quickly looks back at the cross and then down again to the program. It's still there. "DEACONS' MEETING, Thursday night, 6 p.m." Almost choking on the thought, Joe throws a glance to his right and catches a glimpse of one of his fellow deacons. He looks straight ahead a few rows to find another one. In his mind's eye, he looks to the back row. And there he sits, the chairman of the board. Darth Vader, as far as Joe is concerned. "STAR WARS, Thursday night, 6 p.m."

Joe has been a deacon for less than a year, but he's no novice concerning the office. Having grown up in this church, he recalls the many deacons that he admired, godly men that left an impression on him. He observed as the church solemnly installed them into office. He watched their lives, listened as they described their service, and heard testimonies of thanks from those they served. In his eyes, the deacons were heroes of the church, right up there with pastors and missionaries. As a boy, he wondered if God would make him a deacon one day. He secretly hoped so.

But now that he's a deacon, things have changed. He's not sure how or why or if it's his own fault. But the sweet aroma of sacrificial service for the Lord is missing, so is the high regard for the office among some members of the church. In the short time that he's been a deacon, he has come to hate the meetings. He doesn't hate the men, not even Darth Vader. It's the arguing and bickering and the fact that, because of petty differences, they often fail to accomplish anything. They talk and talk and talk as if that's what being a deacon is about.

They talk about problems but rarely solve them. They talk about people but rarely serve them. Joe knows he's not alone in his frustration. He senses there are other deacons who feel the same way, but they don't know what to do about it. Of the seven deacons, two or three seem to have their own agendas. Sadly, the chairman seems to stonewall every effort that does not serve his own interests.

More importantly, Joe senses the pastor is frustrated, as well. He's a good pastor. He loves the flock, and most of the flock genuinely loves him. Joe has listened to the pastor preach and teach on unity, love, and forgiveness, and the Spirit has convicted Joe concerning his own sinful attitudes. Although he doesn't know for sure, Joe thinks the pastor has pulled some of the men aside and talked to them privately. But he doesn't understand why he allows these men to remain on the board and hijack the ministry of the deacons. He's also aware of the fact that he might be part of the problem, and if so, he prays the Lord will make that clear to him.

As Joe sings the opening anthem, "Oh Worship the King," his mind is on the meeting. By the time the pastor prays the benediction to conclude the service, Joe is certain he's coming down with a cold and should stay home Thursday night out of love for the brethren. But he knows Margarette will never let him get away with that, so he resigns himself to the inevitable. "DEACONS' MEETING, Thursday night, 6 p.m.

During lunch Joe is unusually quiet, not because he's still dreading the meeting, but because the Spirit of God is speaking truth into his heart and he's under conviction. He knows that his attitude is wrong and grieves the Spirit. After the last dish has been dried and Margarette and the girls head outside to play, he sits at the kitchen table and thinks about his sinful attitude toward certain deacons and of being critical of his pastor. He resolves by God's grace to do something about it.

But what? Should he resign to avoid the conflict? Should he confront those he believes are hard-headed and causing the deacons to be ineffective? Is that even his place? Should he protest the meeting to make a statement of his discontent? As Joe sits there pondering his course of action, the words of Jesus come to him: "Without me you can do nothing." So, Joe prays. It's a simple but sincere prayer: "Father, I confess my sinful attitudes and thoughts toward these men. Help me to love them as Christ loved me. And You are right—I can't do that on my own. I need Your help. I also pray for my pastor and the other deacons. May we all be submissive to Your Word and Spirit, seeking only to do Your will. Amen."

Joe feels some encouragement as he drives to the meeting Thursday night. He's sure that he is spiritually prepared and looks forward to a good meeting. As he heads home from the church three hours later, he says to himself, "I can't do this anymore. I can't take another meeting." However, he realizes he has fallen prey to some unrealistic expectations. He foolishly thought that, since he prayed about it, God would surely answer his prayer that his own heart would change and immediately change the hearts of the other men as well. But God had other plans.

After pulling his car into the garage, he sits there thinking about the meeting. He knows something has to change. He knows this cannot be God's will for the church. There has to be a way for the deacons to be united and work together for the glory of God and the good of those they were called to serve. Long after the light has gone out in the garage, Joe turns to the Lord. This time he prays for forgiveness, patience, and wisdom. Then he heads into the house to share his thoughts with Margarette.

They grew up in the church together, and Margarette is the daughter of one of the godly deacons that Joe admired as a boy. Just knowing she is in the house waiting for him brings comfort to Joe. She'll listen as he pours out his heart to her, and she will always point him to the Scriptures for answers. She never says, "Joe, my dad would . . ." but he hears her godly upbringing in her counsel. He's thankful for that. As he locks the door behind him, their eyes meet, and she knows he's had a disappointing meeting.

For the next day or two, Joe thinks about what is missing among the deacons of the church. The word that keeps coming back to his mind is "teamwork." At the plant where Joe works, this is a catchword. Everything is about teamwork. The company even brought in corporate specialists to train the employees on the importance and practice of teamwork. They went through team-building exercises to help build *esprit décorp*, a spirit of pride and unity among the employees. As Joe thinks about these things, he gets out the training manual and notebook that he kept during the training sessions. He hopes it might prove helpful.

He remembers one of the trainers explaining that the word *team-work* first appeared in the English language around 1820 to 1830. His notes include *Webster's Dictionary* definition: "TEAM-WORK *n* [team and work] work done by a team as distinguished from personal labor." It comes from the idea of a team of horses or oxen teamed together with a harness or yoked to the same wagon or cart.

"Think of a team of draft horses," the trainer said, "pulling a heavy load of logs in a turn of the century logging camp or pulling a wagonload of fresh cut wheat on the farm." The trainer pointed out that these may have been the very images Webster had in mind as he defined teamwork: "work done by a team as distinguished from personal labor." According to his notes, the word *team* can be traced back to around the year 900 A.D. and means "that which draws" or pulls in the same direction.

In the spirit of teamwork, as if to make the point, another trainer stepped in to point out that currently the main idea behind teamwork is "a group of people collaborating or working together to achieve a common goal." Joe had forgotten this, but in the margin of the page he wrote this note: "Teamwork implies pulling together, unity of effort, and more than one working toward a goal."

At work they insist on teamwork, and Joe is good at it. He's also been able to put some of the principles to work at home. But he hasn't yet learned to apply these things to other areas, specifically the servant ministry of the deacons. This makes him think. Where does the word *teamwork* appear in the Bible, and more importantly, what does the Bible teach about teamwork?

Joe remembers the pastor urging the church to be a unified team of believers working for God's glory. He finds his Bible and turns to the concordance at the back and looks up the word *teamwork*. Nothing. How about "team"? Still nothing. He gets out his copy of Strong's Concordance. Surely, he would find the words there. Not there either. Joe finds that interesting and a little frustrating. At this point, he decides to call Pastor Gary to talk about these things, not just where to find the word *team* in the Scripture, but also his concerns regarding the lack of teamwork among the deacons. He calls the church office and schedules an appointment for Tuesday morning before work.

DIALOGUE

SESSION 1

As they settle into the comfortable leather chairs in front of Gary's desk, Joe has mixed feelings about this meeting. His pastor doesn't know it yet, but Joe has some tough questions in mind and he's nervous about how the pastor will receive them. On the other hand, Pastor Gary has a way of making everyone around him feel comfortable. Gary's a tall guy with a broadcaster's voice and an infectious laugh. Anyone around him for very long feels the warmth of his soul and his love for people. It's what makes him a good shepherd, that and his love for God's Word.

He often mentions his seminary training, and he continues to be a diligent student of the sacred Scriptures. When he opens the Bible, you know that he believes every word of it with every fiber in his body. It's what makes him a good teacher. So, with mixed emotions about opening up to his pastor, Joe begins.

He starts by explaining his dilemma. He wants to know what the Bible has to say about teamwork, yet he couldn't find the word anywhere in the Scripture. He describes the teamwork training he received at work and shows Gary the teamwork training manual he was required to read and bring to the training sessions. He finds the page with Webster's definition of teamwork and reads it to his pastor. He thinks it might somehow be applicable to diaconal ministry, but he isn't sure.

He also musters up the courage to share with Gary where this question is coming from: his frustration with the meetings, the ineffectiveness of the ministry of the deacons, and his own sinful attitudes of resentment, discouragement, and pride.

Pastor Gary begins by commending Joe for his sensitivity to the Spirit's leading in his life and his determination to bring a spirit of teamwork to the deacons. As the pastor speaks, Joe senses the humility of his spiritual shepherd. Instead of being defensive or offering excuses, he confirms Joe's observations concerning the ineffectiveness of the board. He confesses his own failure to deal with some long-standing, unresolved issues concerning some of the men and his reluctance to confront the problems that are preventing them from working together as a team.

Joe knows this has to be hard for him, but he is handling it with grace. Joe finds his pastor's receptiveness both comforting and disarming. As he continues, he even thanks Joe for bringing his questions and concerns to his attention and commends his courage. He acknowledges this has to be hard for Joe. At this point, he suggests they turn to the Lord in prayer. Closing his eyes, Gary quietly leads them in a prayer of confession asking the Lord for forgiveness and a spirit of unity in the church and especially among the deacons. As Gary prays, Joe's heart is filled with both humility and hopefulness.

After praying, Gary begins answering Joe's questions. He tells Joe the reason he couldn't find the word *teamwork* in the concordance is because it isn't there. But he explains that, even though the word is not in the Bible, the concept is definitely biblical.

"Joe, the word the Bible uses to express the idea of teamwork is the word *unity*. I see you brought your Bible. If you would, open it to Ephesians 4:3. When you find it, go ahead and read it out loud."

So, Joe reads, "Endeavoring to keep the unity of the Spirit in the bond of peace."

Gary continues: "The Greek word behind our English word *unity* is *henotes*.[143] It basically means oneness, unity, and harmony. When oneness is put into action, it suggests teamwork. Let me explain. The concept of oneness, along with the terms *unity* and *harmony*, implies *more than one*. There has to be more than one to have a spirit of oneness or a spirit of harmony.

"Oneness is not aloneness. The word itself speaks of more than one. Then, when oneness is put into action, you have two or more working together to achieve a common goal. That's teamwork. Think of the Trinity: Father, Son, and Spirit. One God, yet three distinct persons. Each member of the Trinity exists and works in harmony with the other two. Three, working as one. So then, oneness speaks of a team, and oneness in action speaks of teamwork. As you read the rest of Chapter 4, it seems that Paul has both unity and teamwork in mind."

"That's interesting," says Joe. "Let me see if I've got this. Teamwork *is* a biblical concept; it's rooted in the word *unity* and seen in the Trinity when each member—Father, Son, and Spirit—work in perfect harmony. As you said, teamwork is unity in action."

---

143 *Henotes* is found only twice in the New Testament. There are several other words that convey the concept of unity.

"That's exactly right," responds Gary. "Joe, read Webster's definitions of teamwork and team again."

"Teamwork," reads Joe, "is work done by a team as distinguished from personal labor, and team means to draw or pull in the same direction."

"In biblical terms, then," Gary explains, "teamwork is unity, harmony, oneness, *in action*. To say it another way, teamwork is what unity looks like."

"Hold on," pleads Joe, "those two statements sound important." Taking out a pen, he writes these words in the margin of the manual. As he writes, he repeats them out loud, "Teamwork is unity in action, and teamwork is what unity looks like." Joe thinks about it a second and then asks, "Could we say that unity is the fountain out of which teamwork springs?"

"Absolutely," encourages Gary. "Teamwork flows or 'springs' out of unity. That's good. Now let me make an important distinction. You can have teamwork without unity, but you can't have teamwork without action. Teamwork, by definition, implies action. Teamwork occurs when two or more people or things work together as one."

Gary realizes this is an abstract concept and might be a little hard to grasp, so he adds this illustration. "I know your daughter takes piano lessons from my wife, Bev. Little Rachael started out pecking away with one finger, then two, and before long she was striking notes with both hands. She was learning to play multiple notes in harmony with each other. Technically, the word *harmony* speaks of agreement and accord. In music, it speaks of any simultaneous combination of blended notes, what we call chords. The important words are *simultaneous* and *blended*."

Gary sits forward in the chair and pretends to strike the keys of a piano. While holding the imaginary chord, he says, "More than one note, working harmoniously with other notes. The notes are played simultaneously, and they all blend beautifully." More imaginary playing follows. He's really getting into this illustration. "More than one, yet working together as one."

Gary turns and points toward the door. "Listen. The piano sitting in the auditorium right now is silent. The parts are all there, and together they all make a whole piano, but there is no action. However, when someone strikes the keys and puts the whole instrument into motion, it produces beautiful music: the simultaneous combination of blended notes and chords. The once silent parts are now producing lovely harmonies." With that, he raises his hands and begins playing again. "Two or more working together in harmony." He dramatically runs the back of his right hand across the keys ending with an emphatic downward gesture. "That's teamwork!"

Worried that his air-playing may have gotten in the way of the point, he asks Joe, "Does that make sense?"

With a grin still on his face, Joe cautiously responds, "I think so. Two or more working together is teamwork, while working together in a spirit of harmony is unity. I see why you said that, while the word *teamwork* is not in the Bible, the concept is. Unity, which is in the Bible, combined with the idea of teamwork, speaks of pulling together in the same direction in a spirit of oneness to accomplish a common goal. If I understand it correctly, unity is the inner attitude or state of accord and harmony, while teamwork is the outward evidence. Members of a united group will be *working* together in a *spirit* of teamwork. While that's important for every Christian to remember, it's really important for deacons. Does that sound about right?"

Gary chuckles. "You're a fast learner, Joe. You clearly get the relationship between teamwork and unity. And since you are doing so well, here's an important question for you. What's the difference between the teamwork that you learned about at work and teamwork in the church? Can you think of something that distinguishes what a secular organization accomplishes as a team and what the church accomplishes as a team?"

As Joe struggles to think of an answer, Gary helps him out. "The difference," he explains, "is the person and work of the Holy Spirit. Through teamwork, football teams, architects, and factories can win games, erect buildings and get a product out the door on time. But the purpose and mission of the church requires more than everyone getting on the same page and pulling in the same direction. The church and her calling are spiritual in nature and can only be achieved through the enabling work of the Spirit of God. It is, as Paul states, 'the unity of the Spirit,' which denotes the source. It is from the Spirit. Therefore, the kind of teamwork that the Bible speaks of, the kind of teamwork that brings honor and glory to God the Father, is Spirit-dependent teamwork. In order to achieve biblical, God glorifying teamwork, the church needs the empowerment that only the Spirit of God can give.

"Joe, this is critical; you have to get this. This distinction between human teamwork and Spiritual teamwork is something that every deacon needs to understand. Diaconal ministry is accomplished in the context of the local church. Every ministry of God's church is spiritual in nature and therefore cannot be accomplished without the Spirit of God. Joe, you, as a deacon, and every deacon must see that serving the church, even in the practical affairs, is spiritual work. This is what distinguishes unity and teamwork in the world from unity and teamwork in the church: the enabling of the Holy Spirit. Why else would the apostles insist that the original servants of the church be men who were 'full of the Holy Ghost'?"[144]

Feeling the weight of his pastor's counsel, Joe quietly responds, "Pastor, I appreciate this reminder that we cannot do God's work in the flesh. I know this. I've seen deacons, spiritually minded deacons in this church, serve the Lord in the power of the Holy Spirit, men who fought for biblical unity and teamwork for the glory of God. On the other hand, I've witnessed deacons, even myself, trying to do things in the flesh. And

---

144 Acts 6:3.

obviously, it doesn't work. Like I said, I know this. But it is easy to forget. Though it stings, I very much appreciate the reminder that God-honoring unity and the teamwork that flows from it starts with a humble dependence on the Holy Spirit. So, thank you for that reminder."

Matching Joe's reflective attitude, Gary responds, "You know what, it's been a good reminder for me as well. To be sure, deacons sometimes operate in the flesh with sinful attitudes and actions. But so can pastors. As men, it's a struggle to do what Paul says in Gal. 5:16: 'Walk in the Spirit and ye will not fulfill the lust of the flesh.'

"There's a reason, Joe, that even believers find it so hard to deny themselves as Jesus demands. There's a reason why unity and teamwork are a struggle. This is a symptom of something that we can summarize in one word. What do you think that word is?"

"Well, my first thought is the word *sin*," answers Joe. "But I think you're going to say *pride*."

"Exactly!" confirms Gary. "It's pride. And when pride swells up within us, we are well on the road to being led by the flesh and not by the Spirit. To the church at Corinth, a church of true saints yet a church divided over several serious issues, Paul said they were arrogant, puffed up, full of pride. As a result, Paul chides, 'For ye are yet carnal: for whereas there is among you envying, and strife, and divisions, are ye not carnal, and walk as men?'[145] In other words, even though the church was a temple of the Holy Spirit,[146] they were acting like spiritually immature babies in Christ. It happens. It shouldn't, but it does! And the underlying problem, whether it was the church at Corinth or our church, is the problem of pride. The solution, then, is humbly submitting our wills to the authority of God's Word and the illuminating ministry of the Holy Spirit.

---

145 1 Cor. 3:3.
146 1 Cor. 3:16.

"This brings us back to the thing that distinguishes teamwork in the world from teamwork in the church: the Spirit. One is natural; the other, spiritual. However commendable and even useful teamwork is, whether it be in the church or the world, if it is not Spirit-wrought teamwork," leaning forward now he repeats those last few words, "if it is not Spirit-wrought teamwork, then God is not in it, nor is He glorified. And Joe, we can be sure that God is not in it when we are full of pride." With those words, he sits back in his chair and lets the words hang in the air for both of them to reflect on that thought.

Silently pondering Gary's words for just a moment, Joe responds: "You said, 'Then God is not in it, nor is He glorified.' Pastor, that's a convicting thought. As I sit here thinking about those words, I'm remembering sermons you've preached from the pulpit, and I remember exhortations you've given to the deacons particularly to strive for unity, the kind of God-honoring unity and teamwork you're talking about. But to be honest, I personally struggle with this. I want God to be glorified in my life and in my service as a deacon.

"You know, some of the sweetest moments I've ever experienced in this church have been as a deacon, serving together in a spirit of unity. But it doesn't seem to last very long. All it takes sometimes is a negative comment, a snarky remark, an insensitive attitude, and the meeting is shot. And it's been happening more and more lately. Our pride shows up, and everything goes downhill from there. And even if it comes later in the form of hard feelings and unkind thoughts, it's still rooted in pride. We know—I know—that pride is sin, yet in the heat of the moment, we let it reign in our hearts anyway. Why is that? Why are we constantly struggling with this?"

Gary's heart is stirred within him. He knows exactly what Joe is talking about, and he wants to shepherd this man's heart through this moment so that he ends up in the right place, so that they both end up in the right place. Gary's pastoral instincts tell him this is an opportunity for spiritual growth, not only for him and Joe, but the entire church. He also senses that Joe is feeling discouraged at this moment and does not want him to think that striving for unity and teamwork is a hopeless cause.

"Joe, I truly appreciate your honesty. These are excellent questions. The good news is that God has the answers. Not only does He have the answers—and this is very important—He has already given us everything we need to live in unity and work in a spirit of teamwork: His Son, His Spirit, His Word, His love. But most of all, He gives us the knowledge of Himself. 2 Peter 1:2-3 says, 'Grace and peace be multiplied unto you through the knowledge of God, and of Jesus our Lord, according as his divine power hath given unto us all things that pertain unto life and godliness, through the knowledge of him that hath called us to glory and virtue.'

"Joe, God is not stingy with His grace toward us. He wants us to live in harmony with each other and with His will for our lives. The fountain of life and godliness is knowing God Himself. That is the greatest resource of all, knowing God. But God also gives us everything we need to live godly lives for His glory. It makes sense that God, who created everything and everyone for His own glory, would also give us everything we need to do so. Having given us Himself and all things necessary to live godly and virtuous lives, He expects us to do so. My point is this: we can! We can overcome our sinful selves and live obediently to the glory of God!"

"What you're saying," responds Joe, "and I've heard you say this before, is the very fact that God expects us to do something tells us we can. He took the initiative to make us His dear children, then gives us everything necessary to live in obedience and fellowship with our heavenly Father. When it comes to sanctification, it is our responsibility to cooperate with the Spirit of God and live lives of humble obedience to His Word. So, you're saying we can, and the real question is, 'Will we?' It's not that we can't, but we won't. As I say those words, they sound pretty harsh. 'We won't.' Without taking all the other factors into consideration, am I right? We can, but we won't? I'm asking, but I already know the answer, don't I?"

"Listening to you, Joe," Gary responds, "just hearing you say it so clearly, you've touched a nerve in me, and frankly, it hurts. And it's this: if the leaders of the church *won't* humbly submit their attitudes and actions to the Word of God and demonstrate a God-glorifying spirit of teamwork out of genuine love for God, the church, and one another, then we need to get out of the way and let someone else lead. That's how serious this is! Can we overcome our pride and live and serve in unity? Indeed, we can. That gives us hope, and hope gives us endurance."

"That being said . . ." In the brief pause that follows those words, Joe studies his pastor's face. His countenance tells Joe this is indeed a serious moment. Every word is now chosen carefully and spoken almost reverently. "The church," he continues "needs leaders. The church needs spiritually minded leaders, leaders who are models of humility, unity, and Spirit-empowered teamwork."

Both Gary and Joe sit in silence for a moment, letting these words sink in. In the awkwardness of the moment, Joe fumbles with the pages of Gary's Bible still sitting on his lap. Gary stares off into the space somewhere behind Joe. Although it was only a few seconds, it seems much longer to both men. Gary breaks the silence.

"I sense this might be a good time to stop our discussion for now. But I want to tell you something. Joe, you have no idea how much I appreciate you coming to me with these concerns. I admire both your courage and your desire to fulfill God's will in your servant ministry. Secondly, I think it's important that we continue this conversation. There is so much more for us to talk about, and I don't want to let this opportunity for spiritual growth slip away. And finally, if we're going to see real change occur and experience godly unity and Spirit-empowered teamwork in this church, we need to commit this issue to the Lord in earnest prayer and commit to praying for one another. Joe, would you do that? Let's lock arms in this commitment. I will pray for you specifically, Joe, as you seek to serve the Lord as a faithful deacon, and will you pray for me as the pastor of this church, as I seek to please and serve the Lord? And together, over the next weeks and months, we will work to glorify God in our ministries."

Fighting through some unexpected emotions, Joe takes a deep breath and manages to choke out, "Absolutely. I promise to pray for you, pastor, and thank you for praying for me. I'm honored to join you in the pursuit of biblical teamwork. I'm not only honored, I'm excited about what the Lord has in store for us."

With those words, Gary bows his head and closes with this prayer, "Father, we submit our thinking and all of our actions to you. We confess our sinfulness, our need for continuous cleansing, and our desire to walk in fellowship with You. We pray that this assembly might experience, as never before, the blessings of unified teamwork and experience the joy of walking in obedient fellowship with You. May the words of our mouths and the meditations of our hearts be acceptable in your sight, O Lord, our Savior and Redeemer. Amen."

Before leaving, Gary asks Joe if he would be available to get together again next week at the same time.

"Good," responds Gary. "You asked some excellent 'why' questions a few minutes ago. But I think we need to spend some time thinking about a more fundamental question first: 'Why is teamwork so important?' We'll talk about that and a few more things next week. Come on, I'll walk out with you."

SESSION 2

As Joe drives to the pastor's office the following week, he thinks about two things. First, how incredibly blessed he is to have his pastor praying for him and his spiritual growth. He knows Gary prays for the entire assembly, but the commitment they made to pray for one another has deeply impacted his soul. Second, all week he has been thinking about pride, not everyone else's pride, but his own. He's been meditating on the humility of Christ, and he has memorized Philippians 2:5-8. As he drives, he recites the passage out loud, "Let this mind be in you which was also in Christ Jesus, who, being in the form of God, did not consider it robbery to be equal with God, but made Himself of no reputation, taking the form of a servant, and coming in the likeness of men, He humbled Himself and became obedient to the point of death, even the death of the cross."

Joe spent the last week praying specifically that the humble mind of Christ would indeed be found in him and considering what that might mean as a servant leader of the church. As promised, he prayed for his spiritual leader, Gary. He also prayed for the other deacons, each one by name. By the end of just one week of praying for these men, he sensed his attitude toward them changing: a little less harsh and a little more forgiving.

It was with eagerness and anticipation that he walked into the church. Gary is there to greet him with a smile and a hot cup of coffee. After praying for God's blessings on their discussion, Gary picks up where he left off.

"Last week you asked some probing questions, and we talked about pride. However, I suggested there is a more fundamental question that needs to be answered. The question, 'Why is teamwork so important?' Did you get a chance to think about that?"

"Honestly," said Joe, "I've thought more about pride. I've been thinking about it a lot. I've also been thinking about my attitude toward the other deacons. But yes, I have given it a little thought."

"And what do you think?" asks Gary. "Why is teamwork in the church so important?"

"Well, initially I thought about the obvious fact that more is accomplished by a team than an individual. A few years ago, my boss sent me to a TEAM conference. It's an acronym for 'together everyone accomplishes more.' But you're probably looking for something a little more spiritual. So, I think the answer might be found in the question, 'What is the chief end of man?' If our chief end, or ultimate purpose, is to glorify God, and if God is glorified through Spirit-empowered unity and teamwork, then teamwork is important. Through teamwork, we glorify God."

"That's a wonderful answer, Joe. All of life is to be lived to the glory of God, the Father. We truly exist to glorify Him. The Scriptures resound with that message, and the heavens declare it (Ps. 19:1). So, let's hone in on glorifying God through teamwork. What I want to do this morning is develop a biblical perspective on teamwork, teamwork to the glory of God.

"The specific question on the table is this: why is it so important for the church, and the leaders in the church specifically, to work as a team? Why is it so *fundamentally important* to be *one* and work as *one*? The answer lies in the nature of God. God is one! It is His nature. Oneness and teamwork, which is oneness in action, reflect the very nature of God.

"Last week we talked about the Trinity: Father, Son, and Spirit, yet one God. In the Trinity, there is perfect unity among the three divine persons. The word *trinity* itself means tri-unity. And the basic meaning of unity is oneness. God is one. It is His nature to be one: perfect in unity, harmony, and without division. Therefore, everything that God does, every time He acts—past, present, or future—is a demonstration of divine teamwork, of unity in action. It bears repeating here: oneness is not aloneness. And oneness, by itself, is not teamwork. Oneness is two or more existing in a state of harmony. Teamwork occurs when two or more, existing in unity, work together to achieve a common goal. God is one yet three divine persons existing and acting in harmony. When they act in harmony with each other, that is teamwork, divine teamwork!

"So, the goal of everything that exists, as you reminded us, is the glory of God. And how does unified teamwork glorify Him? Both unity and teamwork reflect His glorious nature, imperfectly, of course, but a reflection of His nature, nonetheless.

"Now, let's think in practical terms. This is when it hits home. Since God is one by nature, everything He does will reflect His oneness or unity.

To reflect anything else would misrepresent who He is and what He is like. This being true, the importance of oneness and teamwork in the church, and in diaconal ministry specifically, cannot be overstated. The Holy Trinity functions as a unified team, as one. Therefore, we—His children, His family, His body, the officers of His church—must function as a unified team, as one (Phil. 1:27-30). Is God honored when the church misrepresents His nature before the world, the saints, or angels? Would the God who cannot be divided have a divided church or a divided office? God, who is one, rightfully expects every ministry of His church to be one and act as one and to be a true representation of His nature. Anything less dishonors His name.

"In the final analysis, there is only one argument for insisting that the church, and every aspect of the church, be one and act as one. It is the fact that God himself is one. If God was divided in unity or action, then there would be little to compel us to be united or motivate us to act as a harmonious team. But God is not divided. He is simply one. And we are compelled to represent His nature in all that we are and all that we do. Anything less misrepresents the nature of God. Teamwork is two or more working together to achieve a common goal. This is true of God, and it must be true of His church.

"Joe, the question I've been answering is, 'Why is teamwork so important?' Because of the nature of God. But here's another question: why doesn't the church, and every individual Christian, strive for God-glorifying teamwork? What do you think?"

"Well," responds Joe, "based on what you just explained, the simple answer seems to be that we don't realize how important teamwork is. Speaking for myself, I guess I never thought about it in light of God's nature. I never drew a line from God's nature to our teamwork, or lack thereof, as the case may be. That makes so much sense to me. God is holy. Therefore, we are to be holy. God is light. Therefore, we are to be light. God is love, and so on. Why? Because of God's nature. Is it really this simple?

We fail to understand how important it is to reflect the nature of God in everything we do?"

"That's very insightful, Joe. Let me put it this way. It is either because we fail to understand the connection between God's nature and our behavior, or understanding it, we do not think it is that important. Which would mean we don't treasure it, don't highly esteem it, don't embrace it as an altogether desirable thing. Let me repeat this." Now Gary leans forward on his elbows that are resting on the arms of the chair. With much intensity, he repeats, "We either fail to understand, or we lightly regard that the nature of God is to be reflected in the nature and activities of the church. Once we know this, then it becomes a question of importance. As you know, we all find a way to do the things that are truly important to us. Is it important to reflect the nature of God in diaconal service?

"Joe, it is one thing to acknowledge this in our heads; it is another thing to embrace it as an all-important reality in our souls! Once we fully embrace the importance of unity and teamwork, both to God and the church, then we are more likely to both strive for and defend the church against anything that would divide or hinder her from working as a harmonious team. The nature of God demands that we take this seriously. We know this is important to God. But is it important to us?"

As Pastor Gary is talking, Joe is listening very carefully to every word. As Gary finishes, Joe speaks up.

"That's a powerful truth. I feel like I've been hit with a theological sledgehammer. God is one, and He expects us to be one. And being one implies working together in harmony. Teamwork! Frankly, these things make me ashamed. I came in here last week with my teamwork manual in hand, demanding to know why we weren't an effective team. It never occurred to me to think about the glory of God or His nature. I'm struck by the fact that I go to work like so many others, and we put our differences aside and work together as a team. We have a job to do, we do it well, we go home, and we start over again the next day. In other words, we get the job done by working together.

"But for some reason, we deacons fail to bring that same intentional spirit of teamwork to the meetings and, beyond the meetings, in our service to the church. But I never thought of it as being a reflection of the nature of God. Or should I say, a failure to reflect the nature of God! And that is always to be the goal for the Christian at work, at home, and at church, especially here at church! Instead of always striving for the oneness and teamwork that reflect the nature of God in myself, I've settled for blaming others. I might desire it, and I know when it's missing, but what have I actually done to ensure that we are reflecting God's nature in our ministry of service? The answer has to do with how important it is to me."

After taking a deep breath, Joe humbly confesses, "I'm sorry, pastor. Please forgive me for not taking this more seriously. I've been more self-centered than God-centered. A few minutes ago, I was quick to point out the chief end of man but slow to seek how to live it out in my diaconal ministry, slow to realize that my relationship with the other deacons and my service as a deacon needs to be a true reflection of the nature of God. That's being hit with a sledgehammer!"

Gary has always known when to let the tension in the air just sit for a moment. No need to ease it too quickly. So, for a moment, they sit together in a silence born of shared brokenness. Joe is concentrating on himself and his own failures, but there are thoughts and emotions going on in Gary of which Joe has no idea. But he's about to find out.

"Joe, your humility is stunning. However, I am the one who should be confessing and asking for forgiveness. The nature of God and our lack of teamwork begs the question, 'Why aren't we, the leaders of this church, a unified team reflecting his oneness?' Well, the finger of God points at me. While we all bear the responsibility to know and obey God's Word, God called me to be the spiritual overseer of this flock. I am the one who will be held accountable for the state of each soul and the spiritual condition of this assembly. If I had been stressing these things more, and not only stressing but insisting on a unified spirit of teamwork as a reflection of God's nature, I might be able to say, 'But Lord, I've done everything I can.' But, sadly, I can't say that. Again, it goes back to what's important.

"This past week I thought a lot about our first conversation. I've also been thinking about the very things we're talking about right now. And this isn't the first time that I've thought about these things, things like unity and teamwork. I see problems, like the lack of teamwork and the sinful attitudes that you see, but I haven't done enough about it. And to be completely honest, I find my lack of action discouraging."

Gary nervously tugs at the bottom of his neatly trimmed beard before continuing. "It's discouraging on a personal level, but mostly on a pastoral level. And this is not the first time that I've been discouraged about this. In various ways I've attempted to address these things in the past, but I don't see any improvement, improvement either in my determination to see it through or a change in the attitudes and overall ministry of the deacons. Providentially, over the past several months, I've known these issues have to be resolved. The Spirit and the Word have been driving me to deal with these things. So, I have been earnestly praying for both wisdom and the spiritual courage to make whatever changes are necessary, *whatever* changes are necessary! And then, after praying over these concerns for several months now, God sent you into my office asking why we don't have a spirit of teamwork among the deacons."

Joe shakes his head and says, "That's amazing. I had no idea."

"No, but God did. I said I was discouraged. But these past two weeks have been so encouraging to me. God used you, Joe, to minister to my soul and, hopefully, to be the catalyst to bring about change in my own life and change in our church. I say that to be an encouragement to you. God sent you to me to be a blessing to His church. I know there are many things I do as the pastor of this church that God is pleased with. He's blessed my ministry here for many years. Thankfully, for the most part, we have been blessed with unity and harmony in our church body. I attribute that to the kindness and mercy of God. But one area of weakness has been my reluctance to deal with issues as I become aware of them, issues that can threaten the unity and teamwork of a church."

"As the pastor teacher of this assembly of believers, my primary tool for dealing with problems is the public preaching and teaching of the Word. I have no problem with that. But that's not all there is to pastoring God's flock. And while I often pull people aside to exhort and encourage them privately, or to arrange Bible studies or teach classes, there are certain arenas and certain people that I tend to draw back from, like the subject we're talking about: the commands to live and serve in unity to the glory of God, to reflect His nature in all we do and to lovingly confront anyone who might be sowing seeds of discord (Titus 3:10, ESV; Gal. 6:1). I sometimes neglect this pastoral duty. It's wrong, and it's discouraging. But, Joe, I believe God is giving me, giving us, an opportunity to lovingly and obediently strive for 'the unity of the Spirit in the bond of peace.' That's what these meetings are about, serving together in unity and manifesting it in a spirit of teamwork, first and foremost among the officers of this church."

While being sensitive to Gary's openness, Joe probes cautiously. "Well, first, thank you for those encouraging words, and I appreciate your humble honesty. But I would like to go back to a couple of words that you used. You mentioned 'reluctance' and 'neglect.' This has me wondering if you have any insights as to why this happens. Not just you, but why do spiritual leaders in general fail to either teach certain biblical truths or, having taught them, fail to make every effort to see that those truths are practiced? And I hope I'm not getting too personal here, Gary, but your reluctance to deal with certain things and certain people, where does that come from? I hope my questions don't offend you. I'm genuinely interested in finding answers because I'm often the same way."

"No," Gary quietly assures, "they don't offend me. They have to be asked." He pauses to find his words. "Joe, maybe it is because I know you've been praying for me, and maybe it's because I believe you're asking for all the right reasons: love for God, love for me, and love for the church. I'm going to be honest and make myself vulnerable with you. The question on the table is, 'Why do we, I, sometimes fail to deal with certain difficult issues?' That's a really good question. I have thought about these things many times and especially in the past week. Our discussion provoked me to prayerfully confess both pride and negligence and to think about the very question you've asked. Years of experience have revealed several weaknesses in my ministry. These are weaknesses that I not only have to constantly guard against, but weaknesses that every spiritual leader has to guard himself against. So, having thought about this question many times, and again in the last few days, here are some of my observations.

"First, there's the potential problem of spiritual laziness. There's a reason Paul exhorts, '[E]ndeavoring to keep the unity of the Spirit in the bond of peace . . .' (Eph. 4:3). We should talk about this verse in greater detail later, but for now, let's just say that endeavoring is hard work. While it would be a shameful thing to admit, some church leaders, both spiritual and servant leaders, are not willing to put in the necessary hard spiritual work to achieve unity in the church. While most of us have an inborn tendency toward *selective laziness*, leaders in the church must have a diligent and self-sacrificing spirit. Otherwise, some of the more difficult tasks of leadership, like 'endeavoring to keep the unity of the Spirit,' will be left unattended. And yes, I do have to be on the lookout for laziness. It's something I must constantly guard against.

"Another potential cause for failing to deal with difficult issues is the fear of man: afraid of confrontation, afraid of rejection, afraid even of losing a job. Like the story of Pandora's box, once you open it up, you never know what evil might come out. Joe, the fear of man can be like a vice grip on an otherwise good man's soul. Try as he might, in his own strength, he just can't shake it off. Whether it prevents him from confronting others or causes him to avoid certain issues from the pulpit or keeps him from bringing up issues in deacons' meetings, he rationalizes it away.

"Though he knows he shouldn't give in to the tyranny of man fear, he bows to the pressure because he longs to be approved of by men (Prov. 29:25; Mt. 10:28; Acts 5:29). As I think of all the potential hindrances to dealing with difficult problems, this is probably the one I battle with the most, not that I always give in to it. The Lord often gives me a holy boldness for the truth. But I often find myself weighing the possible outcomes and asking myself, 'Is it worth the trouble? Will he be mad at me? Will he quit giving? Will they leave the church?' For a person with a fearful nature, these can be debilitating considerations. Only love for God and others can overcome fear (1 John 4:18).

"I also think that indifference can lead to neglect. It might be hard to believe, Joe, but Christian people, even pastors, can stop caring. It happens. In fact, think of our own church. It seems to me we are admitting that a biblical, God-honoring spirit of teamwork has been neglected. To some degree it has to be, because we, or I, don't care or at least don't care enough to do something about it. Take you and the other deacons, for instance. What if you served a church that didn't value your service, where you never saw teamwork modeled or unity insisted on? You might end up with an attitude of indifference. Even if a man is as bold as a lion and works harder than Noah preparing for rain, if he does not believe that his effort will make any difference or that no one will care whether or not he does it, or that in the end it just won't matter, then he probably won't give it his full attention. Eventually, he might stop caring altogether. He thinks, 'If no one else cares, why should I?' In his mind he knows that God cares, but he is seduced into a spiritual apathy, a spiritual indifference.

"Well, these are a few reasons why spiritual leaders might not be willing to deal with issues in the church: spiritual laziness, fear, and indifference. But I have to mention one more. I've already brought it up, and that's the problem of discouragement. Joe, this is a big problem among pastors. We preach sermons. We work hard to be faithful to God and faithful to His Word. We disciple and counsel both members and nonmembers alike. We labor to do the things a pastor should yet, often, with little to show for it. Sometimes, we wonder if anyone is listening, and that includes both men and God. Besides those things, there's our own failings, weaknesses, and sinful natures to deal with. And then, on top of it all, Satan accuses us of every kind of sin and causes us to question everything from our calling to our conversion."

"So," Joe asks, "what do you do when you are discouraged or buffeted by Satan?"

"Thankfully," explains Gary, "the Lord doesn't allow me to wallow in self-pity very long. When I sense a spirit of discouragement, I go to the Word. I can only speak for myself here, but the preciousness of Christ floods my mind and soul, lifting me above the present world and points me back to the Father. A verse that has often sustained me is 1 Peter 2:23, "[W]hen he suffered, he threatened not, but committed himself to him that judgeth righteously." Christ Himself, the Son of God, was constantly entrusting Himself to the Father. Christ knew, and we know, that His promises are sure, and in the end, He will make all things right. That's what we must do every moment of every day: keep trusting the Father, knowing that in the end He will make all things right. This precious thought, of Christ Himself, the God man, trusting the Father, drives me to the Father when I feel discouraged. If Christ Himself trusted Him, then surely, I can trust Him. And there are many more precious promises and truths that lift me up out of my discouragements. Back to my point; discouragement can be a cause for neglecting our duties.

"So, there are a number of reasons why a pastor might not deal with difficult issues. Spiritual laziness, fear, indifference, and discouragement are among the most prevalent. However, with these various reasons stated, let me come back to the fundamental issue. We must understand how important teamwork is in light of the nature of God. Not just important, Joe, it is essential! A passion to reflect God's nature will drive us to mortify the flesh and live our lives, individually and corporately as a church, for His glory."

Suddenly, Joe becomes aware that Gary is on the edge of his seat again. Joe starts to grin. He gets tickled when Gary gets worked up and passionate. Whatever discouragement he might have been feeling a moment ago, it's gone now. He's back in full shepherd mode. He has a member of his flock in front of him, and he has a word of exhortation to give him. Whatever it is, Joe is ready to be fed.

Leaning as far forward as he can without actually getting out of his chair, Gary looks straight into his eyes and says, "Joe, let me put it to you this way. *The measure of how important teamwork is to us will be the measure of our diligence in striving after it.* When we think of the many things that we allow to pull us apart and how little we fight for unity and teamwork, it ought to make us wonder if any of us adequately values reflecting the nature of our God. So, I'll say it again: the measure of how important teamwork is to us will be the measure of our diligence in striving after it." With that said, Gary slides back in his chair.

"As I listened to you explain how important this is generally," replies Joe, "I sensed how important this is to you personally. You obviously care about unity and teamwork in the church. This excites you! So, I have a question. Is it possible I'm overreacting? Is it just me? I was just remembering that I used to enjoy being a deacon. Most of the time we got along, and we actually accomplished some things. Yes, now it seems that some of the men are always bickering and complaining, and all of us get a little heated at times. And it's true that we end up tabling most issues due to a lack of agreement, which is very frustrating to me. Maybe that's it. Maybe it's just me and my pride, and the fact that I haven't understood how important unity and teamwork are to God and the church. What do you think? Am I overreacting?"

As Joe asks his question, Gary is nodding, a quick staccato nod of "I know where you're going with this, so let me answer!" As soon as Joe finishes, Gary quickly starts to answer. "Joe, I appreciate what you're doing. I think you're trying to let me off the hook by taking all the blame. That's commendable. Your observation is that, while there are signs of trouble, there isn't any outright hostility. No punches have been thrown, so let's just forget the whole thing. Maybe it will be better next meeting. Here's something I learned a long time ago. The absence of hostility is not to be confused with unity. They are not the same thing. Unity is oneness, harmony, accord. Biblical teamwork is unity in action. Unity is not simply the absence of trouble, strife, and division. A church can sail along on seemingly united waters, yet beneath the surface there are dangerous rocks and churning turbulence that threaten the unsuspecting passengers. Sometimes the dangers are hidden. They are not always out in the open, like icebergs and sand bars that cry out for attention. We might think that, as long as we're not sinking, everything must be okay.

"To stay with the sailing metaphor, the crew is disgruntled, hungry, and cold, but because there hasn't been a mutiny, the captain stays in his quarters chugging ale. No, I'm not suggesting we all drink ale. My point is this: the absence of hostility is not the same as a spirit of unity and teamwork. This is why the dangers of spiritual laziness, fear, indifference, and discouragement must be scrupulously guarded against. Otherwise, who will sound the alarm when danger arises? This is also why sins like bitterness, brooding, an unforgiving spirit, and sins of the tongue, like gossip and sarcasm, are so dangerous. These inclinations of the flesh can entice us to settle for the absence of hostility when Spirit-filled unity is the goal. When we allow these hidden sins to fester below the surface, we're sure to sail into trouble. While I agree with you that there is no open hostility among the men, I have learned to keep an eye below the surface for signs of trouble. And even if the *dis-unity* is contained, the fact that it is a problem at all should be unacceptable to us. We should always be 'endeavoring to keep the unity of the Spirit in the bond of peace.'

"Joe, herein lies a great danger. If there is a lack of harmony among the leaders of the church, there will be a lack of harmony among the members of the church. And I say these things as one who admits to sometimes overlooking signs of trouble in the hope that it will all work out in the end. I say this to my shame. My point to you, Joe, is regardless of whether great or small, we ought to be alarmed and ever on our knees whenever we find discord, but especially when we find it among the leaders of the church, both spiritual and servant leaders. So no, I don't think you are overreacting.

"Well, you need to get going, and I have some soul work to do. But let's keep our commitment to pray for one another, and let us also pray that God will do a work of grace in the hearts of all the leaders of the church. Next week?"

"I'm already looking forward to it, pastor. Lord willing, I'll see you tomorrow night at the prayer meeting."

Later that night, Joe receives an email from Gary.

Dear Joe,

What a blessing and encouragement our meetings have been. I thank God for you! After you left, I spent some time reflecting on our conversation. Specifically, the hindrances to God-honoring teamwork and my own weaknesses. A certain thought came to my mind that I want to share with you. *We should never settle for the lesser thing, simply because the greater thing is harder to achieve.* Biblical teamwork is hard work. We'll talk about that soon. But we should never settle for anything less. It might be easier, but it will never be better. If you don't mind, I have some homework for you. First, read Eph. 4 at least once a day for the next week. Get real familiar with it. Think about our discussions of unity/teamwork as you read. Second, you brought your Teamwork Manual with you tonight. Do you think it would be okay for me to borrow it for a couple of days? You can bring it to me Sunday. See you then!

SESSION 3

Finally! Joe thought the week would never pass. He loves talking about spiritual things, the things of the Lord and of his church. He deeply appreciates his pastor taking the time to disciple him, but especially the openness and honesty of their fellowship. He always loved Gary, but it's different now. Joe senses a real spiritual bond developing between the two of them. Joe hopes the day will come when he can have the same spiritual fellowship with the entire deacon board.

He's been able to share a few things with Tom, his best friend and fellow deacon. Tom's family moved to the area when he was in high school. That's where they met. Tom's reaction to the things that Gary and Joe are working through has been exciting to Joe. Tom looks forward to when all the deacons are brought into the discussions. Joe knows there will be some trying times ahead, but these last couple of weeks have given him much hope concerning the future.

This week Joe opens the meeting with prayer. Gary gets the conversation going. "Before we get into the Scriptures, I've been looking through your teamwork training manual. There's a lot of good stuff in here. For instance, I really appreciated the chart listing the characteristics of teamwork."

Gary opens the manual to the right page and hands it to Joe saying, "Go ahead and read the traits of a successful team."

As requested, Joe reads the following information.

CHARACTERISTICS OF A SUCCESSFUL TEAM

- Each member is willing to embrace a common goal.
- Each member has the necessary skills to help the team achieve the goal.
- Each member is willing to collaborate with others.

- Each member knows and accepts their individual role on the team.

- Each member is willing to accept and support the role of others.

- Each member is willing to help every other member do their very best.

- Each member trusts other members of the team.

- Each member is committed to protecting the team from division.

- Each member believes that the goal is more important than personal achievement.

When he finishes reading the list, Gary comments, "Though this isn't a Christian manual, I think Scriptures could be found to support each one of these characteristics. Let me give you a heads-up, Joe. At some point in the near future, I think this will be something I'll have the deacons do together. I'll have you come up with Scripture passages to support each of these characteristics. This will get all the deacons thinking about what a good team looks like and, at the same time, force everyone to think biblically. I think that will prove to be a valuable exercise.

"For the most part, this list is descriptive of what biblical teamwork should look like. A team of believers that looks like this would indeed be 'one.' Joe, you've been through this material before, and I may have you introduce this to the deacons when the time comes, so do you have any thoughts or observations about these characteristics that might be helpful to the others?"

Joe does have something to say about the list that he thinks will be helpful. "When the trainers went through this with us, they pointed out two things. First, it's important to know yourself. In other words, successful teams are driven by teammates who know their own strengths and weaknesses (Rom. 12:3). When each one is honest enough to acknowledge his weaknesses as well as his strengths, he can appreciate and utilize the strengths of others on the team. As a result, they will avoid volunteering for tasks that do not match their skills, which will allow someone else to flourish.

"And that leads to the second point. While it is important to know yourself, you must also know your teammates. You have to know what value each member brings to the team. When it comes to evaluating teammates, it's important to focus on strengths, not weaknesses. These two simple things are the starting point for becoming a great teammate: an honest evaluation of self, along with a genuine appreciation for the skills of others.

"There are times when the weaknesses of others have to be addressed, but it's important to do so in a positive manner. A great teammate cares first about the team, but you must also care about people. You probably saw my note in the margin: 'First cast out the beam out of thine own eye; and then shalt thou see clearly to cast out the mote out of thy brother's eye' (Mt. 7:5). In other words, focus on your own weaknesses first, then when the time is right, you'll be in a position to help others. You'll see this in the list. The first five are all about others; the last four are all about the team. The team needs every member to strive to be the best teammate, and that includes both self-evaluation and a positive and helpful attitude toward others."

"That's a great observation!" declares Gary. "When it comes to weaknesses, focus on yourself. At the same time, appreciate the strengths of others (Rom. 12:3-5). The bottom line is the team. Joe, if all of us would have that mindset—my weaknesses and your strengths—what a difference that would make. Think of the difference it would make throughout our church and among the deacons, specifically. That's an excellent thought. Thank you for pointing that out.

"I noticed in your manual a list of examples of what teams and teamwork have accomplished in the past. Examples help us grasp intangible ideas, like unity and teamwork. Do any of these examples of teamwork stand out to you?"

"Sure," replies Joe. "I don't remember all the details, but the great pyramids in Egypt, the great wall of China, and, though it might be less dramatic, the Hoover Dam. It goes without saying that one person could not have accomplished these great projects on their own."

Gary, not willing to let this moment pass, pushes the conversation in the direction of Joe and the other deacons. "As you were mentioning these examples, I was struck by something. God Himself places a premium on teamwork. He has always accomplished His plan and purposes through unified teamwork. The evidence is everywhere: His nature, His creation, His redemption, His church, the human family. Joe, do you see that divine teamwork is everywhere? Not only is it seen everywhere, but it is a pattern for the church! When everyone in the church, from officers to members, are harnessed together as one team, then everyone will be pulling in the same direction for the glory of the triune God. This includes me and my ministry as the spiritual leader of this church, and it includes you and your ministry as a deacon.

"I think the questions we have to ask ourselves are, 'Are we a united team? Are we all pulling together in the same direction in a spirit of oneness? If not, why not?' Maybe, as we talked about last week, the problem is that we don't value it enough, which comes from not understanding how vitally important teamwork is to God. Do you remember the maxim I stated last week? *The measure of how important teamwork is to us will be the measure of our diligence in striving after it.* Are we striving after it? Teamwork is important to God. Therefore, it must be important to us. Giant pyramids, great walls, and energy-producing water dams are great examples of teamwork. But the greatest example on earth," Gary pauses and adds with great emphasis, "*ought to be the church!*"

"Not trying to copy you or anything," says Joe, "but I too was struck by something as you were talking. Growing up in the church, listening to literally over a thousand sermons, sitting through hundreds of Sunday School lessons, and reading through the Bible several times on my own,

I've always enjoyed 1 Corinthians 12. As you were pressing home the point that the church, of all institutions, ought to model its behavior after the unity and teamwork that exists in the Trinity, I thought of the church as the visible body of Christ. Paul speaks of the church as a body having many members, or various parts, yet all the parts make up one body. The hand, the foot, the eye are all part of one body, and they must all work together for the good of the whole church. As Paul explains, it is not God's plan, nor is it good for us, to live and work alone. All the members make up the body, and all the members, as diverse as they are, ought to work together in unity. Working together is teamwork. This is how the body of Christ functions to the glory of God" (Rom. 15:6-6).

As Joe speaks, he's turning to the passage. "Verse 12 reads, 'For the body is one, and hath many members, and all the members of that one body, being many, are one body: so also is Christ.' When I read that, I keep expecting Paul to write, '[S]o also is the church.' But he doesn't. Instead, he writes, '[S]o also is Christ!' It seems that Paul cannot think of the church without thinking of Christ or of Christ without thinking of the church. Nor can he think of the church without thinking of the individual members all working together as one."

Smiling like the cat who ate the proverbial canary, Gary leans back in his chair, folds his arms, and says, "So, apply what you just said to the office of the deacon."

Joe replies, "You're trying to humble me again, aren't you? Okay." Once again, seeming to enjoy the challenge, he continues. "I think the application is fairly obvious. God is glorified when the deacons of a church, the body of Christ, work together as a team, modeling their unity and teamwork after the nature of God. And not only is God glorified, which is the ultimate purpose, but the church experiences greater unity and effectiveness in the world. Every individual member needs all the other members to do their part, and that is especially true of the officers of the church. And . . . I'm a deacon in this church . . . Therefore, the body is counting on me to do my part. Anything less and I—we—fail our *oughtness*. So, thank you very much; I am humbled again!" And the big grin tells Gary it's okay.

Gary sits up straight again and assures Joe he wasn't trying to humble or embarrass him, just trying to force him to make it personal. With a fist bump, Joe assures Gary that it was good for him to own the application. This unpretentious moment quickly passes, but it reveals the sweet relationship that is developing between the two men.

Without skipping a beat, Gary asks, "Do you remember that little saying, 'Two heads are better than one'? That's what came to my mind as you and I sit here talking about teamwork. In a nutshell, this is why teamwork is so important, because two are better than one. In God's kingdom, two working together are better than one working alone. Going back to 1 Corinthians 12, we could say, '[I]t takes a body'. God's plan for His people, rarely, if ever, involves working and serving alone."

This triggers a thought in Joe. "That reminds me of Ecclesiastes 4:9-12. Margarette and I memorized these verses when we were first married.

"'Two are better than one; because they have a good reward for their labor. For if they fall, one will lift up his fellow: but woe to him that is alone when he falleth; for he hath not another to help him up. Again, if two lie together, then they have heat: but how can one be warm alone? And if one prevail against him; two shall withstand him; and a threefold cord is not quickly broken.'"

"Excellent passage for what we're talking about, Joe. The vanity of being alone. Since teamwork is all about everyone pulling together to achieve a common goal, only a vain person says, 'Teamwork? I don't need a team! I'd rather do all the work myself!' I'll never forget what Matthew Henry called the proud loner in this passage: a 'covetous muckworm.' A muckworm! There's a picture for you. Do you know what a muckworm is? I had to look it up! It's the larva of a beetle that lives in the muck of mud and dung! That's what Henry thought of the person who chooses aloneness over teamwork."

With a wry smile, Joe adds, "I can see it now. At the pyramid job site in Egypt, there's a sign that reads, 'NO MUCKWORMS HIRED HERE.'"

They both enjoy a good laugh over that thought.

Striking a more serious tone, Gary says, "This brings us to the passage that I asked you to read, Ephesians 4. I see you have your Bible. Turn to that passage and read verses 1 through 3."

As soon as he finds the passage, Joe begins to read. "I therefore, the prisoner of the Lord, beseech you that ye walk worthy of the vocation wherewith ye are called, With all lowliness and meekness, with longsuffering, forbearing one another in love; Endeavoring to keep the unity of the Spirit in the bond of peace."

"Joe, in this Epistle, unity is not just one subject among many; it is the very heartbeat of the letter. You see the word *therefore* in verse 1? I know you've heard me say it before, but when you see the word *therefore*, you need to ask, 'What is it *there for*?' It signals that a conclusion is being drawn, a conclusion that is based on what was previously stated. In this case, the *therefore* in verse 1 probably points back to everything in this letter prior to Chapter 4. The letter has been gradually and systematically building up to this point. The doctrinal beginning is not simply to astound us, though astounded we are. Saints are chosen, predestined, adopted, redeemed, quickened, united in the work of Christ, and more. But these dynamic theological truths lead us to the main exhortation, which is stated in verse 1. 'Therefore,' based on these dynamic truths, 'walk worthy of the vocation wherewith ye are called,' or as the ESV has it, 'walk in a manner worthy of the calling to which you have been called.' Then, the exhortation comes to a head in the words 'endeavoring to keep the unity of the Spirit in the bond of peace.'

"The natural flow of the letter forces us to conclude that Paul has been laying the theological groundwork of God's profound grace in salvation in order to lead us to the exhortation, which is this: the privilege of *being* the children of God comes with the responsibility of *acting* like the children of God, the responsibility to live lives that live up to the tremendous blessings that have been bestowed upon us.

"Joe, you've been reading these verses all week, so I have a question for you. Does Paul tell us to live in a worthy manner and then leave it up to us to decide what that means, or does he describe what a worthy manner would look like?"

Joe takes a quick look at the verses while Gary waits. "I would say that he's describing what a worthy manner looks like in the two verses that follow. Lowliness, meekness, longsuffering, forbearing in love, and endeavoring to keep the unity in the bond of peace."

"Exactly! They're descriptive. These are virtues that ought to be visible in every believer's life. You know about indicatives and imperatives, right? You should remember these from our How to Study the Bible class. Indicatives are statements of fact. Imperatives, on the other hand, are commands. They tell us what we ought to do. Here in Ephesians, with only one exception, everything in the first three chapters is in the indicative mood.[147] In other words, everything is stated as facts.

"But in Chapter 4, Paul switches to the imperative mood, the commands. In light of God's amazing grace and mercy, which He already bestowed upon us (the indicatives), we are now commanded (the imperatives) to walk in a manner worthy of our calling. The imperative to live worthily contains certain virtues. These virtues lead us to another command found in verse 3, 'endeavoring to keep the unity of the Spirit in the bond of peace.'

---

147 In Eph. 2:11, "remember" is an imperative, but even then, it calls us to remember a past event, which is what God already accomplished for us in Christ.

"You see those books on my desk? If you don't mind, we're going to do a little Bible study right now. Take the top one, and open it at the first bookmark. When you find it, read the section that I've highlighted."

As Joe picks up the book, he takes a quick peek at the cover and sees that it is a commentary on Ephesians. When he finds the marked page, he reads, "These admonitions lead in an ascending line to the goal to be aimed for[—]preserving unity."[148]

After reading it out loud, Joe reads it to himself a few times. He puts the book down and picks up his Bible again. He studies the verses. Gary can see that the wheels are turning, so he lets Joe mull it over.

Finally, Joe says, "So, working backward, Paul is telling us that, if we want to experience peace in the church, we must work at keeping, or preserving, unity in the church, and the steps to unity and peace are the four virtues he listed. Is that right?"

"You're spot on, Joe. Verses 2 and 3 explain what he means in verse 1. In other words, the virtues explain what a worthy life looks like. Okay, turn to the second bookmark in the same book, and when you find it, go ahead and read. This will give us the very important definition of endeavoring."

Joe finds the place and reads, "The verb translated as *endeavoring to keep* means 'be zealous, eager, take pains, make every effort.'"[149]

As Joe reads the definition of the Greek verb, Gary gets up and walks to the bookshelf directly behind his desk and pulls out a few books. As he stacks them on his desk, Joe finishes reading.

"In order to give due diligence and adhere to 2 Timothy 2:15," Gary says, "let's confirm that O'Brien's definition is correct."

---

148 Peter T. O'Brien, *The Letter to the Ephesians*, The Pillar N.T. Commentary, (Grand Rapids, MI: Erdmans, 1999) p. 276.

149 Ibid, p. 279.

For the next few minutes, Gary leads Joe through several lexicons, expository dictionaries, and a good concordance. Joe is having a blast and Gary is a happy shepherd as they search through the various resources. Although Gary clearly knows beforehand what they will find, he believes this will prove to be a good exercise for Joe. Joe's enthusiasm in the process confirms that he is right. With Joe still leaning over the books, Gary continues the teaching moment.

"Because Greek is much more nuanced than English," Gary explains, "the English translation doesn't always communicate the full impact of the Greek text. If Paul was speaking this and we could hear the tone of his voice, we would detect passion, urgency, and perhaps even a tone of righteous impatience with all who would dilly-dally or lag behind. He's saying, 'What are you waiting for? Get busy! It's your privilege and responsibility to be doing this. Empowered by the Spirit who dwells within you, this is something you should always be working at!' And as you pointed out, Joe, this is what he means by living in a manner that is worthy of being called the children of God. As children of a gracious and merciful Father, we must live in a way that reflects our privileged status.

"This, in fact, is why he's writing, to urge us to live in such a way that is worthy of the marvelous grace and mercy that is ours through Christ. And what does a worthy life look like? Humility, gentleness, patience, and bearing with one another in love. But these virtues lead us to the key issue: the *absolute importance* of unity and, by implication, the necessity of teamwork in the local church. Above all else, unified teamwork, or unity in action, is the one thing that will demonstrate we truly understand and appreciate the gracious blessings of God that are ours through Christ Jesus our Lord.

"Furthermore, if we eagerly and persistently pursue unity in the church, it will act as an agent of peace in a chaotic and dangerous world. Living in unity will be challenging. It will be hard work. At times, it will be costly. To ensure that we are able to live and work in unity, God has given us His Spirit to empower and strengthen us for the task. While it is His work, we are responsible to make every effort to maintain it. By a lack of strenuous effort on our part, we will be resisting the work of the Spirit."

As Gary repositions himself in the chair, with a little shrug of the shoulders, his arms are suddenly reaching out and the palms of his hands face each other like a man holding an invisible basketball. Joe instinctively senses he needs to pay attention to this.

"Joe, this is a very important point. The Spirit of God Himself is seeking to promote unity in the church! It is the 'unity of the Spirit.' The Phillips translation reads, 'But if you heed my instruction you will be one with the Spirit and you will be at peace with one another.'"

Gary pauses long enough for Joe to jump in with a question. "Could we say that if we—and I'm thinking now of the deacons—ignore these virtues and the command to strive for unity, it could be an indication of how little we understand or, even worse, how little we value what God has done for us?"

"Great observation, Joe. Go on."

"Verse 1," continues Joe, "speaks of walking or living lives that are worthy of the blessings to which we have been called, living life in light of God's grace. What does it say about us if we do not live out these virtues and ignore this command? It would suggest that all that came before this is," Joe searches for the right word, "is unpersuasive, that the great work of God in Christ to save poor dead sinners by His grace and for His glory just doesn't move us, or at least not adequately. It seems as though Paul writes these things because he expects us to be moved. And being moved, he expects us to do these things, to live these virtues. And considering that we have the aid of the Word and his Spirit, we are without excuse!"

Joe looks like he has more to say, so Gary waits for him to organize his thoughts. Then, as if a light goes on, he continues. "If we are not moved by these things . . . then maybe it's an indication that we either do not have the Spirit of God living in us or we are sinfully rebelling against the leading of the Spirit in our lives. I know there might be other causes, but unbelief and disobedience have to be considered.

"Reading Chapter 4 this week, I was struck by the words *one body and one Spirit* (v. 4) and the command, 'Do not grieve the Holy Spirit of God' (v. 30). Because the Spirit is living in us, He is grieved when we resist His leading to live what God has already made us: one body." Joe pauses again, and his eyes dart back and forth as he searches for the right words to express his thoughts. "As a deacon, not just a Christian, but someone in the church who is supposed to be full of wisdom and the Holy Spirit, my life must demonstrate that I am submitting to, not grieving, the Spirit. And the starting point for demonstrating submission to the Spirit is living out the virtues listed in verses 2 and 3."

"Joe," responds Gary, "I'm humbled by your sensitivity to the Word, the leading of God's Spirit, and the seeming ease you have with making hard personal applications. Look at my arms—goosebumps! I should have been taking notes! You connected the dots from 'one body and one Spirit' to the necessary virtues; then you drew a line to the Holy Spirit and grieving Him.

"Paul contrasts the lives they used to live as Gentiles, or unbelievers, with their new lives in Christ, which he describes as 'created after the likeness of God in true righteousness and holiness' (v. 24). The Holy Spirit not only makes us alive in Christ, He works in us to conform us to the image of Christ in righteousness and holiness. The primary means that the Spirit uses in transforming us after the image of Christ is the Word (Eph. 6:17; 1 Pet. 1:23; Heb. 4:12). The Word is, shall I say, the atmosphere in which the Spirit works. The Spirit leads us to the Word, the Word leads us to grace, grace leads us to humble gratitude, and humble gratitude stirs us to joyful obedience. So yes, you are right. If we are not moved by His great grace in and through Christ, then that would be an indication that either we do not have his Spirit in us or we are not submitting ourselves to the Word. And when that happens, the Spirit is grieved.

"Don't get me wrong, Joe. Every true Christian wants to be like Christ. I know you want to please God, to live in harmony with His will. How do I know that? Because the Spirit of God is in you, creating a desire to be conformed to the image of Christ. As John explains, this is the reason every believer not only does not practice sin, but cannot practice sin. John acknowledges that we do, in fact, sin. We lie if we say we do not. But he means, of course, that sin is not our habit. We are not practitioners of sin. You have your Bible open. Flip over to 1 John 3:9."

When Joe finds it, he reads, "'Whosoever is born of God doth not commit sin; for his seed remaineth in him: and he cannot sin, because he is born of God.'"

"Now read 5:3," Gary says.

"'For this is the love of God, that we keep his commandments: and his commandments are not grievous.'"

Gary explains, "Even though every believer finds it very hard at times to live consistent with his profession, he does not consider it a burden, or as the KJV reads, 'grievous.' Every true Christian loves God, strives to keep His commandments, and doesn't find it a burden to do so. It is what he desires, longs for, and fights for, when necessary. This is how I know every believer wants to live like Christ, to be conformed to His image. And how does John explain this phenomenon? The dead sinner has been born of God (John 3:3; 1 John 2:29, 3:9-11). The Spirit, who now lives within, will not allow the child of God to carelessly live in disobedience. When we do, then what happens? God disciplines and corrects us. Why? Because He loves us (Heb. 12). That's as much a fact as the new birth itself!"

Gary is slowly getting more and more animated. His hands and arms are now gesturing with every word. He's inching closer and closer to the edge of his chair. Joe has often seen Gary get passionate, both in the pulpit and out of the pulpit. He loves it! He loves to see his pastor get stirred up when teaching the Word. As Gary continues, Joe hangs on every word.

"How important is a spirit of unified teamwork in the church? It's everything!" Gary exclaims. "It is a visible, tangible outcome of our redemption. It is how the church expresses that it understands both the nature of God and the inestimable worth of its calling! It's how we demonstrate our love for one another! It's how we make an impact on the lost world! This is the message of Ephesians. This message is found throughout the entire Bible. And once fully embraced, we will never again settle for a *lesser thing*, a splintered and divided body, when the *greater thing*, a unified body, is not only for our own good, but resounds to the glory of the Father who designed it all. We ought to love unified teamwork in the church and hate anything that threatens it. Do you see how important unity and teamwork are, Joe?"

"I feel like a NASCAR driver racing with my head out the window," exclaims Joe. "I'm blown away! I know I need to think about these things to let them soak in, but to answer your question, I'll say I'm learning to understand the importance of unified teamwork in the church. When I say I'm blown away, I mean both my mind and my spirit. In my mind, I'm overwhelmed, and in my spirit, I'm convicted. Oneness and teamwork with others are the evidence of being one with Christ. Since I have allowed sinful attitudes to creep in and cause division between myself and some of the other deacons in this church, I have to conclude I've been resisting and grieving the Spirit of God! Instead, I need to die to myself and live for Christ and others."

"Indeed," responds Gary, "die to self and live for Christ and others. That's a very Christ-like way of living: death to self for the sake of others. Philippians 2:3-8 states, 'Let nothing be done through strife or vainglory; but in lowliness of mind let each esteem other better than themselves. Look not every man on his own things, but every man also on the things of others. Let this mind be in you, which was also in Christ Jesus: Who, being in the form of God, thought it not robbery to be equal with God: But made himself of no reputation. And took upon him the form of a servant, and was made in the likeness of men: And being found in fashion as a man, he humbled himself, and became obedient unto death, even the death of the cross.'"

Joe adds, "Amen to that, but it is so hard, isn't it? An *others-minded-ness*, born out of love."

"Joe, I very much appreciate your own humble spirit. I know you won't give yourself any credit, but I will. When you came to me a few weeks ago, you described the inner turmoil you were going through over the problems you were experiencing in the meetings and the general ineffectiveness of the deacons. Well, that inner turmoil you were experiencing was conviction. That's the same conviction I was under as I prayed for wisdom and strength. The Spirit and the Word were already speaking to you, and you were listening. That's a testimony to you being a genuine child of God and a testimony to the fact that you came in here ready to take the fight to the enemy."

Looking at his watch, Gary tells Joe this would be a good place to end their session. "In the meantime," he says, "let's continue praying for one another. I am extremely thankful to God for this time together, Joe. Also, it's a blessing to know that you are lifting me up to the throne of grace. As promised, I'll continue praying for you as you seek to be submissive to Christ in everything you do.

"I would like to conclude our time this morning by reading a prayer from *The Valley of Vision, A Collection of Puritan Prayers and Devotions*. This one is entitled 'JOURNEYING ON.'"

LORD OF THE CLOUD AND FIRE

I am a stranger, with a stranger's indifference;

My hands hold a pilgrim's staff,

My march is Zionward,

My eyes are toward the coming of the Lord,

My heart is in thy hands without reserve.

Thou hast created it,

redeemed it,

renewed it,

captured it,

conquered it.

Keep from it every opposing foe,

crush it in every rebel lust,

mortify every treacherous passion

annihilate every earthborn desire.

All faculties of my being vibrate to thy touch;

I love thee with soul, mind, body, strength,

might, spirit, affection, will,

desire, intellect, understanding.

Thou art the very perfection of all perfections;

All intellect is derived from thee;

My scanty rivulets flow from thy unfathomable fountain.

Compared with thee the sun is darkness,

all beauty deformity,

all wisdom folly,

the best goodness faulty.

Thou art worthy of an adoration greater than my dull heart

can yield;

Invigorate my love that it might rise worthily to thee,

tightly entwine itself round thee,

be allured by thee.

Then shalt my walk be endless praise.

Amen.[150]

Before Joe leaves, Gary gives him some homework. First, he gives him a copy of *The Valley of Vision* and asks him to pick out a prayer for next week. Second, he gives him a list of verses he compiled that address the subjects of unity and teamwork. He tells Joe, "Just take a look at these over the next couple of weeks. No special assignment or anything. Just read them, and if you want to talk about any of them, we can do that."

Joe takes the paper from Gary and takes a quick look. He sees the following verses and thinks to himself, "Wow, it's a long list:" Ps. 133:1-3; Prov. 27:17, 11:14; Eccl. 4:9-12; John 17:22-23; Acts 4:32; Rom. 12:4-8,16; 1 Cor. 1:10, 10:16-17, 12:4-31; Gal. 3:26-28; Eph. 1:10; Eph. 2:14, 17-22; Eph. 4:3-16; Col. 3:13-14; Heb. 10:24-25, 11:25; 1 Pet. 2:9-10, 3:8, 4:8-11; 1 John. 5:1-2.

Then to Gary, he says, "I might not get them all read by next week, but I'll definitely get them read." With a fold of the paper, a smile, and a warm handshake, Joe is off to work.

The following night, Joe begins to read the passages that were intentionally chosen by his pastor. At first, he reads, thinks on the passage for a moment, and then moves on. But when he reads John 17:22-23, "And the glory which thou gavest me I have given them: that they may be one, even as we are one: I in them, and thou in me, that they may be made perfect in one: and that the world may know that thou hast sent me, and hast loved them, as thou hast loved me," something in Joe changes. Now, instead of just reading through a list, his mind is arrested by the words. Everything

---

150 *Valley of Vision* (East Peoria, IL: Versa Press, Inc., 1975), 108.

slows down. He's more intentional, more sensitive, keenly aware of the fact that he is reading of holy communion between the Son and the Father. As he opens his mind and heart to what Jesus is saying, the Spirit drives the words of Christ deep into his soul, "[T]hat they may be one, even as we are one."

"One . . . as we are one." For the next hour, Joe reads and rereads, meditates on, and is stirred by the entire High Priestly prayer recorded in Chapter 17. He staggers over the words in verse 23, "[T]hat the world may know that thou hast sent me, and hast loved them, as thou hast loved me."

At this point the tears in his eyes prevent him from reading further, so he silently offers up a doxology of praise to the Father, Son, and Spirit for the inestimable treasure of being one with the Father, one with the Son, and one with fellow believers, and for his pastor who cares for his soul as "one who must give an account." Before heading to the family room to share these precious moments with Margarette, Joe resolves that, starting tomorrow, he will go back to the beginning of the list of verses and give them their due attention, which he does over the next few weeks.

Joe doesn't fully comprehend what's happening in his heart and mind, but the Spirit of God is at work. This will become evident to both Joe and Gary over the next few weeks as Joe yields to the leading of the Spirit in his life. But for now, all Joe knows for sure is that he will never look at the office of the deacon, or the church family as a whole, the same ever again.

CHAPTER 8

A DIALOGUE ON TEAMWORK, PART 2

SESSION 4

In the week since their last meeting, Joe has been poring over the Scriptures his pastor assigned him. Being in the Word has stirred his heart, and he is overflowing with love for God, his Son, and the Word itself. He is actually aware that his mind is being renewed and his life is being transformed more and more into the image of Jesus Christ (Ro. 12:2; 2 Co. 3:18).

As he walks into the office and sees Gary, he immediately starts to share what God is doing in his life, and not just his life, but in Margarette's as well. She's been reading the passages on her own, and together they share, and fellowship, and praise God for His grace and blessings on their lives. The list of Scriptures on unity have driven them to their knees as they have confessed their own failure to always strive for "the unity of the Spirit in the bond of peace" (Eph. 4:3).

As their pastor, Gary is both ecstatic and humbled. His heart is full of joy for the spiritual growth he sees in this precious family. As Joe wraps up his comments, Gary impulsively goes in for a big ol' man hug. As they step back, each unashamedly dabs tears from his eyes.

Breaking up the somewhat awkward moment, Gary exclaims, "As much as I enjoy talking about this spiritual journey we're on, we have a lot to cover this morning and you have to be at work by eight, so let's get started. In the previous weeks, we've talked about the foundational truth that motivates us to strive for a spirit of unified teamwork: the nature of God. God is one and expects, even demands, that we live and work as one. Knowing this foundational truth is the beginning point. However, knowing it is not enough. Knowledge is not a magical wand that makes everything right. Even if we know how important teamwork is to God, we must be prepared to work at it. Remember, we are already one in Christ, yet we have to make every effort to maintain unity and teamwork in the church.

"Because of the flesh, unity is fragile, and we must be ready to deal with the challenges that threaten to tear us apart. And, if our unity does unravel, either between individuals or the whole church, how do we pick up the pieces and put it all back together again? These are important questions. It's not *if* challenges come, but *when* they come. So, I think we need to talk about the difficulty of preserving teamwork and the difficulty of restoring teamwork in the church once it is lost. I've hinted at these in our previous conversations, but I think it will be beneficial to focus our attention on them for a few minutes this morning.

"Once again, Joe, we're not able to dig real deep and mine every nugget of gold in our brief Tuesday morning conversations. As you very well know, there are books, training manuals, and seminars that deal with teamwork. Some are very helpful and should be explored. Perhaps as we move forward, the deacons can take advantage of some biblically sound, team-oriented resources. In fact, I would encourage that. However, today's conversation on teamwork will be more focused, specifically the difficulties of preserving and restoring teamwork. You have hinted at these issues a couple of times in our conversations, so I know these are concerns that you have as a deacon.

"As we start with the difficulty of preserving Spirit-empowered teamwork, we have to begin with the big picture. Why is biblical, God-honoring, Christ-centered, Spirit-empowered teamwork so hard for us? After all, if these things were easy, every church would know the blessings of 'the unity of the Spirit in the bond of peace.' But it's not easy. So, we're forced to ask, why? The answer is actually quite simple. Joe, if I ask you, 'What do you think is the single greatest reason that teamwork is so hard to keep, and so hard to fix when it's broken?' how would you answer?"

"Well, it seems pretty obvious," replies Joe. "I would have to say the problem of sin."

"Exactly! Sin. Once we identify sin as the fundamental problem, we then understand why overcoming our self-centered natures and living in unity is so hard. Because overcoming sin is hard work. Mortifying the flesh is painful. And not only painful, but as long as we are in our mortal bodies, it is a never-ending struggle. Furthermore, to add one more degree of difficulty, the whole man has been affected by sin. There is not one part of us that is not fallen and tainted by sin. Charles Spurgeon said, 'As the salt flavors every drop in the Atlantic, so sin does affect every atom of our nature.' Not exactly a recipe for unity and teamwork, is it?

"So, sin is the problem. But let's take it one more step. The reason that sin is so hard to overcome—and we're talking about believers here—has to do with the nature of the battle against sin. It is by nature a *spiritual* battle. In biblical terms, it's *spiritual warfare*. Paul describes the entire Christian life as a spiritual battle between the flesh and the Spirit (Gal. 5:16-18; Rom.

7:14-25). To the church at Ephesus, the letter that calls for strenuous effort to live in unity, Paul warns, 'For we wrestle not against flesh and blood, but against principalities, against powers, against the rulers of the darkness of this world, against spiritual wickedness in high places' (Eph. 6:12). Peter exhorts, 'Be sober, be vigilant; because your adversary the devil, as a roaring lion, walketh about, seeking whom he may devour' (1 Pet. 5:8). The Scriptures declare we are opposed on every side by the world, the flesh, and the devil. Every effort to either *preserve* or *restore* unified teamwork in the church will be opposed. It's the nature of the battle.

"It is exactly because of the spiritual nature of the work that Paul commands us to equip ourselves with the whole armor of God (Eph. 6:10-18). Not physical armor, of course, but spiritual armor that is provided only by God. We can't just run down to the local Army surplus store for battle-ready spiritual uniforms. The weapons of man will not equip us for spiritual battle. No, Paul wrote to the church at Corinth, 'For though we walk in the flesh, we do not war after the flesh: (For the weapons of our warfare are not carnal, but mighty through God to the pulling down of strongholds). Casting down imaginations, and every high thing that exalts itself against the knowledge of God, and bringing into captivity every thought to the obedience of Christ' (2 Cor. 10:3-5). Living and walking in the Spirit is hard because of the nature of the battle against sin. It's spiritual warfare.

"Here is a short spiritual warfare quote that I remember. John Piper said, 'Life is war. That's not all it is. But it is always that.'[151] That's a good reminder that we are always in the battle."

Gary remembers something and crosses the office to the section of his library marked "Christian Living." He pulls out J. C. Ryle's book *Holiness.* As he opens the book he says, "There's a page here in the introduction that I have bent the corner over. Listen to this: 'Is it wise to teach believers that they ought not to think so much of fighting and struggling against sin, but

---

151 https://www.epm.org/resources/2010/Mar/2/quotes-regarding-spiritual-warfare.

ought rather to "yield themselves to God," and be passive in the hands of Christ? Is this according to the proportion of God's Word? I doubt it. A holy violence, a conflict, a warfare, a fight, a soldier's life, a wrestling, are spoken of as characteristic of the true Christian . . . If Christian in *Pilgrim's Progress* simply "yielded himself " to God, and never fought, or struggled, or wrestled, I have read the famous allegory in vain."[152]

"The biblical record is clear, Joe. The Christian life is spiritual warfare!"

Gary pauses for a moment, obviously thinking about something. "It just occurred to me, Joe, that maybe I need to back up for a moment. I'm talking about the difficulty of preserving unity and teamwork in the body of Christ. It starts with recognizing the nature of the battle. But let's not get the cart before the horse. There's another issue that has to be settled first. How do we *achieve* spiritual unity and teamwork in the first place?"

With Gary staring a hole through him, Joe realizes he's supposed to answer. To buy some time, he slowly repeats the question, "How do we achieve unity?" As he thinks about the question, he nervously reaches up and rubs the back of his neck. "How do we achieve unity? That's like asking, 'How or when does our unity begin?' Also, the question assumes that it is something that we achieve. I don't know. I'm thinking of a possible answer, but I'll let you answer first." In an exaggerated serious tone, with a wry smile and a wink he quickly adds, "I'll let you know if you're right."

"Well, it's kind of a trick question," Gary replies. "I'm not surprised you had trouble with it. How do we achieve unity? Actually, we don't! I'd better explain. Going back to Ephesians 4, we are commanded to give every effort or be diligent to do what?"

Joe answers, "Keep the unity of the Spirit in the bond of peace."

"That's right. *Keep* the unity. *Keep* speaks of something that we already have. You can't keep what you don't have, right? Paul assumes we

---

152 J.C. Ryle, Holiness (Hertfordshire, England: Evangelical Press, 1987), p. xvi.

already have unity. But where did it come from? Hold on Joe, this will blow you away. The answer begins before the foundations of the world. Unity *originates* in the eternal plan of the Father to 'bless us in Christ with every spiritual blessing in the heavenly places, even as he chose us in him before the foundation of the world.' The Father's plan is to bless us in Christ, with unity, with oneness. This is according to 'the purpose of him who works all things according to the counsel of his own will' (Eph. 1:3, 4, 11). In time, it is *achieved* in the redeeming cross-work of his Son. Christ Himself has already achieved our unity for us. If you would, Joe, open to Ephesians 2 and read verses 13 to 16."

Joe reads, "'But now in Christ Jesus, ye who sometimes were far off are made nigh by the blood of Christ. For he is our peace, who hath made both one—'"

Gary interrupts, "Stop right there, Joe. Read that again. Has what?"

"Made both one."

Gary then points out, "'Hath made' is past tense. Already one! Already achieved. Keep reading."

Joe picks up where he left off, "'[A]nd hath broken down the middle wall of partition between us; Having abolished the enmity, even the law of commandments contained in ordinances; for to make in himself of twain one new man, so making peace; And that he might reconcile both unto God in one body by the cross, having slain the enmity thereby.'"

"So Joe, when did He make us *one new man in place of two*?" asks Gary.

Joe answers like a man who has just discovered something important. "When he died for us on the cross!" Reading from verse 15 again to continue his discovery, "'[S]o making peace . . . that he might reconcile both unto God in one body by the cross.'"

Gary jumps in to continue the explanation. "It's finished, Joe! Biblical unity, out of which biblical teamwork flows, *originates* with the Father, is *accomplished* through his Son and graciously *applied* through the working of the Spirit. Having accomplished, or to put it another way, having *achieved* our unity for us, a unity with God and all believers that we could not achieve on our own, it is now our responsibility to what? Back to Ephesians 4. Diligently keep it! Preserve it!

"Joe, this is why it is so important for us to work in unity and teamwork. The unity that we are to prize was achieved by the triune God, each divine member working together for our benefit. And think of the great cost to unite us as one body. The Father sacrificed his Son! No wonder the Spirit is grieved when we do not live and work in unity! No wonder Paul is so adamant that we quickly, earnestly, and constantly work at *keeping* unity in the church. Anything less fails to appreciate what it took to *achieve* unity—the death of Christ!

"Think of it, Joe. Unity, our union with Christ and one another, is an ever-present reality. It can't be lost! It can't be destroyed! It cannot even be diminished! What would it say about the Father's love or the cross of Christ if we could lose our unity? No! Unity is simply ours to enjoy. Amazing reality. Amazing unity. But here comes the real challenge. We can only enjoy the unity that is already ours in Christ when we *live* in unity."

Joe waves his hand above his head and says, "Time out! You lost me. If we can't lose it, then why are we exhorted to keep it? You said *keeping* implies we already have it. But doesn't *keep* also imply that it can be lost? What am I missing?"

Gary laughs. "An excellent question! I'm glad you spoke up. Let me see if I can explain this. As an eternal reality, the unity we have in Christ and with one another in Christ cannot be shaken. Because of the finished work of Christ, unity is ours, and we can never lose it. However, perfect unity will not be fully *realized* as long as we are in these bodies of flesh. This is one of the reasons we long for heaven, to fully experience the blessings that have already been won for us. But to experience and enjoy unity as a present reality, right now, we must work at keeping it. And lest we forget, keeping unity alive cannot be separated from the virtues in verse 2 and the diligent effort in verse 3. In other words, we must be practicing those virtues, and strenuously working to live in unity, which is to walk, or live in the Spirit."

"Maybe it's just me," says Joe, "but that's a pretty deep thought. Unity is already ours to enjoy, but we have to work at it. It might take me a while to wrap my head around that."

"Sometimes it helps to hear it from someone else," Gary replies. "I kept a couple of the commentaries from last week on my desk." Gary gets up and sits on the corner of his desk while reaching for the books. After thumbing through a few pages, he says, "Here's John Eadie. Listen to this. He writes, 'And this unity of the Spirit was not so completely in their possession, that its existence depended wholly on their guardianship.'[153] Did you hear that, Joe? The existence of unity does not depend on our ability to guard it. Let me keep reading: 'For it exists independently of human vigilance or fidelity, but its manifestations may be thwarted and checked.'

"It is independent or outside of us. Then what do we have to do with unity? What role do we play? We hinder the 'manifestation' of unity. Through our diligent effort, unity is made visible and is experienced and enjoyed. On the other hand, it is tarnished and its beauty and enjoyment are stiff-armed by our carelessness and neglect. Sin prevents us from enjoying the unity that God graciously provides through Christ."

Gary continues reading Eadie: "'They were therefore to keep it safe from all disturbance and infraction. And in this duty they were to be earnest and forward . . . using diligence . . . for if they cherished humility,

---

153 John Eadie. Epistle to the Ephesians. (Minneapolis: James and Klock Christian Publishing Co., 1977), 271.

meekness, and universal tolerance in love, as the apostle enjoined them, it would be no difficult task to preserve the "unity of the Spirit.'"

"He's saying it is our responsibility to keep unity safe from being disturbed and divided. Again, we keep safe what was already achieved for us. So, unity is pictured as a valuable treasure won by Christ, but it is now in the believer's possession and must be protected, guarded, or kept. And what about this statement, '[I]t would be no difficult task to preserve the unity of the Spirit'? That sounds impossible, until you reread what he says just before that, which is, '*if* they cherish humility, meekness, and universal tolerance in love.' Keep these virtues, and it will not be difficult to keep unity safe. In reality, though, it is very hard to cherish and practice these virtues. Why? Again, because of the spiritual nature of the battle. We must fight for the continued development of every virtue."

Gary puts Eadie down, opens O'Brien's commentary, and reads, "'Without these graces which are essential to their life together, they would have no hope of maintaining the unity of the Spirit.'[154] Maintaining, keeping, preserving the unity which they already have in Christ. But to this Paul adds, 'The "unity of the Spirit" is to be maintained "in the bond of peace," that is, in the bond which consists of peace.'"

Gary's hand skims over the page to another spot and he reads, "'Ultimately, the unity and reconciliation that have been won through Christ's death,'" Gary pauses, "Let me repeat that." "'Ultimately, the unity and reconciliation that have been won through Christ's death (2:14-18) are part and parcel of God's intention of bringing all things together into unity in Christ (1:9, 10). Since the church has been designed by God to be the masterpiece of His goodness and the pattern on which the reconciled universe of the future will be modelled (see on 2:7), believers are expected to live in a manner consistent with this divine purpose. To *keep* this unity

---

154 Peter T. O'Brien, *The Letter to the Ephesians*, The Pillar N.T. Commentary, (Grand Rapids, MI: Erdmans, 1999), p. 279

must mean to maintain it *visibly*. If the unity of the Spirit is real, it must be transparently evident, and believers have a responsibility before God to make sure that this is so.'"[155]

"Wow, that's staggering." Gary pauses for a moment as his voice cracks with emotion and his eyes well up with tears. His heart is stirred as he thinks of Christ who loved the church and gave Himself for her. He stares at the page for a moment before continuing, "'The church is the masterpiece of his goodness, the pattern on which the reconciled universe will be modeled.'" I love that! 'The masterpiece of his goodness.' That thought is absolutely staggering. Joe, one dimension of God's goodness to the church is His gift of unity. And rather than leave it up to us to acquire it, He acquired it for us in His Son and calls on us to guard it, to keep it safe. To say that unity and teamwork are important is an understatement! It's what Paul calls living worthy of our calling. I get the feeling Paul comprehends what unity means to God when he implores us to walk worthy of our calling."

"Joe, the doctrine of unity is so wide, so high, so deep, it's an all-encompassing reality. It reaches into eternity past and stretches out into eternity future. It touches every doctrine of the Bible: from redemption to sanctification to the fruit of the Spirit to body life to fellowship with God. To follow Paul's train of thought, he commands unity in verse 4, then follows that up with a string of realities that have unity, or oneness, at their core. One body, one Spirit, one hope, one Lord, one faith, one baptism, one God and Father of all. Unity is the touchstone of them all! As I said, it's an all-encompassing reality, and here's the thing to bear in mind: it is ours for the enjoying, as long as we work at keeping it.

"Well, we have to move on, but the main things to remember are that unity has already been achieved for us by Christ, and now it is our responsibility to guard it by living a virtuous life that is empowered by the Spirit.

---

155 Ibid, p. 279.

And not only will we have the joy of living like Christ, but we will enjoy the blessing of unity in the present as we wait for its perfect completion in the future" (Eph. 1:10).

Gary thinks Joe needs a little break, so he suggests they walk to the fellowship hall to get a refill on their coffee. A little caffeine sounds good to Joe. No words are spoken as they walk to the kitchen. Each is lost in the wonder of unity already achieved. After filling their cups, Gary gestures toward a table, and they sit to continue their conversation.

Gary starts it up by saying, "Joe, I want to return to the spiritual nature of the battle. That's what we were talking about before I asked how unity is achieved. While every individual believer must be on guard, I believe Satan's most devious weapons and darkest fury are aimed at the church, the body of Christ. It is the church that is in his crosshairs. Jesus said, 'I will build my church and the gates of hell shall not prevail against it' (Mt. 16:18). He's saying that the church, His church, as a mighty army will trample down the forces of evil as they vainly defend their dark strongholds. Yet, Satan will not meekly lay down. He is described as a raging, roaring, bloodthirsty lion, seeking someone to destroy (1 Pet. 5:8). And I think that especially applies to the church's officers.

"Paul writes in Ephesians 3:10, '[S]o that through the church the manifold wisdom of God might now be made known to the rulers and authorities in the heavenly places' (ESV). Do you see that? The multifaceted, multidimensional wisdom of God is being made known to whom? The 'rulers and authorities in the heavenly places.' This speaks of demons, their rank-and-file leadership structure, and it leads all the way up to the top, to Satan himself. In the face of this dark army, there is an institution that is making God's wisdom known to them. And what entity is doing that? The church!

"Think about it. The church is revealing God's power and wisdom to the universe. It's on display for everyone to see. Joe, I love this! This is God's

Word, and He is taunting Satan with it. We get the picture of God saying to the dark tyrant of evil, 'Do not think for a moment you can defeat Me or My church. Look! Watch! Oh, you may trouble them, but try as you might, you cannot defeat them. Did you not hear My victorious Son declare that He would not lose one (John. 6:37-39)? Do you not remember when He paraded His defeated and quivering foes before the courts of heaven (Col. 2:15)?' Doesn't it sound like God is taunting Satan in His Word?

"Do you think Satan will accept this without a challenge? Do you think he's just going to lie down and take it without a fight? Not the roaring lion that the Bible describes. No, not for a minute! It is for this reason that the church is constantly and insidiously under spiritual attack. Satan opposes every aspect of the church. But of all the dimensions of body life, perhaps the thing that he hates the most is our unity. Every time our unity is attacked, every connective tissue of the church body is under attack. This is why the church and her leaders must remain united, to show our enemy that we cannot be divided and we cannot be defeated. We remain one united and mighty army.

"Joe, this is very important. Unity and teamwork reflect the nature of God. And this must drive Satan mad! It must infuriate him! While God has given us an entire panoply to withstand Satan's attacks, unity is one of the most valuable weapons against the kingdom of darkness."

"This reminds me," chimes in Joe, "of the hymn, *Onward Christian Soldiers*: 'We are not divided, All one body we, One in faith and Spirit, One eternally. Onward Christian soldiers, marching as to war, with the cross of Jesus, going on before.'"

"Yes," shouts Gary, as he pounds a fist into his open hand. "One united body of soldiers on the march, taking the fight to the enemy. I love it! And through biblical, spiritual unity, and teamwork, we lock arms and make the line stronger."

Joe still has his Bible on his lap, so he quickly turns over just a few pages and adds, "This reminds me of Philippians 1:27 and 28: '[S]tand fast in one spirit, with one mind striving together for the faith of the gospel; And in nothing terrified by your adversaries: which is to them an evident token of perdition, but to you of salvation, and that of God.'"

"Amen," responds Gary. "Standing fast and striving together pictures a contest." Gary jumps up and grabs another Eadie commentary off the shelf. This one is in Philippians. As his eyes scan the page, he begins reading various relevant statements. "'The Philippians were to stand in one spirit, united in their inmost conviction, and they were to strive with one soul[—]those convictions not allowed to be latent, but stirring up volition, sympathy, and earnest cooperation. Such concord was essential to success . . . the character of true mind and soul, a self-formed *esprit de corps*, what a power it has! As concert is indispensable to victory, should there not be mutual cooperation[—]striving together? But not only are unity and mutual support necessary to this conflict on behalf of the faith[—]there must also be a calm and steadfast courage.'"[156]

He closes the book and returns it to its place on the shelf. "Striving together in unity, and unity in action is teamwork, and it is essential to victory. Locking arms. No weak links. Collective effort. This is the value of teamwork. Teamwork is like a spiritual force field. When it is strong, we are strong together. But when it is weak, we expose the entire church to danger. Okay, I can't believe I just said 'spiritual forcefield.' I went 'Star Trek' on you. Seriously, though, without unified teamwork, we will be weak, vulnerable, and open to attack. We dare not diminish the importance of unity and teamwork in the church. To do so would play into the hands of Satan.

"Here's another thing to think about, Joe. As a deacon in the church, you will want to listen to this. While the entire church is under attack,

---

156 Eadie, *Philippians* (Minneapolis: James and Klock Christian Publishing Co., 1977), p. 72.

no one is in more danger than the officers of the church. It's as if we walk around with a big bullseye on our back with the words, 'Shoot Here.'"

"Speaking of officers getting shot," replies Joe, "I think we all know that, if you take out the officers, you create a leadership vacuum and that can demoralize undisciplined troops. Going back to the American Revolution, the colonists used snipers to intentionally kill British officers. It makes sense that Satan's troops would focus on the officers of the church. They're like Satan's snipers, if you will. Sorry, it was the visual of the bullseye on our backs that made me think of that."

"No problem," says Gary as he laughs over Joe's observation. "Satan's snipers! Nice! If I'm not mistaken, both William Gurnall and John Bunyan said that Satan snipes at the saints. Since you brought up snipers, let me add that Satan also has his spies. This is the tactic of infiltration or, as we call it today, being embedded. Paul warns Satan that disguises himself as an angel of light. It is no surprise then that Satan's minions disguise themselves as servants of righteousness (2 Cor. 11:14-15). Satanic spies! It would be naïve to think there is no mastermind behind false teachers who infiltrate the church, a devious orchestrator whose passion is to destroy the church. The devious dividers of unity have been planted by their captain, the devil. They are, as Jesus stated, 'false prophets, which come to you in sheep's clothing, but inwardly they are ravening wolves' (Mt. 7:15).

"But let's get back to the officers of the church. For our morning devotions, Bev and I are reading *Daily Readings from the Christian in Complete Armour* by William Gurnall. I brought it in this morning. Gurnall seems to have a special concern for church officers. Listen to this from the January 31 reading: 'The more public your place, and the more eminent your service for God, the greater the probability that Satan is at that very moment hatching some deadly scheme against you. If even the cadet corps need to be armed against Satan's bullets of temptation, how much more the commanders and officers, who stand in the front line of battle.' One more. This warning is found under February 4 and is especially poignant. He writes,

'Satan also aims at those in office in the church. What better way to infect the whole town than to poison the cistern where they draw their water? He takes special delight in corrupting the heart of a minister. If he can wiggle into a pastor's heart, then he is free to roam among the flock undetected[—]a devil in shepherd's clothing.'

"Poison the cistern! That's a great picture. So, while every believer is under constant surveillance and attack, the leaders of the church must always be on high alert and prepared to resist every devious temptation to sin. While it is unquestionably true that the church is always on the offensive against the forces of evil, we are at the same time a resistance movement. We are resisting the kingdom of darkness. The moment we let Satan have a foothold among the leaders, we are setting ourselves and our churches up for spiritual trouble, not the least of which is hindering us from enjoying the gift of unity so graciously and sacrificially provided by our heavenly Father.

"Joe, let me speak frankly. This must be taken to heart. This is vital for you and the other deacons of this assembly. A spirit of teamwork, *esprit de corps*, is a powerful thing. Given the nature of God and the nature of the battle, it's absolutely indispensable. But as I've tried to make clear, a spirit of teamwork is not easily maintained. We know what to do, but doing it is just hard work. While we may become more skilled at living in unity in the church, we will never be free from the battle. We must embrace the battle as a way of life.

"For you, Joe, the question is, 'As a deacon, are you willing to embrace the battle and lead the other deacons in the war against Satan and his devious schemes to divide the church?' I know I'm focusing on you and making this personal. The truth is, it will take all of us working together. But God began to work in your heart to find a better way, and you came to me for help. Yes, it begins with me. But I need your help if we are going to win this battle. Will you lock arms with me and resist any and every effort to divide us? I need you, you need me, and we need every deacon to join us."

Gary pauses for a moment and lets this challenge sink in. As they exchange stares, Gary then asks, "What do you think, Joe? Will we embrace the battle together?"

Joe doesn't answer right away. He's thinking, pondering, even praying. He's taking seriously the invitation to join arm in arm to wage war against Satan's schemes to cause division and ineffectiveness in the church. He's feeling and thinking things that he's longed for, and now they are staring him in the face. He says the next thing that comes to his mind.

"'Two are better than one because they have a good reward for their toil. For if they fall, one will lift up his fellow. But woe to him who is alone when he falls and has not another to lift him up . . . And though a man might prevail against one who is alone, two will withstand him[—]a threefold cord is not quickly broken.' I know you're the spiritual leader, and I'm one among several servant leaders in the church, but whatever it takes, count me in. With God's help, let's put together a threefold cord that is not easily broken."

Gary, being an emotional person, struggles to keep the moisture in his eyes from turning into tears. He considers what a privilege it is to have a man like Joe by his side as they fight the spiritual battle that lies ahead.

"Joe, this will take all of us working together: me, you, all the deacons, and the entire church. I'm reminded of Philippians 1:1: "[T]o all the saints in Christ Jesus which are at Philippi, with the bishops and deacons." There is the threefold cord: saints, overseers, and deacons, all working together in harmony. Praise God!

"Well, our time has gone by quickly, but I think it is important to point out one more thing about protecting unity in the church. Protection is not just defensive. It involves an aggressive offense as well. Every resistance movement knows you have to promote, spread, and pass on the cause to others. It has to grow to survive. Likewise, unity and teamwork must be promoted to survive. And how are they promoted? They are promoted best by those who practice the virtues that lead to 'the unity of the Spirit in the bond of peace.' More than anyone else, the leaders must practice humility, gentleness, patience, and loving forbearance. Furthermore, as we submit ourselves to the leading of the Spirit in our lives, we will also be living out the fruit of the Spirit found in Galatians 5: love, joy, peace, patience, kindness, goodness, faithfulness, gentleness, and self-control (5:22-23). As we practice these virtues, we will enjoy the unity that God has provided, others will be recruited to join us, and together we will live and serve in 'the bond of peace.'"

Gary pretends to catch his breath like a swimmer coming up for air. "Okay," he loudly exclaims, "that's enough for today! In fact, that's enough for several days." Then he asks Joe, "Did you get a chance to find a prayer in *The Valley of Vision* to conclude this morning's session?"

As Joe pulls the book out of the backpack he carries to church, he says, "I did. In fact, I picked several. I wasn't sure which one to read, but this prayer entitled 'Almighty God' seems to be appropriate."

ALMIGHTY GOD,
I am loved with everlasting love,
clothed in eternal righteousness,
my peace flowing like a river,
my comforts many and large,
my joy and triumph unutterable,
my soul lively with a knowledge of salvation,
my sense of justification unclouded.
I have scarce anything to pray for;
Jesus smiles upon my soul as a ray of heaven
and my supplications are swallowed up in praise.
How sweet is the glorious doctrine of election
when based upon thy Word

and wrought inwardly within the soul!

I bless thee that thou wilt keep the sinner

thou hast loved,

and hast engaged that he will not forsake thee,

else I would never get to heaven.

I wrong the work of grace in my heart

if I deny my new nature and my eternal life.

If Jesus were not my righteousness and redemption,

I would sink into nethermost hell

by my misdoings, shortcomings, unbelief, unlove;

If Jesus were not by the power of his Spirit

my sanctification,

there is no sin I should not commit.

O when shall I have his mind!

when shall I be conformed to his image?

All the good things of life are less than nothing

when compared with his love,

and with one glimpse of thy electing favour.

All the treasures of a million worlds could not

make me richer, happier, more contented,

for his unsearchable riches are mine.

One moment of communion with him, one view

of his grace,

is ineffable, inestimable.

But O God, I could not long after thy presence

if I did not know the sweetness of it;

And such I could not know except by thy Spirit

in my heart, nor love thee at all unless thou didst

elect me,

call me,

adopt me,

save me.

I bless thee for the covenant of grace.[157]

To this prayer Joe added his own, "Amen," and left for work full of joy.

SESSION 5

Before leaving the house for his meeting with the pastor, Joe looks at the calendar: May 30. He thought he might be mistaken, but he's right. Somehow, they have managed to get in five sessions between the monthly deacons' meetings. He takes the calendar down and quickly flips through the year. He discovers there are four months that have five Tuesdays. Not that unusual. Then he eliminates July because of their family vacation to the cabin on Little Birch Lake in Minnesota. Then he scratches January because of the overtime he has to put in every year. There's no way he could meet every Tuesday morning in January.

"Margarette, is it in October that Pastor Gary takes two weeks off every year?"

"Yes, one week for the pastors' conference and one week to go see his parents in Oklahoma. Why? Is he changing it this year?"

"No. Just wondering. It is interesting, though. May is the only month in the entire year that Gary and I could meet for five consecutive Tuesdays between deacons' meetings."

As she kissed him goodbye, Margarette said, "Well, then, I guess the Lord knew you needed another meeting with your pastor to get you ready for the deacons' meeting. I'll be praying that your meeting goes well this morning. Don't forget tonight is Hannah's kindergarten graduation. You

---

157 *Valley of Vision* (East Peoria, IL: Versa Press, Inc., 1975), p. 51.

have your list, right? I have to be there early, so I'll meet you at the school at seven."

There are four framed documents hanging on the wall behind Gary's desk in his office. He's a bit of a history buff, and he has copies of the Constitution, the Declaration of Independence, the Bill of Rights, and the Emancipation Proclamation. As Joe walks into the office, Gary has his back to him as he stares at a copy of the Declaration of Independence. Without turning around to acknowledge Joe, Gary says, "I've been thinking about this document all week. Have you ever been to the National Archives building in Washington, D.C.?"

"I have."

Still standing behind his desk, he turns to face Joe. "Two weeks ago, we talked about the importance or value of teamwork. And do you remember what we talked about last week?"

"I do. You explained why it is so hard for a church to stay in a spirit of biblical teamwork."

"Go on," prods Gary.

"As I recall, it is because of spiritual opposition. Diaconal work, like every function of the church, is spiritual in nature and will be opposed by the world, the flesh, and the devil. You described it as a spiritual battle. By the way, those thoughts left an impression on me, especially the idea of Christianity being a resistance movement—I think that's the language you used. I've read Bunyan's *Holy War*, and I like the image of resistance. It reminds me of what Paul writes in Galatians 5 and the conflict between the Spirit and the flesh. Resistance! Resisting the forces of evil, resisting the prince and power of the air, and even resisting the sinful nature that we still wrestle against. I think the main point was that we must work at keeping, preserving, maintaining the unity that God has already given through our union with Christ."

"Very well stated. That's a good summary. I'm impressed."

"I owe some of that to Margarette," confesses Joe. "Every Tuesday night, after we get the kids in bed, she wants to know about our discussion. As I share with her what I'm learning, it forces me to review what we talked about and restate it in my own words. Usually, she repeats it back to me and asks follow-up questions that she wants answered. I really appreciate her interest in spiritual things and her desire to see me grow in the Lord and as a deacon. It's been great to include her in our discussions. There's an interesting thing that I've realized. Through these meetings, I'm growing closer to my wife, my pastor, and also the other deacons who don't even know about these meetings or my increased love for them."

As Joe speaks, Gary is struck by what he's hearing. Without any conscious effort, he smiles a bit and has the look of a proud parent. What he's hearing gives him a great deal of pleasure.

"I'm so excited for you and Margarette, Joe. What a tremendous blessing a godly wife is. It's wonderful that you talk these things over with her. Your wife can play an important role as you carry out your duties. She can pray for you, give you good advice from a woman's point of view, help you with delicate situations, and so forth. You know that our church has deaconesses, and sometimes a deacon's wife serves in that capacity. As you know, we have two couples right now who serve as deacon and deaconess couples. But at other times, as in the case of you and Margarette, she doesn't have the title, but she nonetheless assists you as you serve. So that's great. I'm glad to hear that you have a spiritual partner in Margarette. She's such a blessing to the entire church.

"Now, getting back to our discussions, I want to pick up where we left off last week: the problem of keeping the unity that God has already given."

Turning around to face the Declaration of Independence again, he says, "You say you've been to the National Archives building?"

"Yes."

Gary continues. "Some of the most important documents ever written are housed there. Among them is the original Declaration of Independence. I've been there several times, and each time I learn a little more about how this document is preserved. It is displayed in a dimly lit public viewing room under green-tinted glass in a custom gas-filled display case, each visitor carefully scrutinized by security cameras and ever-vigilant guards. Then, after inspiring thousands of visitors every day, it spends the night in an amazing vault. But it hasn't always been so carefully preserved. For more than hundred years, it was rolled up, carried around, wrinkled, torn, faded, spilled on, nibbled on by a bug, and spent forty of those years tacked to a wall."

"Seriously?" Joe replies. "I didn't know that."

Still staring at it, Gary goes on. "Someone finally said, 'Maybe we should preserve this thing.' You think? I learned that the price tag for just the three cases that frame the Declaration, the Constitution, and the Bill of Rights was $5 million. Who knows how much the annual budget is to preserve these national treasures? Do you know why they go to so much trouble to protect these historical documents?"

Joe isn't sure if that's a rhetorical question or if Gary is expecting an answer, so he just waits.

Almost as if speaking to the document hanging on the wall, he says, "It's simple really. *That which is of great value is worth great trouble to preserve.*" Turning his head toward Joe, he adds, "My point is this: if we value something, if it is truly important to us, we will make every effort to preserve it." With that, he walks around his desk and sits opposite Joe.

"Two weeks ago, we talked about the importance of teamwork. And from there, we talked about keeping a unified spirit of teamwork. That discussion is what led me to think about the documents on the wall, preserving what is important. Quiz time. Why are unity and teamwork so important to the church?"

Joe, without any hesitation, says, "I know this one! Because unified teamwork reflects the nature of God. I'll never forget that lesson. I had my own private brain tsunami when you said that. It was great! God is one; therefore we must be one. We must be one inwardly as a state of being, but also outwardly in all that we do. Teamwork, by definition, is oneness in action. If we hope to glorify God in all that we do, then we must be a unified team."

With a look of astonishment on his face, Gary informs Joe, "Don't be surprised if I have you teach this to the church! I think you're somehow getting more than I'm giving. And your commitment to internalize these discussions and get spiritual profit from them is truly a work of grace. I'm so proud of you, Joe. You clearly understand what I've been talking about the last few weeks. Unity is *from* God, *through* the Son, *by* the Spirit. Also, by the empowering work of the Spirit, we are responsible to preserve the unity that Christ already won for us. And even though He has given us His Spirit to both enable and empower us, preserving unity and teamwork is our responsibility.

"Take the originals of these documents on the wall. The Declaration of Independence, for example. Preserving this document and its words because they are important is one thing. But believing they are important enough to live and fight for is another thing. If we do not practice these ideals, in time they will be lost.

"As believers, our document is the Word of God. It is our responsibility not just to say that the Word contains many important truths, but to embrace those truths, to own them, to live them, to fight for them. My point is this: unity and teamwork are taught in God's Word. If they are to be preserved in the church, they must be valued, lived, and fought for.

"This past week, I spent several mornings thinking about the difficulty of practicing teamwork in the church. All I can give you this morning in the few minutes we have left are kernels of thought. Over the next few weeks, I will be teaching these things to all the deacons, and from there, I'll teach them as part of a series on unity and teamwork to the entire church. But for now, I'll trust that you are able to see the value of these things as they relate to the subject of *preserving* teamwork. Based on what I've heard from you so far, I have no doubt you will profit from this brief discussion.

"I've condensed my thoughts on preserving teamwork down to three words. I believe these words represent three key issues in the fight to keep teamwork alive: submission, diversity, and sovereignty. The word *submission* represents an attitude of humble, submissive obedience to the Lordship of Christ over our lives. It really does boil down to this: will we submit to Christ, or will we rebel against His will for us? And where do we find His will? In the pages of the Scriptures.

"Let's return to Ephesians 4:1-2. The chapter begins with a call to live worthy of our calling. Then, to briefly explain what he means, Paul gives us those four virtues that ascend like a stairway leading to the grand theme of the Epistle, endeavoring to keep the unity of the Spirit in the bond of peace, or as the NASB has it, 'being diligent to preserve the unity.' Here they are again: lowliness (or humility), meekness (or gentleness), longsuffering (or patience), and forbearing one another in love (or loving tolerance).

"Endeavoring means making every effort, being diligent, eager to do. Combined with the idea of keeping, it gives us the picture of a diligent centurion standing guard over unity. Generally, guards either watch a prisoner to make sure he doesn't escape, or they protect a prisoner or a valuable asset from outside attack. It's all a matter of focus. They're either keeping an eye on the valuable asset or keeping an eye out for the enemy. Sometimes, however, they have to do both: one eye on the asset, one eye on the enemy."

Joe speaks up and offers this thought, "That makes me think of Nehemiah and rebuilding the wall. A sword in one hand as they kept an eye out for the enemy, and a trowel in the other hand to build a wall around their beloved city. For us, we keep one eye on Satan and his evil minions and the other eye on the valuable asset, unified teamwork."

"Excellent application," responds Gary. "Here in Ephesians God is clearly telling us that if we value His marvelous grace—a grace that reaches back into His eternal plan to redeem us out of the slave market of sin and death, a plan that springs out of a Father's eternal love for His children—and if we are concerned about living lives that resound to the glory of the Father and the Son, lives that are led by the Spirit, then practice these virtues and you will preserve unity in the church. This is God's will for the church and every individual believer. I know I am being quite simple here, but it really does boil down to this question: will we humbly submit ourselves to Christ, who is the head of the church, and His Word? We cannot claim to care about unity and teamwork if we do not practice the virtues that we already know will preserve it in the church. So, the first key word to preserving unity in the church is submission.

"Second, is the word *diversity*. This is interesting. The thing that we often think of as the problem to keeping a spirit of unified teamwork alive in the church is diversity. We're all different. We have different likes, dislikes, tastes, opinions, aspirations; we're young, old, male, female; we're from different ethnic and cultural backgrounds, etc. How can such a diverse group possibly work as one? How could we ever hope to work as a team?

"But, Joe, diversity is not the problem. Accepting diversity is the problem. Or I could put it this way: not accepting God's unique design for the church is the problem. Once we accept and embrace the diversity of people and gifts in the church, we are well on our way to preserving unity and teamwork. If ever there was a church having problems with teamwork, it was the church at Corinth. Yet, isn't it interesting that Paul preaches this kind of diversity as profitable to the church? Within the one body of Christ, God has given a variety of gifts. Joe, would you open your Bible to 1 Corinthians 12? Read the entire chapter to yourself. Go ahead; I'll wait."

Gary waits for Joe to read. When he is sure that Joe is finished, he continues. "Joe, to what end have the gifts been given? What does the passage say? I'll give you a minute to find the answer."

It doesn't take Joe long. He already knows the answer, but he takes a moment to find the verse. "Verse 7 says, '[T]hat all may profit.'"

"That's right," agrees Gary. "God gave a variety of gifts for everyone's good. In fact, the ESV reads 'for the common good.' So, rather than being a hindrance, the assortment of gifts is good for the entire body.

"Now read verses 24 to 26. Begin in the middle of the verse with the word *but*. And this time, read the three verses out loud."

Joe reads, "'But God hath tempered the body together, having given more abundant honor to that part which lacked; that there should be no schism in the body; but that the members should have the same care for one another. And whether one member suffers, all the members suffer with it; or one member be honored, all the members rejoice with it.'"

"Joe, just one Greek word is translated as 'tempered the body together.' It can be translated as 'composed.' It speaks of compounding various elements together. One writer says it implies a deliberate mixing and blending process.[158] And why has God done this mixing and blending in the church? Verse 25 tells us. The word *that* indicates a purpose or aim is about to be stated. Here's the purpose: *that* there should be no schisms or divisions in the body. God composed, compounded, blended diversity into the body so that there would be no divisions!

"This is exciting, Joe! We see the wisdom of God unfolding before us in the way that He brings the church together. Let's keep reading. 'But that the members should have the same care one for another.' The less honorable are, as it were, thrown into the same mixing bowl with the more honorable, and they are so blended that there is no distinction between them. Without distinction between them, no preference will be shown by them. They all get the same treatment. They all get the same care. No divisions, only unity. Oneness. That way, if one member suffers, all the members suffer together.

---

158 Garland, *BECNT*, (Grand Rapids, MI: Baker Academic, 2003), p. 569.

If one member is honored, all the members rejoice together with the one being honored. They all suffer together. They're all honored together. They all rejoice together. No resentment, no jealousy, no hard feelings. All working together as one! Working for the mutual good of the body. That's beautiful! And who gets the glory? God! He designs, achieves, and empowers unity in the church (Rom. 15:6-7). That's the second key word: diversity.

"We're now ready for the third word, *sovereignty*. I know you already embrace and love the doctrine of the sovereignty of God, that God *actually* rules His universe. So, for the sake of brevity, I will limit my comments to something here in 1 Corinthians 12. Just a minute ago, I said, 'God gets all the glory for designing it all.' Listen to verse 11 again. 'But all these worketh that one and the selfsame Spirit, dividing to every man severally as he will.'"

Gary leans over and takes a look at Joe's Bible. He sits up and says, "Joe, in your Bible there are numbers next to the words *dividing* and *severally*. What do those two words mean?"

Joe acknowledges the numbers, and then reading the notes in the center column, he tells Gary, "Dividing means distributing, and severally means individually. So, God does what? He gives gifts to each one individually. It creates this image in my mind of God handing out gifts to every member of the church, but then saying, 'This isn't for you; it's for everyone.'"

"That's right," Gary tells him, "but more to the point are the words *as he wills*. Without getting into the details right now, when Paul writes 'as he wills,' he is telling us that God is sovereign over the distribution of the gifts. Whatever they are, however they are given, they are distributed as He wills. Joe, would you read verse 18?"

"'But now hath God set the members every one of them in the body, as it hath pleased him.'"

Gary continues. "Now what Paul means by setting the members in the body . . . I'll leave for another time. The point is, God is sovereign over the church! Whatever He does, He does it 'as it pleased him.'"

"If you don't mind," interrupts Joe, "a couple of verses come to mind. Psalm 115:3: 'But our God is in the heavens; he hath done whatsoever he hath pleased.' That's sovereignty for you. And I thought of 1 Corinthians 4:7: 'For who maketh thee to differ from another? And what hast thou that thou didst not receive? Now if thou didst receive it, why dost thou glory, as if thou hadst not received it?' The first passage declares the sovereignty of God, the second implies it."

"Good verses, Joe. By the way, I'm not missing the fact that you are quoting these verses from memory. Good job. Yes, both confirm that God is sovereign over His church.

"Joe, let me make a pastoral observation. Many of the problems that lead to divisions and disunity in the church are interpersonal relationship problems, in other words, people problems, like the church at Corinth. Many of their problems were relationship problems. They were upset with each other for various reasons. For some, it was over their favorite teacher. Others looked down their noses at the poorer members. Some took their brothers to court to settle matters, and so on.

"A large part of the solution to people problems in the church is to accept the fact that every person in the church is gifted by God and has a contribution to make for the good of the whole body. And this arrangement of people and the gifts that God distributes is according to God's sovereign will. The spiritually mature thing to do is Ephesians 4:1-3: 'Walk in a manner worthy of the calling to which you have been called, with all humility and gentleness, with patience, bearing with one another in love, eager to maintain the unity of the Spirit in the bond of peace.' But it starts with a right view of God. He is sovereign over everyone and everything, and His sovereignty certainly extends to the church. This doctrine is paramount to serving in unity and teamwork.

"There is so much more that I would like to say about each of these three key words: submission, diversity, and now sovereignty. Hopefully, I've said enough for you to understand the relationship between these things and preserving unity and teamwork in the church. If we would constantly submit ourselves to the Lordship of Christ in our lives, if we would always remember that diversity in the body is for our common good, and if we would surrender to the fact that God's sovereignty extends to every detail in the church, we would be, shall I say, less inclined to insult the wisdom, love, and goodness of God to His church.

"Well, I see our time is up."

"Actually," Joe says, "I forgot to tell you that I took the morning off today, so I have a little more time. Tonight is Hannah's graduation ceremony, and I'm helping Margarette get ready with a surprise party for her. I have to pick up some party favors and a Bible we're having engraved. The school is hosting a reception, but we thought we would surprise her with a small family party at home. So, since I'm going in late today, we can take a little more time this morning. Unless you have somewhere you need to be?"

"No, I don't. This actually works out great. As you know, we have a deacons' meeting in a couple of days, and I would like to cover one more thing with you before then. Let me just quickly add a few thoughts on restoring a spirit of teamwork, once it is lost.

"Briefly stated, biblical restoration comes through two words: love and repentance. Maybe I should say something about biblical restoration of unity in the church. Let's turn to 1 Corinthians 1:10. Paul writes, 'Now I beseech you, brethren, by the name of our Lord Jesus Christ, that ye all speak the same thing, and that there be no divisions among you; but that ye be perfectly joined together in the same mind and in the same judgment.' The word translated as divisions is the Greek word *schismata*, from which we get the word schism. When used literally, it means to tear or rip up. As a metaphor, it represents disagreements and divisions that tear people apart.

How are we to respond when a *schismata* occurs? How do we fix it? The remedy is restoration.

"The words *perfectly joined together* are a translation of the Greek word *katartizo*, which means to repair, mend, restore, put in order. It's used in the New Testament for the mending of nets, bones, dislocated joints, and even fabric (Mt. 4:21, 9:16; 2 Cor. 13:11; Gal. 6:1; 1 Pet. 5:10). Think of a fisherman repairing the nets, a doctor setting a broken bone, or a seamstress mending a tear. The word speaks of putting things that are broken and torn back together again. What Paul is exhorting then is that there be no tears or breaks in the church's unity. And if any exist, they need to be restored, 'perfectly joined together.' Here's the point. The church must not suffer divisions, and when the unity and teamwork of a church has been ripped apart, it must be restored.

"That brings us back to the two words I mentioned: love and repentance. I'll start with repentance. I'm sure you know this, but confession, such as we find in 1 John 1:9, basically means to acknowledge or agree with. When we confess our sins to God, we agree with Him that we are sinful and in need of His ongoing cleansing. As we receive His cleansing and forgiveness, we restore our fellowship and communion with Him.

"We do the same thing when we confess or acknowledge a sin against another person. We own it. We go to the offended person and agree that we sinned against him (Mt. 5:20-26, 18:15ff). Then, with a repentant heart, we resolve by God's grace to never do it again. The resolve to never do it again is repentance. Repentance means to turn. When we repent before God, we turn from our sin to Him. When we confess our sin against someone else, we own the sin and resolve to turn our back on that sinful behavior. That's repentance. At that point, the burden falls on the offended person either to forgive or hold on to the offense. If they choose to hold on to the offense, then they become the offender and must confess and repent to restore the relationship (Lk.17:3-4).

"Joe, offenses happen. We're sinful people, and we often make a mess of things. If we ignore it or proudly insist that the other person is in the wrong, we leave it unresolved and open the door for division. But if we deal with offenses, either as the offender or the offended (Heb. 12:14), then we are free to let it go and restore the relationship. When we restore the relationship, we restore the conditions for unity and teamwork. Paul wrote in Ephesians 4: 'Do not let the sun go down on your anger,' because in doing so you 'give Satan a door of opportunity' (Eph. 4:26-27; 2 Cor. 2:10-11). An opportunity for what? For all kinds of evil, but specifically an opportunity to create division in the church.

"What I've just described is more about the process of restoration: repenting, confessing, acknowledging. Remembering the three key words for preserving unity and teamwork are helpful as well: submission, diversity, and sovereignty. I think there are times when a rip occurs in the fabric of the church, and healing and mending start by remembering submission to Christ and the Word, accepting the diversity of individuals and gifts, and acknowledging the sovereignty of God. However, most of the time, we must humbly repent in our hearts, confess our sin to God, and acknowledge the sin to the offended party, the key word being repent, turn our backs on the sinful behavior.

"There is one more word that is fundamental to keeping and restoring a spirit of unified teamwork: love. Sometimes love is reactive. It covers a multitude of sin and is always ready to forgive. When a tear divides the church, love is ready to step in and mend the divide. But love is also proactive. By its constant presence, love can keep the tear from happening in the first place. Joe, you turn to Ephesians 4:16 and 1 Peter 4:7-8. I'll turn to 1 Corinthians 13. When you get them both, go ahead and read the verses."

Joe reads in the order they were given without break. "'From which the whole body fitly joined together and compacted according to the effectual working, maketh increase of the body unto the edifying of itself in love . . . But the end of all things is at hand: be ye therefore sober, and watch unto prayer. And above all things have fervent charity among yourselves: for charity shall cover the multitude of sins.'"

Before reading 1 Corinthians 13:4-8a, Gary tells Joe he is going to substitute the word *love* for *charity*. "'Love suffereth long, and is kind; love envieth not; love vaunteth not itself, is not puffed up, Doth not behave itself unseemly, seeketh not her own, is not easily provoked, thinketh no evil; Rejoiceth not in iniquity, but rejoiceth in the truth; Beareth all things, believeth all things, hopeth all things, endureth all things. Love never faileth.'

"These passages tie a number of things together, don't they?" added Gary. "I'm sure you've heard me say it before, but Paul didn't write Chapter 13 so we would have something to read at weddings. It must be kept in mind that this chapter on love comes right between his instructions concerning gifts and the problem of chaos and division in worship. Practice Christian love, Paul is saying, and you won't have these problems. Through love, you will both restore unity and prevent division. Someone once said, 'Unity does not always lead to love, but love always leads to unity.' I don't remember who said it, but I've always remembered the saying. So, the two key words for the restoration of unity and teamwork are *repentance* and *love*."

Joe doesn't say anything, but a little knot is developing in his stomach. Joe might even say that the knot has a name: Tony. Tony is the chairman of the deacons and the man that Joe has the most problems with. He hasn't always had issues with Tony, just in the last six months or so. As Joe listens to his pastor speak of restoring teamwork, of repentance and love, he knows he will have to talk to Tony. Repentance, love, unity, teamwork—these are the words creating the knot named Tony. Joe's silent turmoil is interrupted by Gary.

"Now, that's a very brief summary of those themes." He then offers this challenge. "If you don't mind, I would like to see if you were listening.

Can you summarize what I just said about restoring unity and teamwork, and can you do it in just one sentence?"

Joe's eyebrows shoot up like a man who has just been shocked. "One sentence?" He squirms a little in his chair to buy some time. He's trying to refocus. It doesn't take very long, and he's ready. "How's this? Concerning the restoration of unity and teamwork in the church," he pauses, "we repent and confess both to God and the other person, but most of all we love, because love covers a multitude of sin! And let me add something that we've all learned from you, pastor. Love is the sacrifice of self to promote what is good for the other person." Joe's thoughts flash back to Tony, but he continues. "We see it, of course, in the life and death of Jesus. In a passage that I memorized many years ago, Paul said, 'Let this mind be in you which was also in Christ Jesus: Who, being in the form of God, thought it not robbery to be equal with God; But made himself of no reputation, and took upon him the form of a servant, and was made in the likeness of men: And being found in fashion as a man, he humbled himself, and became obedient unto death, even the death of the cross.' The ultimate sacrifice of self to do what is good for others." *The knot growls.*

"Excellent summary," praises Gary, not knowing what's going on in Joe's mind. "Now my turn. We have covered a lot today, so let me just remind both of us what this meeting has been about. First, *that which is of great value is worth great trouble to preserve.* That has been the main theme of our meeting. If it's important, we'll do it. And teamwork is so valuable because it reflects the nature of God. Then, I talked about three key words and their relationship to preserving unity: submission, diversity, and sovereignty. I followed that up with two key words concerning the restoration of unified teamwork: repentance and love. Restoration begins with repentance, as we submit ourselves to God's Word and turn from anything that could cause a division in the body of Christ. Also, repentance often requires confession to the wronged individual. And finally, the all-encompassing word *love.* It begins with love for God—Father, Son, and

Spirit—and extends to everyone around us. As John said, 'Beloved, let us love one another; for love is of God: and everyone that loveth is born of God, and knoweth God. He that loveth not knoweth not God; for God is love' (1 Jn. 4:7-8).

In a thoughtful and reflective mood, Joe adds, "I remember the man who asked Jesus how to inherit eternal life. Jesus turned the question around and asked the man what does the law say. The man correctly answered, 'Love the Lord your God with your whole being, and love your neighbor as yourself.' And Jesus said, 'You are not far from the Kingdom of God.' First, love God. Then, love everyone else. Going back to something you said earlier, Gary . . . For the believer, the commandment to love is like all the other commandments. It might be hard, but it's what we do. More than that, it's what we want to do. God loved us; we love others. I hope I can live that out as a deacon, among deacons, for the sake of the church and for the glory of God. That's my prayer anyway."

For Joe, that means Tony.

"Amen, Joe. Amen. Before you go, I want you to know that I am planning to go over all of these things with the entire board in the very near future. I mean everything we've talked about the last month. In fact, I'm planning on beginning this Thursday night. I've already taught a lot of these things through the years, but because of your prodding and the discussions we've had, I'm putting these things into a series of lessons that I can first teach to the deacons and then the entire church. I plan to begin by addressing the elephant in the room: the lack of unity and teamwork that often exists here among the leaders. The reaction might tell me where we need to go next. Hopefully it all goes well.

"Please pray for me. The first meeting will be especially hard for two reasons. First, I have to confess my sin of negligence to the board and seek forgiveness. That won't be easy. I'm a proud person. Second, I have to confront several issues head on: sinful attitudes and behaviors that must change as we move forward, not the least of which is the sin of not serving the body as Christ intends, as we all promised to do. And I have to keep watch over my own attitude to make sure I do this with gentleness and humility, so that, if possible, I encourage, not discourage, every deacon to serve as Christ served (Gal. 6:1). I don't know if that's realistic. I expect some pushback. And if necessary, I may have to do the hardest thing of all: ask for a resignation from the office. But I'm hoping and praying that won't be necessary."

Joe thinks to himself, "So am I, pastor; so am I."

"Honestly, Joe, I am full of fear as I think about this. Please pray for me and every deacon as we go into this meeting. Pray that the Spirit and Word would reign in our hearts, that we would experience 'the unity of the Spirit in the bond of peace' and that God would be glorified before, during, and after this painful process."

Joe's heart is gripped with the need to pray right now. He asks Gary if he can take these things to the Father before leaving. So, he prays. He prays with a sanctified fervency that he has rarely felt. As Gary adds his "amen" at the end of the prayer, both men are moved and encouraged. It takes a few moments of silence for Gary to compose himself.

"Thank you, Joe. While it would be great to linger in a spirit of prayer for a while, I've taken up enough of your time this morning, and I have to leave myself for another appointment. I hope Hannah's graduation party is a huge success! We can walk out together." As they stand up to leave, Joe puts his arms around Gary in a big bear hug and whispers in his ear, "I love you, pastor. I'll be praying for you every day."

Gently grabbing Joe by the shoulders, Gary warmly responds, "I love you too, brother, and I will continue to pray for you as well!"

EPILOGUE

As Joe collects his children from their various Sunday School rooms to gather for worship in the auditorium, he notices a spirit of joy and excitement in his own soul. It's been a good morning. The drive to church was uplifting as Margarette led the family in the singing of choruses. Joe likes the idea of the family SUV being a "Spiritual Utility Vehicle" unto the Lord. There was a noticeably good spirit in the adult Sunday School this morning. Joe was especially grateful for that. As his family slips into the pew, his eyes are once again drawn to the stained-glass cross behind the pulpit. As preparation for worship, Joe often looks on the cross as a reminder of Christ and the privilege of coming to the Father through His Son. A good morning indeed!

As Joe looks at the worship bulletin, there it is in black and white, and his heart rejoices. "DEACONS' MEETING, Thursday night, 6 p.m."

Joe looks up at the cross again. He then throws a glance to his right and catches a glimpse of one of his fellow deacons. He looks straight ahead a few rows to find another one. And in his mind's eye, he looks to the back row. There he sits, his dear friend Tony, still the chairman of the deacons. "DEACONS' MEETING, Thursday night, 6 p.m." And he thinks, "A good morning indeed!"